D.

CONTENTS

'Dangerous Faith'

CHAIRMAN'S INTRODUCTION

The title of our week came to us very quickly through the two Bible reading themes. In retrospect we were right, and there was a challenge not only through the Bible readings to this kind of risking in faith. Donald English with his Bible readings from Galatians brought home some of the practical theological challenges of that red-hot letter. We need never be ashamed to be evangelicals; but we must be sure that we live out the implications biblically and honestly. Alistair Begg took us to the early chapters of the Book of Daniel which inevitably call for courageous holiness. He would emphasise consistently how the four leading Jews in Babylon were involved in the life of that community and yet were utterly separate. That age-old Keswick theme of holiness within the world and not of the world was marvellously expounded.

Throughout the various messages of a very busy and encouraging fortnight there was this tone of excitement at the prospect, as well as humility before God's word. The regular World View meetings had a very deep response to the challenge to service, demonstrating our 'dangerous faith' in the world.

There was a comparatively younger element about the platform, which had a new look with fewer participants on it. Nigel Lee and Mark Ashton were with us for the first time and we much appreciated their ministry. There were new ventures in other ways with more informality in welcoming new people as well as in the traditional missionary reception.

The first week of the Convention took on its own children's work this year and this was very well supported.

There was a significance about this year because some months before, Keswick had been involved in collaboration with Proclamation Trust, UCCF and Spring Harvest with a venture at Pwllheli called Word Alive. It was Spring Harvest with a difference and yet with much similarity. It was a venture in collaboration which in its own way was dangerous faith. This was very well received and very well supported; among those who came were 1,200 students. It was almost certainly the beginning of a regular annual event. Keswick happily has stepped out in faith believing that it would not be a rival attraction but an added opportunity for biblical exposition. Certainly our numbers this year were by no means affected adversely, rather the reverse. God is on the move and Keswick is not lagging behind.

I end my nine years as Chairman of the Keswick Convention Council with much thankfulness and looking forward to serving under Keith Weston who will follow me. I do believe that within the last nine years there has been development, we have taken steps in dangerous faith without in any way affecting the depth and application of the message of scriptural holiness. The added value of the written page is enormous, although print can never convey the warmth, love and friendship of Keswick. I trust that these pages may not only reward your study but stimulate you to join us within the fellowship of Keswick in 1994. Come and exercise dangerous faith with us.

> *Philip Hacking*
> *Chairman of the Keswick Convention Council*

EDITOR'S INTRODUCTION

This year's Keswick book reflects several minor changes in the Convention, one of the most significant being the number of evening meetings with a single speaker instead of two as in earlier years. My own (short-lived) reaction was one of disappointment, for one of the joys of editing this material over the years has been the interplay, unscripted and unforeseen, between two speakers arriving on the same platform with little opportunity beforehand to compare notes; there have been numerous occasions when God clearly divided the same message between two speakers. I need not have worried. You will find in the present volume much conscious and unconscious integration by speakers in the fortnight's ministry as a whole, where a theme introduced by one is taken up and developed by others who could not have seen each other's notes. This is especially true of one of the overarching themes of this year's teaching: the vital necessity of Christians going into the secular world and holding out the gospel truths.

There is a comment somewhere in Augustine in which he regrets that being absorbed in the beauty of a preacher's style he quite forgot to listen to the message. Working so closely to the text, this is an error to which editors are particularly prone. Yet it was especially striking this year what a wide variety of preaching methods was in evidence, and in how many different ways the speakers unpacked and illuminated the passages they were expounding. I would hate to see

Keswick regarded merely as an display of preaching techniques and skills, but I would certainly urge readers to make use of the tape library (see p.238) where all the messages in this book, plus the ones that could not be included, can be found in their entirety; the video library (p.239) offers an even more vivid record that is especially suitable for group meetings.

I have to remind readers once again of the editorial policy; particularly out of fairness to the speakers, few of whom have had the opportunity to read and check the edited text for themselves (though a representative of the Keswick Council reads the entire book in proof before it is printed). This book is the edited transcript of a pulpit occasion, not the revised, polished and expanded text that the speakers would certainly have produced had they been preparing for book publication.

The reason for the above is the very tight schedule that Christmas publication demands. For the same reason, though all Bible quotations have been verified, not all the other quotations have been tracked down, though I have supplied as many footnotes as I could. The other constraint —space—has meant that as in previous years I have assumed that readers will have a Bible open as they read, and in some cases I have provided only a verse reference where the speaker originally read the passage out in full. One speaker demurred, pointing out that it was God's word not his own that ought to be given prominence. I hope he and his colleagues will forgive me. The aim has been to preserve the teaching intact, and provided the open Bible is not regarded as optional, readers will have every Bible text available to them that the speaker quoted. Where speakers have paraphrased, this is made clear by the context, by the omission of a reference, by the insertion of 'cf' before a reference, or by the use of capitals for pronouns referring to the Persons of the Trinity (the latter is the Keswick preferred style; but as is usual in editing, all quotations are left in the original style. Hence no capitals in AV, NIV etc.). For the same reason I have, as always, had to be ruthless with many amusing anecdotes, jokes and illustrations. The principle, as in previous years, has been to preserve all the teaching, and enough of everything else to preserve the flavour of the event.

Greek words are transliterated following W. E. Vine's *Expository Dictionary of New Testament Words*. I would like to thank Peter Cousins and Barry Seagren particularly, both of whom have helped me with a number of queries. The editing has this year been a family project, for my wife Tricia has transcribed all the tapes. Consequently I am particularly grateful to my daughters Eleanor and Lauren, who shared their parents, for part of the summer, with a galaxy of preachers.

David Porter

THE BIBLE READINGS

The Life of Faith:
Paul's Letter to the Galatians

by Rev Dr Donald English

1. Obeying the Gospel Truths
(Galatians 1–2:14)

Our aim in these Bible studies is to ask ourselves each day
two questions. What was the Spirit saying to and through
Paul, to the people of his day? And what is the Spirit saying
to us today through that same writing from Paul? The
principles are the same in both, though the applications may
be very different.

I feel that the letter to the Galatians may be like a time-
bomb ticking away below much modern Christianity. I would
ask you to resist the temptation to enjoy watching Paul
knocking the spots off an unknown group of people whom he
was criticising, for if you do I think you will miss the point
entirely. We must ask: What is God the Spirit saying to you
and to me today, through this letter of Paul to the Galatians?

The greeting (1:1–5)

Paul uses the traditional greeting. That is, he says who is
writing and to whom he is writing, and he makes some
comment about it. We Christians are not called to be apart
from the world. We are called to be different from the world,
but within it. And right from the very beginning Paul uses
the normal greeting of people of his day. But, as we shall see,
he Christianises it; he infuses it with Christian meaning. And
that, I think, is our calling today; to be in the culture—in a

sense, of it—yet not dominated by it but dominated by Jesus Christ our Lord.

Some of you may have been listening to the BBC Reith Lectures, which this year were about the task of the intellectual.[1] The lecturer, Professor Said, made an impressive statement: he said that the intellectual is always somewhere between loneliness and alignment, somewhere between being totally separate from the culture and being wholly accommodated within it. As I listened to him, I thought it was a good description of the Christian: we may never be wholly of our culture, but we must never entirely separate from it. So Paul says to the Galatians at the very beginning, 'I'll start the way everybody starts.'

'Paul'—that's just to be sure they know the letter comes from him and is not some kind of copy—'Paul, an apostle.' What a lot of difficulty we've had with the word 'apostle'! Let us look again at what the New Testament says about apostles. The word is first used of the twelve disciples: Matthew 10:2; Mark 6:30; Luke 6:13, 17:5, 22:14, 24:10. They are called apostles. Luke, in Acts, usually gives the word the same meaning: Acts 1:2, 26; 2:37, 42, 43; 4:33 and so on. 'The apostles' often means 'the Twelve' because they were with Jesus, they were called by Him, they observed what He was about, they became in a sense foundational to the growth of the church.

Sometimes one or two outstanding names are added. For example in Acts 14:4, 14, Luke says 'the apostles Paul and Barnabas'. So now the list has grown a little. And in Galatians 1:19 and 1 Corinthians 15:7, James the brother of Jesus is referred to as an 'apostle'. So the list is still growing. And you may remember, in 1 Corinthians 15:7–9, Paul says, 'last of all he appeared to me also, as to one born out of due season [NIV: as to one abnormally born]. For I am the least of the apostles' (though he adds, 'I worked harder than them all'!).

So it's the Twelve, and then sometimes it's this larger group. But thirdly, the word we translate as apostle is used in a number of places to describe a whole category of people. In Luke 11:49, Jesus says to the lawyer that God sent prophets and apostles. In John 13:16, He says that 'messengers'—

apostles—are not greater than their sender. In Philippians 2:25, Epaphroditus is described as an apostle. In 2 Corinthians 8:23 it means the representatives of the churches. In Romans 16:7 it refers to those two well-known apostles Andronicus and Junias (if you know anything at all about either of them, please speak to me afterwards!).

I think there's a warning here about how we should use Scripture. We do wish that Scripture had made things clearer than it does!—because that would be more comfortable for us, particularly if we could then say that our own denomination had got it right. But the Holy Spirit in the Acts and in the growth of the church was not enabling us to build a structure. He was not enabling us to define status. The Holy Spirit, in telling the story, was seeking to enable us to see how God's work grows through a variety of people, needed at different times. Don't turn the New Testament into the kind of home that is so tidy that you daren't sit anywhere! Like the vicar's wife who wondered why the bishop visiting their home left the towels in his room unused; she discovered later she'd forgotten to remove a note she'd attached to them for the family's benefit: 'If you use these, I'll kill you . . .'

The Scriptures are God's gift of life through the Spirit. Don't expect them to be tidy. They are alive, just as we are alive!

But I think we can say that apostles can mean that small group who were deeply privileged to be called by the Lord and to be special witnesses for Him. We can go on to say that God calls at different times those whom He needs for whatever He wishes them to do. And we can certainly say that the apostolic succession is that succession of people all over the world who have been faithful to the gospel and have proclaimed it, whatever their status. Paul says (I think some people must have been questioning it), that he is 'an apostle —sent not from men nor by man.' You can feel already an undercurrent to this letter. What is being said about him that makes it necessary to say, 'sent not from men or by man'? If you are in conversation with a doctor and he keeps saying 'Of course, as a doctor I have to say . . .', you begin to think: Why are you so anxious I should know you are a doctor?

Now Paul explains that whatever he is claiming as an apostle is not man-made. It is something that Jesus Christ has called him to: 'and God the Father, who raised him from the dead'. He wants to ensure that these people know that what he is about to say to them, and which they are not going to like, does not come from him or any group surrounding him or any group of people from the past. These are the words of Jesus and God the Father who raised Him from the dead.

'And all the brothers with me.' Who are they? Well, Stephen Neill suggests that Acts 13:1–3 might provide a reasonable list—'Barnabas, Simeon called Niger, Lucius of Cyrene, Manaen (who had been brought up with Herod the Tetrarch)'—wouldn't you love to know about those people? How many people in the New Testament we don't know about, who are just names! And how many more are not even named—and yet where would Paul be without them? My sisters and my brothers, we've become somewhat worldly in the church, with our league tables of speakers and the people who we choose to honour; and I think Heaven is going to be a very great shock for many of us, not least for those of us who occupy the platforms of the world. It's not like that here: without these people Paul could not have been what he was. Think for a minute, who has helped you? Who in your journey has been important?

'To the churches in Galatia'—I wish we had time to expand on that. It's either the old kingdom of Galatia, centred in modern Ankara in Turkey; or it's the Roman province of Galatia which was much larger and included the old kingdom but also in the south Pisidian Antioch, Iconium, Lystra and Derbe, places Paul visited as a missionary in Acts 13 and 14; and for what it's worth, that's what I think he's talking about. We do know that there were Jewish and Gentile Christians there, and we do know from the letter that Paul is addressing the question: Is Christianity a version of Judaism, or is it something brand new? And if it's brand new, how do you defend it?

'Grace and peace to you from God our Father and the Lord Jesus Christ'. I said to you that Paul uses the normal form of greeting. But this is where, I suggest, Paul is infusing into it some of the Christian gospel. The Greek word Paul uses for 'grace' is *charis*; the normal greeting began with *chairo*: 'Be happy'. 'Joy and peace to you' was the normal greeting: Paul substitutes grace for joy, for there is no joy without grace. So those who first read the letter would see a normal greeting until they discovered that Paul had inserted that attitude with which the prodigal was received by his father; that attitude by which the vineyard owner paid all the labourers what they needed, irrespective of their work; that attitude which received the man praying at the back terribly aware of his own sin and his difficulty, and received him because he had need.

The gospel is not about 'Be happy—oh, and by the way, have peace.' The gospel is about the grace of God, which first comes in order that we might know peace. And peace isn't just the absence of war, the corner in which a boxer sits between rounds: it's an inner sense of well-being based on the fact that God is in control. And peace relates very closely to Keswick, because the search for peace is the search for perfection, for being whole, holy, healthy within.

'. . . Who gave himself for our sins to rescue us from the present evil age'. Paul is rejecting any picture of the loving son standing in front of an angry father. That little boy who prayed, 'Lord, I like Jesus but I don't like God'—there's none of that here. The word 'rescue' has to be taken in its full sense. One of the awful things about watching television pictures of former Yugoslavia is to see people desperately trying to climb up on to lorries and escape. They want to be rescued. But, says Paul, that's what our gospel is about. Although the precise meaning of the preposition 'for' our sins is still much discussed, what is clear in what Paul is saying is that what Jesus did for us on the cross rescues us from our sins.

> What can wash away my sins?
> Nothing but the blood of Jesus;
> What can make me pure within?
> Nothing but the blood of Jesus.

'. . . From this present evil age . . .' Now, we need an

illustration here. In the New Testament there are two ages. The 'present evil age' begins, in biblical terms, with the Fall and goes on to the end of the created world. It is dominated by the powers of evil, because of men and women's co-operation with the powers of evil. But at a particular time during this present evil age, God acted in Jesus and introduced the age to come, which begins with Jesus and goes on out beyond the end of this present evil age, beyond the end of this world out into eternity. To illustrate it, I would need to borrow the television commercial's picture of the apparently endless toilet roll which that little dog keeps running away with!

Now, Paul says, Jesus died: He gave Himself to rescue us from this present evil age so that we may be part of the age to come. But the two ages run side by side. That's where all our problems as Christians come from: we are living in the new age, but we are living alongside the other age. Many Christians spend their lives hesitating. Which age do we belong to? Where are we at home? Keswick, and holiness, is about learning to be permanently and totally rescued by God.

That's what he hopes for, for them.

'To whom be glory for ever and ever. Amen.'

How the Galatians have erred (1:6–10)

Usually Paul follows his greeting with some statement about the people he's writing to. He normally says some nice things about them and then tells them what he's praying for them, which is a gentle way of telling them what he expects them to become. For example: Romans 1:8, Philippians 1:3, Philemon 4, 1 Corinthians 1:4, 1 Thessalonians 1:2, 2 Thessalonians 1:3. He introduces his writing in the same way in all these passages: 'I'm glad to write to you, I'm grateful for you, I thank God for you with every memory, I'm grateful to the memory of this and that, I'm praying that you'll grow in this, and this, and this . . .'

Now if the Galatians had known about those other letters (which they wouldn't have, because this was written first), they would have wondered what had gone wrong here. Paul intends them to wonder, as we can see from verses 6–10.

Paul's word 'astonished' is a strong one. It's used of the
crowd's attitude in Luke 1:63, when Zechariah was cast
dumb: they said to him, 'What's your baby going to be
called?' He wrote on a slate, 'John'. They said, 'There's
nobody in the family called John.' They were 'astonished'. A
good modern translation would be 'gobsmacked'!

'I am astonished' says Paul, 'that you are so quickly
deserting the one who called you by the grace of Christ.' The
word is *metatithemi*: it's what a soldier does when he deserts,
what a person does when he changes from one philosophy to
another. It's used in the Greek version of the Old Testament
about Ahab, every time Jezebel changed his mind. It can
mean conversion to something good, but that is not how it is
being used here. 'How on earth could you desert'—not 'the
philosophy', but 'the one'—notice that; Paul doesn't say 'I'm
astonished that you are so quickly deserting the faith/the
church/the fellowship/the views I gave you', but 'the one
who called you by the grace of Christ'.

Some of the versions of the New Testament don't have 'of
Christ'. It may be that some later scribe felt we had better
make it absolutely clear and slipped it in. It's even stronger if
'of Christ' isn't there: 'He who called you by grace.' That's
what this letter is all about.

'To a different gospel'. There are two New Testament
words for 'different'. *Allos* means 'another of the same kind'.
If I said in Greek 'Bring me another Bible' and I used *allos*, I
would mean I wanted another NIV. If I used *heteros*, I would
mean an NEB or a Good News Bible—another of a different
kind. Paul uses *heteros*, and then quickly corrects himself
—'which is no gospel at all. Evidently some people are
throwing you into confusion.' That's *terasso*, the lovely Greek
word for stirring up something. When you put a stick into a
pool and stir, it's *terasso*. The word is used in John 5 about
the Pool of Bethesda. Paul is saying, 'It seems to me, I hear
that there are people who are stirring you up against the
gospel.'

'Gospel' originally didn't mean 'a story', as in 'the gospel
of Christ'. It didn't mean 'a book', as in 'the Gospel of
Mark'. The gospel, the *euangelion*, originally meant 'an
epoch-making event'. The birth of the emperor Augustus

was described as an *euangelion*. And Paul, following the New Testament writers, says: 'Somebody is messing about with what God did once for all in Jesus, and I'm amazed that you have bothered to listen to them.' May I in passing just remind you of the implication of that word *euangelion*? It means that what God has done in Jesus is the gospel. It means that the world can never be the same again. The living and dying and rising of Jesus puts all history into a different perspective. That's the gospel—God acting in Jesus before we were even alive, in order to do for us what we could not influence and what we cannot change because it is written into history.

So beware of making the gospel suit your inclinations. There are Christians deeply committed to evangelism—but, bit by bit, the gospel is bent to serve the evangelistic task. There are people who are deeply committed to social caring—the same thing happens. The struggle for justice —the same thing happens. We take the gospel and we bend it to our passion. And then it's so easy to exclude everybody else. 'No,' says Paul, 'it's the other way round. God in Jesus has acted once in history. *You* bend to *that*.'

It was, you remember, the message sent from John the Baptist in prison: 'Are you the one who was to come, or should we expect someone else?' (Luke 7:19). Jesus sent back the reply, 'Go back and report to John what you have seen and heard: The blind receive sight, the lame walk, those who have leprosy are cured, the deaf hear, the dead are raised ... Blessed is the man who does not fall away on account of me.' The gospel is meant to be our foundation. We are not the gospel's foundation. Somebody, Paul says, is changing, is perverting, the gospel. And then come these awful verses: 'But even if we or an angel from heaven should preach a gospel other than the one we preached to you, let him be eternally condemned! As we have already said, so now I say again: If anybody is preaching to you a gospel other than what you accepted, let him be eternally condemned!'

Paul could be simply saying, 'Any other gospel will not rescue you from eternal condemnation, and therefore if you follow these false teachers you will be eternally condemned.' But I think he's making a stronger point. I think he's saying that this gospel is such a matter of life and death that we are all committed permanently to the defence of it. And they are perverting the gospel of Jesus Christ. How he goes about dealing with that we will see shortly. It may be a shock for some of us.

Verse 10: 'Am I now trying to win the approval of men, or of God? Or am I trying to please men? If I were trying to please men, I would not be a servant of Christ.' Once again he is being personally attacked. It is being said that Paul is trying to be a man-pleaser; and Paul is saying, 'Listen, if you want to know the difference between the gospel and the not-gospel, it's simple: the not-gospel appeals to human preferences. The not-gospel is a D-I-Y gospel. It says you can do something about your salvation. That's man-pleasing. The real gospel says that nothing you can do will save yourself. The real gospel is dependent entirely on what Jesus Christ has done for us. That's the true gospel; and anything other than that is not the gospel. So how can they accuse me of pleasing men? If I were pleasing men, I would not be a servant of Jesus Christ.'

So the next question is: How did he get his gospel?

Paul's apostolic pedigree (1:11–24)

'I want you to know, brothers, that the gospel I preached is not something that man made up. I did not receive it from any man, nor was I taught it; rather, I received it by revelation from Jesus Christ' (verses 11–12). Literally, it is 'not according to man'. Now there is a difficulty here of which those of you who know the New Testament will I am sure be aware. The two problems are Acts 9: 17–19, where Ananias was sent to the blind Saul in Damascus, and even more serious, 1 Corinthians 15:3–8, where Paul says 'I passed on to you what I first received.' The words 'received' and 'passed on' are both words that come out of the idea of a tradition of being given something, cherishing it, looking after it and passing it on as you received it. And the whole impression in 1 Corinthians 15 is that he received it from somebody else. So how can Paul say 'I received it and I passed it on', where there's no time for him to have received it from people in the story of Acts; and how can he have been visited by Ananias who told him some things, and then have gone out and immediately preached the gospel, and yet have said 'I received it only from Jesus Christ'?

Well—what did Ananias teach him? Look at Acts 9:17. He taught him the reality of the body of Christ ('Brother Saul'); he taught him the continuity of God's work ('Jesus who appeared to you on the road has said to me'); and he taught him something about the Holy Spirit ('I am come that you may see again and be filled with the Holy Spirit'). What Paul says he received in 1 Corinthians 15:3–8, as you will remember, is Christ's birth, His dying, His rising and all the appearances of the risen Christ. So what was it he received direct from Christ that does not include those things?

I think it must be what he himself describes in verses 15 and 16. 'But when God, who set me apart from birth and called me by his grace, was pleased to reveal his Son in me so that I might preach him among the Gentiles . . .' *The essence of what Paul received on the Damascus road in Acts 9 is that God's grace in Jesus is entirely free and sets us entirely free.* I think that is the essence of the gospel.

What Ananias taught him was the outworking of that. The things that Paul refers to in 1 Corinthians 15—the birth, death and resurrection of Jesus, the appearances to the disciples—these are all the stuff of the gospel; but the gospel itself is that God's grace in Jesus is offered to us entirely free and it sets us entirely free. John Stott paraphrases Paul as saying it like this: 'In my fanaticism'—this is the Damascus road—'I was bent upon a course of persecution and destruction, but God, whom I had left out of my calculations arrested me and changed my headlong course. All my raging fanaticism was no match for the good pleasure of God'. Hold to that very tightly. That's what this battle is about. It's not actually about theories of Christology. It's not actually about doctrines of the atonement. It's not our best explanation of how He could be raised from the dead or of how He could have ascended or how and when He will come again (I'm choosing all the things about which Christians notoriously fall out with one another). The essence of the gospel is that grace is given free in Jesus Christ and sets us wholly free.

And that's the one thing that Paul received on the Damascus road which nobody else taught him. Everything else follows from that freedom.

So in verses 13–20 he expands on this. 'I am telling you,' he is saying, 'exactly what happened. I was met on the Damascus road and after that I really did not depend on other people for the understanding of the gospel. And I assure you before God that what I am writing you is no lie.' That last sentence, from a Jew, was a very serious affirmation indeed. Then verse 21: 'Later I went to Syria and Cilicia'—was that back to Damascus again?—'I was personally unknown to the churches of Judea that are in Christ. They only heard the report: "The man who formerly persecuted us is now preaching the faith he once tried to destroy." And they praised God because of me.'

I think that last verse is beautiful. Picture it. Here's this rogue-elephant evangelist careering around the world, claiming to be a Christian and an apostle, and people are sending messages back—'You'll never guess where he is now! You'll never guess who he's talking to now! You'll never guess what he's doing now! What are you going to do about it?'

Paul says, 'They praised God because of me.'

I wish we had that kind of generosity, my sisters and my brothers. Because of my work I have become engaged ecumenically in situations I never dreamed I would be in. I notice the look on fellow evangelicals' faces when I tell them that. I see the incredulity when I tell them about some great Roman Catholic preacher of the gospel. And I can see them thinking, 'Er . . . I'm not so sure . . . Er . . .' Or they come back with some answer about Rome's history and all of that, about which as a historian I happen to know already.

But Paul says, they had the grace to hear about this rogue evangelist, and to say: 'If he's winning people for Christ, thank God for that.' I'll never forget a prayer meeting in a nation-wide initiative in evangelism, which was of course all the denominations working together. And Lewis Misselbrook, whom many of you will know, said as we all bowed our heads: 'Lord, I don't know why you keep blessing the wrong people.' I just ask you to be open to the possibility that in our determination to defend what we treasure so greatly, we have made the gospel more than it actually is for the purposes of excluding other people; that we've not accepted what I think Paul is saying here—that the gospel as God's free grace is offered to us freely in Jesus Christ and sets us solely free; and that all who preach that word deserve, in John Wesley's phrase, the words 'Give me your hand'. I know I am treading on very delicate ground. I'm trying to tell you what the gospel is saying here in Paul's letter to the Galatians. 'And they praised God because of me.'

Paul's accreditation by the apostles (2:1–10)

'Fourteen years later I went up again to Jerusalem, this time with Barnabas. I took Titus along also.' Oh, I wish I had time to tell you about Barnabas! Let me just give you the Bible references and you'll see. In Acts 4:36–37 he's a generous man. In Acts 9:27 he's a bridge-builder. In Acts 11:19–26 he's an ambassador. In Acts 11:25 he's enabling somebody else. In Acts 13:13–14:28 he's a missionary. In Acts 15:36–40, because he doesn't agree with Paul about John Mark, he leaves Paul in order to give John Mark a chance to do what he really should have done the first time round. In 1 Corinthians 9:6 and Philemon 24 they are obviously reconciled; here is Barnabas, a Cypriot Jew from the church in Jerusalem, and going along with him is Titus, an uncircumcised Gentile. That's what Paul is trying to say about this gospel that sets us free: 'The two workers I took with me were a Cypriot Jew and an uncircumcised Gentile.'

He says that he went in response to a revelation (verse 2). That's important. He's trying to tell them that the authorities at Jerusalem didn't summon him. He wasn't being called for an interview about how he was getting on. 'I went by revelation.' Maybe we need to remember that Paul, the great intellectual of the faith, was not averse to charismatic experience; that some of the most crucial things in Paul's ministry came in ways about which some of us might have some reservations. 'Are you sure, Paul, that you actually saw what you saw? Are you sure that voice said "Come over to Macedonia and help us"? I mean—it's a bit odd, it's not what we were planning, is it!' I heard John Drane say in a conference a while ago that the challenge is to worship the Lord our God with heart and soul and mind and strength, but that too often we go for one or other of those to the exclusion of the rest.

Even the great Paul, the intellectual thinker of the faith, was ready to go by revelation. Was it Agabus's revelation about going up to Jerusalem and doing something for the poor and the needy? 'I . . . set before them the gospel that I preached among the Gentiles,' he says, 'but I did this privately'—it wasn't a public examination—'to those who seemed to be leaders'—you see how careful he is about their standing—'for fear that I was running or had run my race in vain. Yet not even Titus, who was with me, was compelled to be circumcised, even though he was a Greek.' Titus may have been circumcised, for all we know. The text doesn't say he wasn't, it simply says he wasn't compelled—that's important for Paul. I think he wasn't, but the text doesn't settle it absolutely. 'This matter arose because some false brothers had infiltrated our ranks to spy on the freedom we have in Christ Jesus and to make us slaves. We did not give into them for a moment, so that the truth of the gospel might remain with you.'

Let me tread delicately again. It has become a characteristic of much evangelical Christianity that when we don't get our own way in a particular church, we leave and we form our own group, where—since we all left together—we do agree. I ask you seriously: Is that the way of the Lord? Paul says, 'This mattered so much to me I wasn't going to run. It mattered so much to me I stayed to fight it out.' And the more you look through Paul's writings, you'll see he's fighting everywhere. The idea of Paul having a wonderful evangelistic wander around the world, preaching the gospel without difficulty, is nonsense. Almost every one of his letters is written to correct somebody about something.

So you don't say, 'All right—if you're going to believe that, I'll go off somewhere else.' You say, 'Hey—just a minute; what is the gospel? Let's talk about it.'

'We resisted them,' says Paul, 'we didn't give way for a minute. Of course we didn't! Because the gospel mattered to us, so that the truth of the gospel might remain with you.'

The degree to which a thing matters to us is the degree to which we should stay and fight it until we are thrown out—that's my judgement, for what it's worth. Paul says, 'I stayed there and I fought them about it, because the gospel is too important to allow people to get away with things that aren't the truth.'

'As for those who seemed to be important—whatever they were makes no difference to me' (verse 6). It's lovely to see a man in a position of power being derogatory about power. It's lovely to hear a man like Paul—who was of course one of the big cheeses—saying 'Well, they seemed to be important' —this is Peter, James and John!—'but God does not judge by external experience—those men added nothing to my message. On the contrary, they saw that I had been given the task of preaching the gospel to the Gentiles, just as Peter had been given the task of preaching the gospel to the Jews. For God, who was at work in the ministry of Peter as an apostle to the Jews, was also at work in my ministry as an apostle to the Gentiles.' Remember—verse 9—Paul would not be there if it were not for Barnabas, who had gone and got him when they needed somebody. But now Barnabas is taking second place to Paul, and James and Peter and John are giving him the right hand of fellowship: 'They agreed that we should go to the Gentiles, and they to the Jews.'

Here's the other thing about people who are different from us. We need the grace to recognise in other people their faithfulness to Christ's call, even if it is different from ours. We need the grace to see that there are others who are called to serve Christ in different ways from those we choose. But if their pedigree goes back to Jesus we have no right to exclude them. The question then is not 'Do I agree with her or him?' The question is 'Does her or his pedigree go back to Jesus? Is what they are doing built on the free grace given by God in Jesus? Imagine how hard it was for Peter and James and John, the great pillars of the church. Imagine how difficult it was to hear reports of this man whizzing around all over the place when they've hardly seen him. But he comes; and they listen to what he has to say. And they say, 'It's quite clear. God has called you to the Gentiles just as He's called Peter to the Jews. We give you the right hand of fellowship.'

When that happens, something takes place in the Christian family. As the psalmist says, 'Where the brethren—everybody—dwell together in unity, there the Lord bestows the blessing' (cf Psalm 133). The Christian church has never taken the Lord up on that promise. Never. Imagine what a team it would be running on to the field, if we were all wearing the same strip, and going in the same direction!

They gave Paul the right hand of fellowship, and only asked 'that we should continue to remember the poor', which strengthens my feeling that it's Agabus who's called to go up to Jerusalem with money for the Jews there. Why did it take me so long as an evangelical to see verse 10? Why did I not see right at the beginning that Paul was committed to mission alongside the poor? Because I wasn't taught it. I was taught that Paul was about preaching the gospel. But Paul was about social caring for the poor also, if I read this aright.

The disagreement with Peter (2:11–16)

In these verses we really see a duel of the champions! Peter has been eating with the Gentiles. He was the first missionary to the Gentiles—do you remember Cornelius? So obviously when Peter came to where they are here—to Antioch—he started to eat with the Gentiles; of course he did. That probably means ordinary food, the agape love meal and the Lord's supper. But then people of the circumcision came, and later (Acts 15) they sent the message out (Acts 15:24–29), James the Lord's brother said, 'Some people purporting to come from us have been troubling you.' They came from Jerusalem and they said that James had sent them. They said to Peter privately 'It isn't appropriate for you to be sitting and eating with these Gentiles.' So Peter withdrew.

Paul says, 'I said to Peter in front of them all'—here he's fighting again for his corner—'Peter, you should be ashamed of yourself. You live like a Gentile now; you don't depend on the law for salvation any more; so if you live like a Gentile, why are you trying to make Gentiles live like Jews? It doesn't make sense.'

And Peter has to back down in front of Paul, to whom he's

given the right hand of fellowship and said it's all right for Paul to be a proper apostle.

To my final point. That expression 'circumcision'. It may not mean just a group of people, it may mean an attitude of mind within a group, which prevents people from being free. It may mean that the *peritome*, the circumcision group, represented a group mentality that wanted to add things to the freedom of the gospel, such as circumcision, food rules, sabbath laws and so on. They wanted to add them all as extras, to make them properly the people of God.

So I leave you with this thought. Think about the fellowship to which you belong. If a stranger came into that fellowship and stayed awhile and you were then to ask him, 'What do you perceive to be the secret of this fellowship?', would he say 'God's grace is offered freely in Christ and sets us wholly free', or would he say, 'The secret of this fellowship is: We believe in Jesus. And these are the things you've got to do to stay in the fellowship . . . I don't mean that people stand up and say you've got to do them, I just mean everybody knows.'

I ask you: who of us in our fellowships is free as Christ set us free? And how many of our fellowships have built up so many rules over the years that it's rather like the corrosion that happens to a constantly dripping tap, until the supply of water gradually starts to run dry—and we've not even noticed how many requirements we've added to the gospel? I ask you, my sisters and my brothers, to think about that before we continue tomorrow. And I ask you, pastors, deacons, elders and leaders—don't sit there thinking 'My fellowship isn't like that.' Ask your members!

Note

1. 1993 BBC Reith Lectures: Edward Said, 'Representations of the Intellectual'.

2. Making the Crucial Choices (Galatians 2:15–3:29)

Paul has now gone beyond Peter in this letter to the Galatians. He is gathering into the argument any of those who are his opponents. Plainly in this letter his opponents are Jews who are now Christians but are trying to add a little more to what people must believe and accept.

So Paul takes the typical Jewish line about the Gentiles. 'We who are the Jews by birth'—*phusei*, by nature—'not Gentile sinners.' The Jews regularly referred to Gentiles in this way, I think for two reasons. One, the Gentiles didn't have the law; so how could they be as good as Jews? Two, the Jews were quite clear that the Gentiles were less moral people anyway. And if you read Romans 1:18–32 you will get Paul's account of that. Paul picked up what every Jew really believed about Gentiles; they are Gentile sinners, and that is why they call them Gentile dogs. But I think he is being somewhat sarcastic, for he says, 'We ourselves who are Jews by birth and not Gentile sinners, we know that a man is not justified by observing the law.' In other words, Paul is saying to Peter publicly (if this is still his speech) and to all his readers if they are listening to what he is saying, 'We Jews who became Christian, we know that you never get to be justified by keeping the law.'

That is the start of his argument.

'But by faith in Jesus Christ.' Now you will have noticed I am sure that the word 'justified' occurs four times in this short reading. This is the great New Testament Greek word which is related both to 'justification' and 'righteousness': *dikaiosune*. And in the whole of the Bible God is spoken of as *dikaios*—'just'. And God being 'just', means three things. God only always *is* right; God only always *does* right. Those are the two fundamental things about God, and He is the only being in the universe about whom you can say them. And thirdly, God has the power to put us into the right. He can take those who are in the wrong and put them into the right. That's justification.

Paul doesn't explain how, here. But he does explain in Romans 3, where he talks about 'This righteousness [that] comes from God . . . through faith in Jesus Christ to all who believe. There is no difference, for all have sinned and fall short of the glory of God, and are justified freely by his grace'—remember what I said yesterday—'through the redemption that came by Christ Jesus. God presented him as a sacrifice of atonement, through faith in his blood' (3:22–25). How does God put those who are in the wrong into the right? Through the blood of Jesus. How does that happen? The blood of Jesus is a 'redemption', a ransom price. The ransom was the price paid in the Old Testament by the man whose ox had gored another man to death. Under the law he should have died himself, but he was allowed to pay a ransom price. In New Testament times the ransom price was paid to set a slave free. Paul is saying, 'God who always is right, who always does right, looks upon sinners who can't get themselves right and puts them in the right through the blood of Jesus who paid the price for our sins.'

> In my place condemned He stood,
> Sealed my pardon with His blood—
> Hallelujah! What a saviour.

He also says, it's atonement. This is another great New Testament word: *hilastrion*. It means either 'expiation'—that which covers over our sins—or 'propitiation'—that which bears upon itself the wrath against sin. Either way, it's Jesus doing for us what we cannot do for ourselves and therefore enabling us who are not in the right to find ourselves in the right before God.

Law can't do that. In a cricket match you cannot say to the umpire, 'I was only out by an inch—can't you let me stay in? I was out by four yards last time.' With the law, such distinctions make no difference. You're out both times, and you can't put it right. I remember accidentally breaking a gift that was to be given that evening at my cousin's twenty-first and engagement party. Whatever was I to do? If only I could replay the incident! But the replay is always the same, the result never changes. And sin is like that, says Paul. 'We Jews know very well that there's no replay that puts it right when you've got it wrong. You're just wrong. So you need somebody to put you in the right.'

He points to the solution: 'faith in Jesus Christ' (verse 16). This could be what is called an objective genitive: 'I put my faith in Christ'. Or it could be a subjective genitive, meaning 'the faithfulness of Christ'. It may be focusing not so much on the strength of my faith or my ability to have faith, it may be emphasising His faithfulness in redeeming us. Well, that's wonderful! If it depends upon my faith I'm still a bit unsure that I'll always manage it; but if it depends on His faithfulness, then that's like a rock. 'No,' says Paul, 'we know very well that Jesus delivers.'

I'm sure you know the story of the fleet that was making its way through stormy seas one dark night. The flagship saw a vessel out in front and a message was sent, 'This is such-and-such a ship—move over.' And the reply came back, 'This is such-and-such a place; move over.' The admiral in charge of the fleet became very angry. He signalled, 'I am an admiral—*move over.*' The message came back: 'I am a midshipman, move over.' The admiral responded, 'We are an aircraft carrier. MOVE OVER.' And the reply came back. 'I am a lighthouse.'

Don't trust your own aircraft carrier! Look to the lighthouse which is Christ, whose faithfulness is our atonement, the source of our justification.

Law and grace (2:17–21)

Now if you read verses 17–21, you will see that the argument that's coming back at Paul goes like this. If you neglect the law, you are going to be rejecting the grace of God. And then you will be behaving unfairly, not playing your part. And if you reject the law, don't you make Christ the agent of sin?

No! says Paul. Not at all; by ignoring the law I do not ignore sin, for Christ has died for my sin. I'm not ignoring it, I just know how to deal with it. 'If I rebuild what I destroyed'—that is, if I start going for the law again—'I prove that I am a law-breaker', because I'm going back to the old keep-the-law days, which can never keep me in the right. 'No,' Paul says, 'I have been crucified with Christ.'

Some people tell us—particularly some theologians, but many others too—that the kind of doctrine of atonement that I was spelling out for you, which sees Jesus as dying for our sins—'In my place condemned He stood'—they say that that is immoral, that it isn't right for God to do for us something that we will not or cannot do for ourselves. It makes the immoral moral, they argue, and that's not moral, it's not right. C. K. Barrett rightly warned against manipulating theological counters like a game of chess: you know, 'I am a sinner', 'There is God', 'I'm under judgement', 'Ah—there is Jesus dying; He dies for me', 'Thank God, I'm a Christian! Boom, boom!' But you see, that isn't what the New Testament says. The New Testament doesn't say that we look from a distance and observe the drama and say 'Thank God, Jesus died for our sins, now I'm saved.' Not so: I have been crucified with Christ. We are actually gathered into that drama.

When I was a young undergraduate I was told in the Christian Union that they were holding an open-air meeting in Leicester market square. So I thought I'd go and watch. There was quite a large crowd, some of them my friends and others I didn't know. One of the leaders came and stood beside me—I thought he was going to evangelise me! But he leaned over and said to me, 'You're on next.' I said, 'Pardon?' He repeated, 'You're on next, keep it short—about three to five minutes.' That was my introduction to open-air speaking. I went to watch, but I was gathered into the drama.

You see the drama of Jesus Christ is not something you watch 'over there', you are gathered into it. Putting your faith in Christ is not just like signing a cheque or signing an agreement. You put faith in Christ by giving yourself, and you give yourself into what He did for us—which is dying for us. So Paul says, 'I have been crucified with Christ.' You don't add anything to the death of Jesus by being crucified with Him. His death is all that's needed, but faith in Christ means to be crucified with Him, which means that you and I die to everything He died to. Whatever Jesus died against —all that is contrary to God's will, all that is sinful and hurtful and harmful in the world, all that pulls people down—you and I, if we put our faith in Christ, die to all of that. That is what your baptism meant, whether you were sprinkled or washed or plunged. Dying with Christ: what a wonderful picture that is! How can it be immoral when I'm gathered into the very thing Jesus died to do for me? And yet I don't add anything to it, I just enter into it by His grace, and life is entirely different on the other side.

'But,' he says, 'it is no longer I who live, but Christ lives in me. The life I live in the body, I live by faith in the Son of God.' I think that some Christians misread this. They take 'I no longer live' to mean that you've got to suppress yourself, that your own being has to be played down so that you don't matter any more. Quite the opposite is true. I remember a speaker who used to speak from this platform who said that he drove all day to address a meeting, and at the meeting the chairman stood up, thanked God for the speaker and then said to God, 'Blot him out!' The speaker thought, 'Have I driven all the way across England in order to be blotted out?'

Some Christians are like that. They keep repressing themselves as though who they are isn't important. But quite the opposite is true. Paul goes on. He says 'I no longer live'; but look at the number of personal pronouns he uses after that: 'I no longer live, but Christ lives in me ... I live ... I live by faith,' and so on; 'God, who loved me and gave himself for me...' When you die with Christ, you learn for the first time what it is to begin to develop and to grow. He doesn't depress you, repress you or dilute you; He makes you free. The point Paul is trying to make is that Jesus is in the driving seat. Paul usually talks about us being 'in Christ'—*en Christo* is Paul's great theological description of the Christian life. But this time it's the other way round: Christ in us. And he's describing where the motivation comes from.

And he goes on, 'The life I now live in the body.' The New International Version could be just a little misleading there, because the word isn't *soma* which is the word Paul usually uses for 'body' in a kind of neutral sense; it is *sarx*, which means 'humanity in all its susceptibility to temptation'. Paul is reminding us that even though Christ dwells within us, we are not somehow free from the battle. Just because Christ is at the centre of our lives, we are not free from temptation, we are not free from falling into all kinds of sins. It's our mortal body that he's talking about, and therefore we have to trust every day, trust, trust, trust, if we are going to go on growing in the way this Convention reminds us to do.

You can say the last part however you like. 'The SON OF GOD, who loved me', 'The Son of God, who LOVED me', or 'The Son of God, who loved ME.' 'Son of God' draws attention to the loyalty of Jesus Christ to His father; sonship in the Bible is about obedience.

So, having wonderfully rejected the idea that he should set aside the grace of God, Paul announces quite the opposite: he's accepted it warmly and died into it with Christ.

The law cannot save you (3:1–5)

Now Paul turns to the Galatians themselves. 'You foolish Galatians!', he says. He's now turning to the text of experience. There are only three times in the New Testament in Paul's writing when he uses the name of the people to whom he's writing: 2 Corinthians 6:11; Philippians 4:15; and here. Preachers who have ears to hear, let them hear: there's a three-point sermon ready-made. Every time Paul names the people he's speaking to, he does so full of emotion. J. B. Phillips translated it: 'Oh you dear idiots of Galatia, surely you can't be so idiotic?'

'Before your very eyes Jesus Christ was clearly portrayed'--placarded--'as crucified.' He says 'I almost painted a picture for you.' How important that we have people who perform Christian drama for us today, who can placard, portray the story! 'Oh' he says, 'how can you possibly have been so bewitched? Who bewitched you?' Then he asks them this question: 'Did you receive the Spirit by observing the law, or by believing what you heard?' That's the fundamental question, back again. 'How did you receive the Holy Spirit?' I hope you see how the Trinity slips into Paul's writing. I don't think he sits down and says, 'I'd better put a bit of Trinity in now; I'd better make sure they're sound on the Trinity.' He just tells the story of salvation; and as he tells it—why, God the Father loves us, stands over against sin, provides a way for us; Jesus the Son comes willingly and offers Himself for us and to us, we put our trust in Him; and the Spirit enters into our lives. He's just describing how it is, how it was and how it is; but it's trinitarian. And if you unbalance any of that trinitarian teaching you are in great danger, because you will then become a God-heretic, or a Jesus-heretic, or a Holy-Spirit-heretic. And we need to watch that in our Christian thinking and living. The Trinity are all involved in how we live as Christians and Paul tries to spell that out for the Galatians now.

'How did you receive the Spirit? Are you so foolish? After beginning with the Spirit, are you trying to attain your goal by human effort? Of course not. The Spirit was given because you believed in Jesus Christ. But after beginning with the Spirit—are you now trying to attain your goal by human efforts? Have you suffered so much for nothing?' (If the word is translated 'suffered' as in the NIV, Paul's reference point might be Acts 14:19. But if it is translated 'experience', as it could be, the reference is Acts 14:10.) 'Have you suffered so much for nothing—if it really was for nothing?' Paul still has hopes for them. For those of us who are pastors, who have to care for other people, it's always easy to err on the side of harshness and judgement. But the true pastor is always fed by hopefulness. 'Love always hopes, love never gives up hope' (cf 1 Corinthians 13:7). You parents who wonder about where your children are and where they will be—never give up hope. Paul says, 'You are in a terrible state, you Galatians. You are idiots, listening to those people who are misleading you. But it surely can't be for nothing. Does He give you His Spirit and work miracles among you because you observe the law, or because you believe what you have heard?' You see, the contrast all the time is between these two: Are you working your salvation? or are you receiving your salvation?

And which way does blessedness come? Does it work by your working salvation, is that how you are blessed? Or are you most blessed when you trust our Lord Jesus Christ and all that follows? Paul rarely refers to the working of miracles. Romans 15:19, 1 Corinthians 12:10, and 1 Corinthians 10:28, 29 are, I think, the only time Paul talks about miracle-working. He says here, 'Do you get your miracles by working the law?' Now, I pause for a moment, because I have a feeling that many of us who are pastors and ministers, who tell people Sunday by Sunday and day by day that the grace of God is free and that we are forgiven in Christ, are too often dominated by an evil conscience about the work we have not managed to do. We are too often oppressed by the things undone, and actually judge ourselves not by grace but by law. And our congregations collude with us in this deception, by expecting us to be such wonderful people that of course we will be able to do everything. Are we saved by keeping the law, or are we saved by trusting in the grace of Jesus? We pastors and ministers and elders and deacons and lay-assistants who care pastorally; let's make sure we are living by grace and not by law ourselves, or we may be so wrapped up in our own sense of failure and guilt that we are not free to tell the good news to others with conviction.

There are churches that are destroying themselves by trying to do everything. Their members want their church to do everything that can be done for young people, for middle-age people, for old people; they want to be socially caring, to struggle for justice, to do evangelism, they want their premises to be used by everybody, they want to be sending their people out always, but they also want them to be witnessing among their friends who they never have time to see anyway. And at work they are so tired out from what they do at church that they can hardly do their job properly, and the pressure mounts and mounts and mounts. We ministers are great at telling people that more and more needs to be done. Is that what Paul says here? Do you find the miracles happen when you are constantly trying to keep your targets?

Do you find the Spirit comes to you when you say, 'Didn't we do well today'?

You see, we've got to keep going back to the source. I don't mean it's wrong to evangelise, to engage in social caring, to struggle for justice and do all the other things. I'm simply saying that bit by bit we move from where we're standing and we find ourselves standing somewhere else. And then we wonder why our members become depressed, why ministers have breakdowns, why people go empty and dry and lacking in enthusiasm, why the world doesn't respond to us. Why should they, if what they find when they get into church is a set of workaholics singing about grace? 'Wonderfully free—but don't forget all the meetings next week; wonderfully free—have you given enough money? Wonderfully free—did you bring your neighbour tonight?' I'm exaggerating, as I think you know.

The same is true of evangelism. Parents, who long for your children to be the very best they can, how easily that becomes a prison out of which they not only can break but *should* break, or they'll never be themselves; they'll never be free if you impose the prison on them, if at every turn they feel you're saying 'Mm ... we like that ... we don't like that.' It's grace, it's freedom. Let me say it, and I hope we can all hear it: in Christ we are loved, we are understood, we are forgiven, we are affirmed, we are enabled, God loves us more than we can imagine, and He understands our difficulties more than we ever will. And He says, 'I am a loving parent whose Son died to show My love for you.' Let's be free in the gospel.

The Jewish heritage considered (3:6–9)

This passage represents a very clever move by Paul, because he's writing to contradict Jewish Christians who may well be saying to some Gentiles, 'Of course we've got all the force of Old Testament law behind us: I mean, we've got all the things you never had, poor souls. How could you know that we've got to add all these things about the law, if you don't know the story of our history? So we'll tell you the story.'

Paul says, 'I'm interested in our history too. Why don't we

go back right to the beginning? Not just to Moses and the law—let's go back to the very beginning. How did all this show ever get on the road?' Well, consider Abraham: He believed God, and it was credited to him as righteousness.' This is a quotation from Genesis 15, where God says to the aged Abraham, 'You're going to populate the world.' Can you imagine Abraham saying, 'Me, populate the world? We can't even have a child!'

Well says Paul, 'Consider Abraham: "He believed God and it was credited to him"—that's a lovely word, credited —"as righteousness. . ." so those who believe are children of Abraham. The Scripture foresaw that God would justify' —there it is again—'the Gentiles by faith, [there it is again] and announced the gospel in advance to Abraham: "All nations [that must include the Gentiles] will be blessed through you". So those who have faith are blessed along with Abraham, the man of faith.'

Why, Paul says, it was faith from the start: and if you want an image of what kind of faith I'm talking about, imagine a man well on in years, with a wife who's well on in years, having to accept that he will be the source of blessing for all the nations through his seed. Can't you imagine Abraham saying, 'You'll have to do it, because I can't'; I'm helpless to keep Your promise, Lord, it will have to be all Your doing.' And God says, 'That's a reasonable deal, Abraham.' And Paul says to these people in Galatia: 'If you want a model of saving faith, that's it, because Abraham was a no-hoper in terms of peopling the world: he hadn't a chance. But he believed God and it was credited to him for righteousness. If you want an example, try that!'

Now, back to some theology again, in verses 10–14, and you will see once again that lovely trinitarian statement at the end of the passage: God, Christ, Spirit. The reference in verse 10 is to Deuteronomy 21:23—'Anyone who is hung on a tree is under God's curse.' But Christ, Paul says, became a curse for us. Remember Paul's words in 2 Corinthians 5:21, 'God made him [Jesus] who had no sin to be sin for us, so that in him we might become the righteousness of God.' Jesus knows that the curse of the law is against all who can't keep it. So He becomes a curse for us, and in so doing redeems us. The word for 'redeemed' is 'buys out'; it's what a soldier does when he buys himself out of the Forces. Christ in becoming a curse for us has bought us out of the law, out of our sins:

> In my place condemned He stood,
> Sealed my pardon with His blood.

Such a high price for salvation! Christ bought us back. He took the curse of the law on Himself, emptied it of power in Himself and set us free. How can you build anything on that other than what He has done for us? How can you add to that by saying, 'Well I'll do this . . . I'll do that . . . I'll do the other.' There's nothing to be done; it's all been done, thank God, for us.

The law, the covenant and the coming of Jesus (3:15–25)

From verse 15 onwards Paul applies the point about Abraham: 'Let me take an example from everyday life.' He uses the example of a covenant. Verse 17: 'What I mean is this: The law, introduced 430 years later'—that is, 430 years after what happened to Abraham—'does not set aside the covenant previously established by God.' God made His promise to Abraham, a covenant, a will-and-testament. Nothing that happens through Moses 430 years later can change that. The original way of God was by grace through faith. The law is an interim. 'Well,' they say, 'what is the law for then?' Verse 21, 'Is the law, therefore, opposed to the promises of God? Absolutely not!'—*me genoito*, one of the strongest phrases Paul ever used. How *can* the law be opposite to the promises of God? Not at all. Verse 23: the law locked us up 'until faith should be revealed. So the law was put in charge to lead us to Christ.' The idea here is not what has sometimes been suggested, that of a tutor or teacher. It is rather that of a quite lowly servant whose job is to look after the children of the nobility. The lowly servant's job was just to make sure they were looked after, kept reasonably well fed and clothed and so on. It wasn't a high teaching responsibility, it was more a caring responsibility. Paul is saying that if God's promise to Abraham was by faith, then what the law did was to help us to see who we were and where we were. We needed to be saved, and the law kept us in that sort of prison until Christ would come. But verse 25: 'Now that faith has come, we are no longer under the supervision of the law.' Thank God, we are set free.

Sons and daughters through faith (3:26–29)

One last passage: 'You are all sons'—and daughters, and the word could easily be rendered 'children'—'through faith in Christ Jesus,'—here's the strong affirmation now—'for all of you who were baptised into Christ have been clothed with Christ.'

That's a lovely picture. The early Christian custom was that when they came up out of the water, they would put on a spotless white robe. 'You ... have clothed yourselves with Christ.' From 'Christ in us', he's now moved to 'us in Christ', which is his normal way of describing the Christian life. We are clothed as by a pure white robe, we are clothed in Christ. What is the result? 'There is neither Jew nor Greek, slave nor free, male nor female, for you are all one in Christ Jesus.' That could be translated, 'You are all one *person* in Christ Jesus'.

'If you belong to Christ, then you are Abraham's seed, [Jew or Gentile] and heirs according to the promise.' In the last minute or two I simply ask us to take with absolute seriousness the implications of that statement of Paul.

It is one of the foundational statements of the New Testament, that the one thing that divides Christians from the rest is being 'in Christ'. There is only one inclusive or exclusive circle for the Christian, and that's 'in Christ' or 'out of Christ'. Therefore we who are in Christ must constantly be asking how that circle may be widened, so that more and more may become 'in Christ'; but within the circle, we have to learn a harder lesson—that all who are 'in Christ' are one person; all who are 'in Christ' are in one person: Christ.

Now: if you can find your way to say, 'Only evangelical Christians are in Christ', you don't have a problem. If you can reject all other kinds of Christianity except evangelical Christianity as not Christianity, you don't have a problem. But if you are willing to admit that there are those who aren't evangelical Christians (however you define that) who are in Christ, however wrong you know them to be, then they are part of the one person in Christ. So think of the zaniest Christian groups you know, that group about which you think 'Please Lord, let me never have to worship with them'—they too are in Christ. Think of those from whom you strongly differ doctrinally so that you find it difficult even to be with them; the question is, Are they in Christ? However misled they may be.

I think they just may think we haven't got everything right. Have we? If you have everything right, see me afterwards —I'd like a little conversation with you! No, the one circle is 'in Christ', and in that circle, says Paul, what's this Jew and Gentile stuff? What's this male and female stuff? What's this master and servant stuff? And if he'd been writing today, he'd be saying what's this rich and poor stuff? What's this developed world and developing world stuff? And what's this black and white stuff? And what's this clever and simple stuff? And what's this leadership and led stuff? And what's this Methodist and Baptist and Anglican stuff? What *are* you talking about?

In Christ one person. Because only in Christ is there salvation and He has borne the sins of all who will come—all.

Now, there are many points at which we Christians have to say to one another, 'I'm sorry my sister, my brother, I can't walk that bit of the journey with you, it's very sad, it breaks my heart, but that's how life is.' But here I'm talking about our attitude, I'm talking about whether we are willing to be biblical Christians, I'm talking about whether we are willing to take our Bible seriously and allow Paul's words to get right to us. In Christ one person; all in Christ one person. The NIV has a lovely translation of Romans 12:5: 'So in Christ we who are many form one body, and each member belongs to all the others.' Every member belongs to all the others. I wonder whether we have the courage to let that sink in to our minds and hearts today?

The other side of that coin is there will be increasing pressure in this decade and beyond for Christians to talk more about God and less about Jesus, because the talk about God allows us to get on better with other faiths. Evangelical Christianity will resist that as firmly as we possibly can. We are Christians because of Christ. If you take away the centrality of Christ, if you make what Christ did negotiable, you've thrown the gospel out. So don't be led down that road. And those of you who are strongly charismatic, be careful that the emphasis on the Spirit doesn't wander away from the centrality of Christ. It is He who is at the centre of all that we have and are. He opens God to us, He is the instrument whereby we receive the Spirit. All one in Christ Jesus, and only in Christ Jesus.

3. Preserving the Family Characteristics (Galatians 4:1–5:6)

The question with which Paul in our study today is still trying to wrestle, for the benefit of his readers and, by the grace of God, for Christians ever since, is this: Why would God, who established a relationship with Abraham on the basis of faith, give a law through Moses so many years later?

As a speaker I am greatly encouraged to see Paul starting with what the NIV translates as 'What I am saying is. . .', for anybody who knows about speaking knows that you should never say, 'what I'm saying is. . .' But Paul understands what all of us who are speakers have to learn: that just because you say something, it isn't necessarily crystal clear to everybody who hears you say it. He knows he's already said it, he knows they should be able to understand it. But he says 'What I am saying is. . .', and he provides an illustration. I think that Paul is picking up his picture of the very young child—the baby, in verses 1–3 and then the more adult concept of 'sons' in verse 4—from what he has been writing a little earlier about God sending His son Jesus Christ.

In all this male-dominated language it's necessary to bear in mind that Paul wants to talk about inheritance; and in the first century inheritance could only pass down the male line. That is why there is so much emphasis on males in the verses we are reading. But his point in verses 1–7 is an obvious one. The child may be the heir to the entire estate, but as a child he has no right of self-determination; certainly not in the

44

first century. He's under guardians and trustees. Lightfoot translates, 'controllers of his person and property'. This is not quite the same as the guardian tutor of 3:24; now it is the person who administers the estate and doesn't ask the child what his opinions are. What the child is waiting for (verse 2) is 'the time set by his father'. In other words, there is a moment when this boy comes of age. It was usually his fourteenth birthday, but in fact legally the father had a certain amount of discretion over when the boy was allowed to become the full owner of the estate and get rid of the guardians and trustees. It's quite clear that this is linked in Paul's mind with verse 4 and 'the time had fully come.'

Now, pause for a moment. Paul is affirming here something that we Christians must never forget. Our God is a God who engages Himself in history; and we understand our God as we see Him against the context of the whole of history. That's how the last chapter ended; Paul was talking about Abraham in the past; now 'you are Abraham's seed' in the present (3:29), and because you are his seed you look to the promise which God promised through him. So we Christians don't need bifocals, we need trifocals! We need constantly to be able to look back to our history which is the foundation and affirmation of all that we are; we need constantly to be looking at the present and all that God is now doing for us and among us; and we must never forget that, as John Wesley said, 'The best is yet to be.' We must never, we Christians (and we evangelicals who love Scripture so much are perhaps in greater danger), we must never allow ourselves to be locked in the past. There is no way you can go back to your favourite period in history. God is relentlessly moving forward. But we Christians are the most broad-minded people in the world. Our vision is from beginning to beyond the end. I don't know why they call us narrow-minded—you can't get broader than that! But we have to be sure that our trifocals are working, that we properly balance the past (with all its wonderful tradition), the present (with all our experience), and the future (with all that we're hoping for).

That demands that we should be open to the question, What is God doing in history now?

Slavery to the basics (4:3)

In verse 3 Paul says, 'So also, when we were children, we
were in slavery under the basic principles of the world.'
That's a very difficult verse. You may not think so, but it is,
because it prompts the question: Who are 'we', in 'when we
were children'?

A large number of Paul's readers were obviously Gentiles.
So they weren't under the law as the Jews had been, and
which is the context in which this little metaphor seems to be
being developed. Is Paul saying 'we' in the sense of 'we
Jews'? And if he does mean 'we Jews', then why does he talk
about being under the basic principles of the world—which
is usually a phrase used about being subject to trees and days
and sun and moon and stars and so on? That sounds more
appropriate to Gentiles. So I conclude that 'we' means
'everybody who is reading the letter, Jew or Gentile', and that
Paul is saying, 'We *all* were in slavery under basic principles
of the world.' For the phrase can be translated 'rudimentary
learning', the basic alphabet, as it were (cf Hebrews 5:12,
'elementary truths'). And though it's very difficult to imagine
Paul putting the law on the level of submission to trees and
hills and so on, he is able to compare and contrast them as
inadequate ways of bringing salvation. Whether you are
coming by the route of the law, says Paul, or whether you'll
be coming by the route of serving whatever it was you saw in
nature to be served; both of those are rudimentary, elementary things that will never get you to where you want to be.

So he can say, 'We were in slavery under the basic
principles of the world, but when the time had fully come
. . .' This is the moment in history that divides two ages, the
moment when God steps in with the epoch-making event of
the coming of Jesus. 'When the time had fully come, God
sent his Son.'

This whole letter is about sending, you will recall. Right at
the very beginning, Paul wanted to establish who had sent
him. 'I don't come on behalf of man. I come on behalf of the
Lord Jesus Christ and God our Father who raised Him from
the dead. I am sent.' Then he describes himself, do you
remember, as an apostle, a 'sent one'. So the idea of being

properly sent and authorised is very much at the centre of the letter. And there arises now what I think is one of the most important truths of the New Testament. I will put it in terms of this letter: 'All forms of apostolic ministry, whatever they are, have as their model the sending of Jesus.' There is only one eternal apostle, and that is Jesus Christ. 'God sent his Son'—the verb shares the same root as does 'apostle'.

Jesus, the model for our calling (4:4–7)

So if we want to test our call, our sense of being sent, if we are asking 'Is it genuine, this call I'm feeling?'—then that's the model, there is no other. Not how your minister felt his or her call; not how preachers tell you you should or should not feel a call; there's only one model, and the model is Jesus Christ. There are books and books written about the question of priesthood, of the priesthood of parsons, of the priesthood of all believers. But there's only one priesthood because there's only one high priest, Jesus Christ our Lord. So the test of all ministry, with or without clerical collar, is this. Does it cohere with His priesthood, is it in harmony with His ministry, is it a shepherding that fits exactly His shepherding? That's the test: and you could go through a whole list—priesthood, ministry, mission, service, sonship —the New Testament is full of themes, but every time you ask for their source you're back to Jesus Christ.

My sisters and my brothers, we disagree needlessly about lots of things, but this is the one thing we all need to get absolutely clear. It is the pattern of holiness.

'Into Christ'; that's the test of the ministry, and of every ministry. He is the focal point for everything. Read, if you will, that well-known passage Philippians 2:5–11, and let it become for you the model of your whole Christian life. And the point I want you to grasp from that passage is that it is not a description of a series of events. It is a single movement. It's not a series of jerky steps, it's a single smooth progression, from glory to glory via lowly serving love. That my sister, my brother, is the model of Christian service; and there is no other.

Jesus among us (4:4–7)

At the moment God chose, Paul says, Christ was born: 'God
sent his son, born of a woman' (4:4). He was truly human.
The meaning of it is incarnation. Would you believe it? At a
moment in time, like the great moment when the boy
becomes the heir, at a moment when all the world's empires
thought they were in power, God sent His son born of a
woman, and the Godhead was among us: John 1:14, 'We
beheld his glory full of grace and truth.'

The Godhead in our midst is the pattern for our mission.
As John Stott said at the Nationwide Initiative in Evangelism
conference in Nottingham many years ago: 'Presence pre-
cedes proclamation'. If you're not there you can't tell them
the good news. But being there means incarnation among
people. I sometimes wonder whether we evangelicals don't
get too quickly to the proclamation before we've properly
explored the presence. Before people actually feel we mean
it, that we are among them, we are proclaiming. That isn't
our Lord's way, you notice. How could it be? He was born as
a baby, it was years before He could even begin to proclaim,
but all those years were the times when He was being
present among us. We need to learn the patience of God in
our mission.

An artist completed a sketch in a dozen strokes. Somebody
saw it and asked, 'How long did it take you?' The artist
replied, 'About thirty years.' How often the Old Testament
prophets and psalmists cried out, 'How long, oh Lord, how
long?' In 1 Peter 1:12 we are told that they were not
prophesying for themselves, but for us who would come
later. We are so anxious, are we not, to start something, to
carry it through to completion in our own lifetime? But so far
as I understand it, that is not how God does His work. Our
task is to contribute what God asks us to say or do and to
allow the results to be His responsibility. We are not called to
be successful, we are called to be faithful. And part of the
faithfulness is the patience which says, 'If my Lord took all
those centuries to get ready for the most significant event in
history, why am I in such a rush? Why can't I patiently trust
Him?'

We are born 'under law'—not *the* law, notice, but born under law. God's character was revealed in the law, we heard that beautifully the other evening from Charles Price. I need to remind you of something else in this context: that God's character is also revealed in everything He has made. That's what Paul says in Romans 1:18–20, one of those passages that people have great struggles with—when he is talking about how the Gentiles could be to blame for not knowing God; he says, 'The wrath of God is being revealed from heaven against all the godlessness and wickedness of men who suppress the truth by their wickedness, since what may be known about God is plain to them.'

But the Gentiles would respond, 'Paul, you're a Jew—*why* was it plain to us?'

'"Because God has made it plain to them."'

'How has God made it plain to us?'

'"For since the creation of the world God's invisible qualities, his eternal power and divine nature have been clearly seen."'

'How have they been seen?'

'"Being understood from what has been made, so that men are without excuse."'

God reveals Himself, of course, particularly in *the* law. But God is also revealed in what we see around us, if only we had eyes to see. That is the point that Paul is trying to make here: born under law, 'to redeem those under law, that we might receive the full rights of sons.' 'Redeem' is that word we've used a few times already: buying back, buying out, the soldier getting himself out of the army. It's the same word. The point to notice, which I think some modern speakers and theologians deliberately miss, is that Christ's death as a buying-back, a buying-out, is not just a demonstration of the love of God. It is not merely an act of love that moves our heart so that we respond to it. The dying of Jesus actually changes things. There is a different situation in operation after the dying of Jesus—the price has been paid, the sinners may go free.

'That we may receive the full rights of sons' may well be a reference to a first-century tradition in both the Greek and

Roman worlds where a rich childless person could actually
make a slave his heir; he could actually give somebody who
owned nothing the full rights of inheritance to the entire
estate. Can you imagine what he would have felt like? To be
raised as a slave, to have nothing but a bundle of clothing, to
have no money, to have no possessions, no rights, no
freedom to go anywhere—then suddenly the owner of the
entire estate calls you in? You would say, 'Oh dear—what
have I done wrong now?'

And then to hear the owner say, 'I've been thinking. I'd
like you to inherit it all.' Can you feel the excitement of that?
That's what Paul says has happened to us. It's as though God
calls each of us in individually and says, 'I'd like you to have
it all.' We have the full rights as sons, but we have no right to
it. But by God, we got it; we are given the full rights as sons,
because Jesus came and died for us.

Verse 6, 'Because you are sons, God sent the Spirit of his
Son into our hearts, the Spirit who calls out, "Abba,
Father." ' Notice again the lovely trinitarian teaching here:
Father, Son, Holy Spirit. They just move around in this
description of our experience. I hope we may learn two
lessons from that. One I've suggested already: the New
Testament writers didn't sit back and say 'Let's give them a
little more Trinity.' They just described how you have a full
Christian experience with the obvious implication that you
can't have it unless you relate to Father, Son and Spirit. So
my sisters and my brothers—is the doctrine alive that you
teach and are taught? And do those who hear you teaching it
say, 'Wonderful! My word, let's get out and live that.' Or do
they say: 'Uh-uh, here comes another bit of doctrine—old-
fashioned, academic, out of the books, needing a degree to
understand it . . .' That's not how it is here. It's lively, this
doctrine of the Trinity. Of course we can't understand it.
Which of you who is in love with your wife can understand
your love? Explain to me, you wives, how you love your
husbands—how do you love them? Of course we don't
understand it. But we know it and feel it make sense within
ourselves. And it doesn't stop us loving.

The second thing is (and I'm sorry if I seem almost always

to be talking about balance, but balance matters in the kingdom of God and is important in our experiencing and teaching the Trinity), that Father, Son and Holy Spirit are *all* part of full experience. The moment we begin to over-emphasise one or other, there are effects on the ministry and the life of the church itself. I leave that for you to work that one out for yourselves.

'. . . into our hearts, the Spirit who calls out, "*Abba*, Father." ' Well, there's no doubt that 'Abba', as I expect we all know, can be translated 'Daddy', but it leaves me uneasy for two reasons. Firstly because my sons, aged 29 and 27, no longer call me 'Daddy'; and I think that's probably right, because they're grown up. And there is something about that word 'Daddy' that can, if you are not careful, turn you into a perpetual Peter Pan of the Christian faith. Because He's our loving warm heavenly Father doesn't mean we haven't got to grow up and take some responsibility for ourselves. I was once in a meeting which was about to divide up into separate groups. The leader said, 'Now we are just going to have a few minutes of quiet while God tells you which group to go into.' I had thought that perhaps God was trusting *me* with that decision. Perhaps I was wrong, but it all seemed too 'Daddy-ish' to me.

Secondly, God isn't just a warm cuddly daddy. He is the awesome, transcendent maker of heaven and earth. Never lose the sense that you would do well to remove your shoes, when you call Him 'Daddy'. He's more than 'Daddy'. But thank God, He is warm and close to us. 'So you are no longer a slave, but a son; and since you are a son, God has made you also an heir.' That's a lovely word, 'since'. It can either mean 'as a proof that you're a son or an heir, or, 'as a result of your being a son, you're an heir'. I think it probably means both.

Paul's concern for the Galatians (4:8–20)

It is one thing to become an heir to the kingdom and a child of God: it's another to live appropriately. And that's why Paul has just said (verse 6) that because you put your trust in Christ for salvation, 'God sent the Spirit of his Son into our hearts'; it's one thing to accept the status, it's another thing to live appropriately. Paul is saying, 'I'm quite sure you have become sons and daughters of God, I've no doubt of it. I'm quite sure that you are heirs of the promise, I've no doubt of that either. The question I'm asking you is: Are you living like those who are the heirs of the promise?'

When people wrote to John Wesley about the great new experiences they were having, he always wrote back and asked for the evidences. Had anybody noticed that this great new spiritual happening had taken place? Were people aware of it? And this is Paul's question now. Verse 8: 'Formerly, when you did not know God, you were slaves to those who by nature are not gods.' It's hard to believe that he said that to his fellow Jews. Were they not (Genesis 18, Exodus 33, Deuteronomy 9) in a covenant relationship with God? But in Philippians 3:8 Paul, as his personal testimony, explains what he means by knowing God. He says he counts all this other stuff as rubbish, 'compared to the surpassing greatness of knowing Christ Jesus my Lord'. So this knowing God is not 'I know that I'm in covenant with Him', and it's not, 'I know I belong to the people who are His people'. It's 'I know Him personally, I have met Him by the grace of Jesus Christ and the power of the Holy Spirit.' Paul says: 'If that's been your knowledge, how can you go back to these other ways of living, how can you allow yourselves to be enslaved by rules again?'

You're free. Try telling yourselves that, in relation to the things that happen in your church. Just keep saying to one another, 'You're free' and see what happens. I suspect that you'll discover that gathered around you and carried on your shoulders are a whole set of rules and regulations that nobody ever mentions. Nobody actually *says*, 'We should do this, we should wear this, we should sit like this, we should be here or there'—but somehow we all know it. And when strangers come in, they are totally puzzled by it, like the little boy who said to his mother half-way through the sermon, 'Mummy, what will we do if that man gets out of that box?'

Paul is saying, 'For heaven's sake—for God's sake, for Christ's sake—stop living under rules. You are free, the world is ours.' It's the meek who inherit the kingdom, the earth belongs to us. But we don't live like it. We live like people who need to hide in churches lest the world should reach us. This is my Father's world! I'm free in Christ Jesus, free to inherit the kingdom, free!

I'm sorry, I'm getting excited! But how can you possibly settle for anything less than freedom? Why don't people join us? Because they can see we are tied up in chains.

'I plead with you, brothers,' he says (he would have written 'sisters and brothers' now), 'become like me, for I became like you.' Well, that's one translation. It can mean, 'be frank with me as I'm being frank with you.' It can mean, 'be open to me as I'm trying to be open to you.' Or it can mean, as it is translated here, 'become like me for I became like you,' meaning (he is thinking of the Gentiles now), 'I, a Jew, have stopped trying to save myself through the law in order to be saved through Christ. So I've become like a Gentile. What on earth are you doing trying to become like Jews? Why are you Gentiles now taking the law on board? That's not the way to be saved at all.'

Verse 13, 'As you know, it was because of an illness that I first preached the gospel to you.' I have no idea what that illness was. Luke tells us nothing about it in Acts, just as he tells us nothing about a lot of things that we'd like to know about. It would enable us to become more and more antiquarian. If only we knew all the details! Who are all these people? Where did they live? Who did they marry? Who were their children? What jobs did they do? It would be wonderful, we could be there for ever! But the New Testament is written on a need-to-know basis. We are told what we need to know, and I therefore need to know that Paul evidently wasn't too well when he first preached the gospel; and beyond that I have no idea.

'Even though my illness was a trial to you, you did not treat me with contempt or scorn. Instead, you welcomed me as if I were an angel of God, as if I were Christ Jesus himself.' Now, whatever was that illness? (You see, I'm going to fall into the trap I've just described!) Was it what he refers to in 2 Corinthians 12:7, the 'thorn in the flesh' that kept on making him humble? If it was, I still don't know what it is. Was it malaria? At that time there were swamps in Pamphilia.

Was it his eyesight? In verse 15 he says, 'You would have torn out your eyes and given them to me'; in 6:11 he says, 'See what large letters I use as I write to you.' Was it epilepsy, I wonder? He points out that they might have been put off by it. Or was it just fair wear and tear, which any of us who travel around conventions know all about? Read 2 Corinthians 11:23–29 sometime and ask whether you wouldn't feel ill occasionally if you had all that done to you!

John Ziesler comments, 'In fact all speculation is fruitless, if more than a little addictive.' But in fact, what Paul is revealing here is the extreme vulnerability of the Christian leader. He said, 'Last time I came to you you would think I was Christ Jesus Himself.' Imagine Paul writing that: '. . . You would think I were Christ Jesus Himself, the way you dealt with me. Why, you would have plucked out your eyes and given them to me' (cf verse 15).

Verse 15a: 'What has happened to all your joy?' Arndt and Gingrich translate that, 'The frame of mind in which you blessed yourselves.' That's beautiful. 'What happened to that lovely open attitude you had to me, through which God blessed you again and again?' Verse 16: 'Have I now become your enemy by telling you the truth?' You preachers, just savour that for a minute or two. It is possible as a preacher never to upset anybody. I know, because I've heard it done often. But the preacher who tells the truth will have to face the point where he sees in the eyes, even at a convention as big as this, the questions, the resentments. 'Have I become your enemy by telling you the truth?' What a hard question that is! That's how vulnerable the preacher, the pastor is. Every new sermon is a risk. And the most risky ones are the ones you have preached before—especially if they went well last time, because then you are in danger of trusting to yourself or your material and not to the Lord.

And you who are not preachers; cherish (I'm sure you do, but I say this in case you don't), cherish your preachers. Not because we are a special race, but because we are especially vulnerable, because we need the love and the support and the correction of the congregations. 'Oh,' says Paul, 'I feel so vulnerable writing to you people, I thought you loved me and now you are treating me like an enemy.'

We need not spend too much time on verses 17–20, but at their centre is something very deep. Paul is saying that the trouble with 'those people'—we don't know who they are—in their zeal (a many-sided word which could mean 'jealous', 'pampering' or 'making a lot of') are either jealous of the Galatians so are trying to make them like themselves, or are pampering them in order to get them to join them. But the real aim is sectarian. They want to take them away from the main body of the Christian church for themselves.

Professor Bosch, a South African Calvinist church historian and theologian, wrote a very significant paper some years ago in which he remarked that the different major denominations in Christian history can each be characterised by a particular emphasis within the single gospel of Jesus Christ. The Anglican Church, for example, characteristically lays great emphasis on incarnation. It's characteristic of the Lutheran Church to emphasise the cross. The Orthodox Church emphasises the resurrection. The Pentecostal Church, obviously, makes much of Pentecost. The Seventh-Day Adventists, he says, emphasise the second coming, and so on. He continues, 'I remain a convinced Calvinist. But if I remain a convinced Calvinist in a way that excludes everybody else, I have become a sectarian-convinced Calvinist.' That is a very significant statement, from a Calvinist theologian. I speak as an Arminian Methodist. And I ask you to ponder it. If I hold to what I hold, that's fine and good before God. But if I hold to it in a way which is meant to exclude everybody else, to snatch as many as I can to my way, I become sectarian. And Paul says, that's not the right way to use your zeal.

The story of Hagar and Sarah (4:21–31)

In these verses we have the lovely story of Abraham, Sarah and Hagar. Paul is taking his readers back again to their Jewish history, because it seems that his opponents made a lot of their Jewish background and particularly of Moses and the law. So Paul says: 'Well, let's make a little journey back down into our history', using this story which you can follow in Genesis 15 onwards.

It's about two women: Hagar the slave woman and Sarah the free wife.

It's about two sons: Ishmael born by Hagar and Isaac born by Sarah.

It's about two ways in which a child is born: Ishmael, *kata sarka*, 'according to the flesh', which I think means Abraham taking matters into his own hands in order to make sure he had an heir; Isaac, 'according to the promise', which is Abraham saying, 'It's impossible but I'll trust you.' It's not a comment on Abraham's sexual life, it's about whether you say, 'I'll do this even though I'm not sure it's the right way to do it—the end will justify the means', or whether you wait for the promise of God to be fulfilled.

It's about two covenants: Sinai which produces slaves, and has as its equivalent modern Jerusalem ('earthly' Jerusalem, as Paul puts it); and the Jerusalem above, the heavenly Jerusalem, which is free (cf Hebrews 11:10, 12:22; Revelation 3:12, 21:1-27).

It's about two powers (verse 29): the flesh and the Spirit, the child of the flesh persecuted the child of the Spirit.

It's about two results: one enters into the kingdom and the other does not.

And at the bottom, it's about two attitudes: the unbelief whereby Abraham tries to arrange things for himself, and the belief by which he believes God's promise.

And at the centre of all of that, the expression twice appears, *gegraptai gar*, 'it has been written'. The Jewish scribes and Pharisees would use 'it is written' as their argument, and the phrase was one of the things that the Christians took over as reliable tradition. If you know your Gospels at all you'll know why. When Jesus was tempted by Satan, again and again He said, 'it is written'. The Scriptures are not meant to be interesting commentaries on the Christian life. They are not meant to be a set of helpful reflections by those who were there which will guide us on our way, though, of course, from time to time it will be necessary to say how wrong Paul got it, or Peter got it . . . No! That's not what the Scriptures are. They are God's breathed word to us, so that we may say, 'It is written'.

That doesn't mean that our interpretations of it are always infallible, but it does mean that our attitude to it should be 'This is God's word to me. I take it, I learn it, I love it, I obey it, I take it with me when I seek to understand what God is doing in the world, and if I can say "It is written" then I'm on a firm foundation.'

Paul says 'it is written'. It's the difference between Hagar and Sarah. 'And I'm inviting you now,' he says, 'to make up your mind which way you want to go.'

Now, I hope that we evangelical Christians don't doubt that this is God's word, and that God's mission is His mission to the world. We are privileged, if we will, to join that mission, Scripture in hand. And our privilege as part of the mission of God is to make sense of what God is doing in the world, in the light of what He has said in the word. Every preacher should be seen to be standing on two feet, one in the first century and one in the twentieth, and should be seen to be taking the strain. I've heard a lot of right-footed preachers; I've heard left-footed preachers; and I've heard 'rockers'. The biblical preacher tries to understand the subject he's talking about and the world in which he's living, and he won't allow himself just to stick texts on it as some sort of a solution. The question is: How do the principles that emerge from this wonderful book now apply, in a world so different from that in which the principles were written? Sometimes the applications in the first century no longer apply to the twentieth century. I don't have a lot of trouble in Cheam with meat offered to idols; it's not a great problem going to the butcher. But the underlying principle is, how will my behaviour affect the conscience of my brother? That was, and is, a very important principle. And we who love the word must learn so to understand world affairs, and the affairs around us, and the affairs in our own home and family, that when we speak, 'it is written', we are standing on two feet. Then those who are looking (as many desperately are) for some kind of solution will be able to say, 'At last, here are some people who understand God's will and can relate it to the modern world.' When people ask me why I am a Christian, the greatest possible reasons are a) 'because it is true' and b) 'because it makes sense'. My sisters and my brothers, we are called to make sense.

Christ's gift is freedom (5:1–6)

Now lastly, 5:1, 'It is for freedom that Christ has set us free. Stand firm, then, and do not let yourselves be burdened again by a yoke of slavery.'

There's a lot of controversy in there. When we come to Christ, how much do we have to work in order to stay with Christ? The Calvinists and the Arminians argue over it; and it's so unnecessary. It's like taking a flower apart and saying 'Now there's a sepal, there's a petal, there's a stamen and there's a stem . . . ' The trouble is, when you've done all that you haven't got a flower any more, you've just got pieces.

It's as if somebody were to explain to you in precise detail how to walk or how to breathe. But we need both the left foot and the right, we need to breath in as often as we need to breath out, and if we forget that, we become ill. A reasonable equality is required all the time. And in just the same way we need God's grace to keep us, and we need to be supporting and serving Him every minute of the day. Both are needed. Don't let's argue about which is most important—let's do it! Paul says, 'You've been set free, now stand firm.' Don't let anybody steal it from you. Left leg, right leg; in, out; be healthy, be free.

'Mark my words! I, Paul, tell you that if you let yourselves be circumcised' (he's talking to Gentiles now) 'Christ will be of no value to you at all.' Look on to verse 4: 'You who are trying to be justified by law have been alienated from Christ.' Look at verse 5—it's an absolute Pandora's box of jewels —'But by faith we eagerly await through the Spirit the righteousness for which we hope.' What a verse that is! We could have spent an hour on it alone. By faith—we wait—eagerly—in hope—for the righteousness that is to be revealed. It's not all tied up for us. We have to live by faith. We haven't got everything yet, so we hope for it.

But it also means we haven't seen the best yet. The preacher and scholar Arthur Skevington Wood went to

Washington to preach. As his cab passed a famous statue he noticed that it carried the inscription, 'All history is prologue.' He said to the cab driver, 'What does that mean —"All history is prologue"?' And the driver thought for a while and then said, 'I guess it means, "You ain't seen nothing yet".'

'By faith we eagerly await through the Spirit the righteousness for which we hope' . . . 'It is for freedom that Christ has set you free . . . do not let yourselves be burdened again.'

4. Displaying the Spirit's Fruits (Galatians 5:7–6:18)

The passage for our last study ended on a verse about which I hadn't time to talk in detail: Galatians 5:6, 'The only thing that counts is faith expressing itself through love.' That's a remarkable statement, and I believe that the rest of the letter is virtually a commentary on it. How does faith express itself through love?

Paul begins in a somewhat negative way, because he is aware that the people to whom he is writing are being hindered in their attempt to express their faith through love. Verse 7, 'You were running a good race. Who cut in on you' (a rather liberal interpretation of the text, but very good in the racing context!) 'and kept you from obeying the truth?' The Christian faith is a race, it's not a ride. It's not about getting on board and being safe for ever after, it's about starting up on the race track. 'Who cut in on you and kept you from obeying the truth?'

The trouble-makers (5:7–12)

Notice that Paul's commentary on the race is very special and specific: 'Who . . . kept you from obeying the truth?' I ask you to take that with very great seriousness. 'Obeying the truth'. A large part of the Christian life is obedience. We are not called just to receive, believe and claim the truth; we are called to obey the truth. In 1 Peter 1:14 there's a lovely phrase translated as 'obedient children'. The text says 'as children of obedience'. If God is our father, obedience is our

60

mother. Jesus said, 'If you love me you will keep my commandments.' And one New Testament scholar wrote, I think very daringly, 'Eighty percent of love in the New Testament is obedience.' I stress this because we are in danger in our day, both religiously and in terms of our culture, of interpreting love as warm feelings within us; or of interpreting love as liking people, things, verses, passages or teaching. Love in the New Testament is about obedience to His will. I beg you to notice that, before we go any further.

'Persuasion' in verse 8 is a kind of pun, for it's from the same root as the word 'obeying' in verse 7 and the word for 'confidence' in verse 10. So, you see, this obedience runs through the passage deep down, even when you can't see it.

Verse 8: 'That kind of persuasion does not come from the one who calls you.' Let me interpolate something else here. The God we serve is a consistent God. He works consistently, He works in keeping with what He has been in the past. It isn't possible for God now to declare something that is out of harmony with what He once declared. And in His dealings with us God is a consistent God. I worry sometimes, because there is growing among us a kind of spirituality which affirms that the most bizarre things that happen to us must be the things most clearly from God. Our God is a reasonable God. He gave us the gift of reason; our God is a consistent God.

I worry about young people who are always looking for dramatic signs of God's will, when what He's actually saying is, 'Why don't you just get on and do what I've got you doing now?' In Paul's journeys, as we see from the Acts of the Apostles, he normally went where it was logical to go next. He went to the cities, because that's where most people were. When he got to a city he went to a synagogue, because that's where the Jewish people were. It was the most logical thing to do. But occasionally he would have a vision or a dream, or would be stopped from going somewhere. And then he said, 'All right Lord, I've plainly not got this quite right. What *am* I supposed to be doing?' If he's not allowed into the synagogue, well—he goes anywhere else where he can find groups of believers. But basically Paul's affirmation is in a God who is consistent, consistent with what He has been, consistent with what He now is, and consistent with what He will be.

Let's lean confidently on our consistent God. And that ties in very much with what we have heard already in this Convention about the importance of the mind in the Christian faith.

Verse 9: '"A little yeast works through the whole batch of dough."' You'll notice that that is in inverted commas, I think because it was a saying that Paul often used. Even Paul evidently repeated himself! You'll find him expressing the same thought in 1 Corinthians 5:6.

And yeast was important. It was forbidden in sacrifices (Exodus 34:25). And you remember from 1 Corinthians 5:7–8 the care with which the house was gone through at the time of unleavened bread, so that all leavened bread might be removed. Paul is saying: 'These people who come in and tell you that you've got to do other things than believe in Christ—it's like having yeast in your dough; let a little in and you never know what's going to happen.' Once let into your Christian thinking the idea that other things are required in addition to salvation by grace through Christ and faith in Christ alone—and who knows where you'll end up?

Verse 10, 'I am confident in the Lord that you will take no other view.' That might mean either, 'My judgement is in the Lord', or it might be, 'I am united with you in the Lord, and so am confident.' And since these people, the true followers, are trying to get away, maybe that's Paul's meaning; he is re-affirming his confidence in them in the Lord. They are one in the Lord, and therefore he is confident that they won't take another view. There's the hopefulness of the pastor again.

'The one who is throwing you into confusion will pay the penalty, whoever he may be.' Was it, I wonder, somebody highly placed in Jerusalem? Are we thinking about somebody who actually was quite near to James the Lord's brother, since in Acts 15 James has to say that certain people went out 'from us'? Perhaps somebody quite high up was getting matters badly mixed up. 'He'll bear God's judgement,' Paul says. And that word 'bear' is the same word used in John 19:17 for the bearing of the cross to Golgotha. He will bear the judgement of God.

In verse 11 Paul is defending himself yet again. 'Brothers, if I am still preaching circumcision, why am I still being persecuted?' That word 'still' is interesting. When did Paul preach it before? It may be a reference to his pre-Damascus Road days, though it's odd that he should be using the word 'preaching' for that. It may be that his critics are saying, 'Well of course, Paul believes in being all things to all men.' He was going to write that later in 1 Corinthians 9:20, and later, you recall, he was going to allow Timothy to be circumcised. Maybe they were misinterpreting Paul's flexibility, and are saying, 'Well—Paul is still preaching circumcision.' Maybe, they even genuinely believed that Paul agreed with them.

I think that of the three the first is most likely; that Paul was saying 'There was a time when I would have told you to be circumcised, because I believed that was the way through, but no longer. And the sign that I am no longer preaching it is, that I am being persecuted up hill and down dale by Jewish people.' And he asks, 'If I am preaching what they like, why are they persecuting me? It's obvious. They know that what I am preaching is the end of any addition to Christ's death and resurrection for our sin. In that case, the offence of the cross has been abolished. Anything you add to it will take away from it. It's as simple as that.' And then verse 12, I have to tell you, is really rather coarse: 'As for those agitators, I wish they would go the whole way and emasculate themselves!' I think Paul actually means 'castrate'. He is so angry about people who would lead others away from the truth that he allows that explosion of anger against them.

The abuse of freedom (5:13–15)

In these verses we come to what is really the abuse of freedom. Paul is aware of two difficulties. On one hand, there is the difficulty that people will slip back into the law.

On the other, there is the difficulty that being free of law, the new believers will use their freedom to indulge themselves.

It has been a danger from the beginning that antinomianism—the rejection of discipline of any kind—would slip in once one preached freedom. That's the risk we take. So now Paul, having warned again against adding things to the law, now warns against the indulgence that might come the other way. 'You, my brother, were called to be free. But do not use your freedom to indulge the sinful nature.' It means, do not use your freedom as a spring-board for the flesh ('flesh', you remember, means the whole of a person susceptible to temptation); don't use your freedom as a spring-board from which to launch yourself in all kinds of indulgence. So Paul is saying that on one side we are not to add anything new, and on the other we are never to allow ourselves to become indulgent. This relates to something I said yesterday. It's one thing to become an adopted heir, it's another thing to know how to behave like one. Do you remember how Paul affirms that the Spirit is given within us, by whom we cry, 'Dear Father' to God, in order that we will not go down the road of indulgence. But now Paul adds something. We have to co-operate. We have to be minded to go down that way. Christianity is about mind and will as well as about emotion and faith, and Paul is reminding these people that even though we are made heirs of the kingdom and the Holy Spirit is given within our lives, we will not be dragooned into being holy. We are called with body, mind, strength and will to give ourselves to living like the heirs of the kingdom. And that means, not using our freedom as a way of indulging ourselves.

So, 'Serve one another in love,' he says: love your neighbour as yourself—'The entire law is summed up in a single command.'

He's now focusing on the danger of being libertine, on the danger within the congregation. He is telling them that a real test for the way they love everybody outside is their love for one another. 'If you keep on biting and devouring each other, watch out or you will be destroyed by each other.'

We need to spend a few moments on the words, 'the entire law is summed up in a single command'. 'Summed up' has the sense of 'summing up an argument'. But the word also has the sense of 'carrying out', of 'putting into practice'. Paul is saying that the single command 'Love your neighbour as yourself' will do, as love expressing itself Christianly; faith expressing itself in love is enough.

So we are not dominated by rules, we are dominated by relationships. In this new way of living, our self is given an affirmation, not a denial. God is saying to us, 'I do not discount you, I account you. I am not saying "You are called to be the children of the inheritance; I give you My spirit so your self is somehow destroyed in this experience." Quite the opposite. I am asking you—your mind, soul, body, will—"Give yourself, because you matter".' Somebody put it to me at this Convention, 'We have to learn to accept the view of ourselves that our heavenly Father has.' He was using the argument that it's known that we actually define who we are by the way we are treated by the people who love us most from the earliest days; they give us our sense of who we are. And this person was saying to me that what Paul was talking about here is that we are called to accept God's view of us, the loving heavenly Father who says, 'You can't save yourselves; I save you. You can't have the strength to live the life of heirs of the kingdom, I give you My Spirit. But I also say to you, you matter so much that I want you to know that you are loved and affirmed, and are part of this deal. You won't make anything happen. But I ask you to be lovingly part of it.'

And if we say 'What does that mean?', the answer is that our attitudes and actions are to be determined by love: 'Was that a loving thing to do—to say—to think?'

Now we touch on something that may worry people. What I have just said does *not* preclude absolutes of good and evil. Certainly the Christian knows that some things are wrong and other things are right; but as we shall see, the reason wrong things are wrong is that they're unloving, and the reason that right things are right is that they are in harmony with love. What it *does* preclude, I believe, is the cult in our present culture that life is all about self-development, about 'my', about building up 'myself' as fully as I can, to enjoy as much of the world as is available and if other people get in the way—that's just too bad. Paul's teaching is wholly opposed to that view.

But it does give us freedom to face new challenges that Christians have never faced before. It gives us a way of picking our footsteps through some of those complex problems we face. The Medical Seminar in this Convention has been addressing some of them. We desperately need some guidance as to how to respond to these new situations. And this law of love, if I may so put it, calls us to that. And because it is a law of love which calls us wholly—being affirmed to play our part—it means we've got to be ready for the hard praying, hard thinking, hard fellowship together, when we discover together how love will respond to new situations that are developing, not only in medical ethics but in almost every area of our lives.

The church, says Paul, is meant to be the model for how the world could be. God wants to say to the world, 'Look at that fellowship. Wouldn't it be wonderful if all the world were like that?' Would you like God to write that in the sky over your fellowship, just at the moment? 'Wouldn't it be wonderful if all the world was like the church he or she belongs to?' That's how it's meant to be. They are meant to know who our God is, what our God intends through who we are day by day.

Now, Paul says: Which way do you want to go, my sisters and brothers? Do you want to go to glory with Jesus, or do you want to keep trying to add bits and pieces which means you'll lose the way all together? You'll never find it. Make up your mind now which way you want to go. I ask you: Are you in the business of being free? Are you in the business of relying on Christ alone through faith? Then—for God's sake—be it; and don't fiddle about with any other ways that promise things they can't deliver. Trust yourself to Christ alone.

The flesh and the Spirit (5:16–18)

Now Paul puts it in slightly different language. Here are the main combatants in the struggle: the flesh—human nature susceptible to temptation—and the Spirit. John Stott says, 'We may say the flesh stands for what we are by natural birth, the Spirit what we become by new birth, the birth of the Spirit. And these two, the flesh and the Spirit, are in sharp opposition to each other.'[1]

Paul makes it abundantly plain. There is no sudden annihilation of the flesh, because the flesh is us: we are the flesh. You can't annihilate my flesh without annihilating me, because the flesh is not merely a part of me—if only it were! Then we could amputate it. But the flesh is the whole of me, in my weakness, temptation and susceptibility to temptation and sin. That's WHAT the flesh is. But the Spirit who is given by the Father occupies this body, which can be flesh-controlled or can be Spirit-controlled. And Paul says the battle goes on and on day after day.

You will remember what Charles Price told us about the law of gravity and the law of aerodynamics.[2] What is it that stops you from falling from an aeroplane? The law of aerodynamics. What is that will cause you to fall in the Christian life? The law of gravity, the flesh. What will keep you rising in the Christian life? The Spirit. But in flying there is no point at which gravity isn't working. It's always happening, all the time. And therefore the Keswick teaching has always been—as I understand it from reading through the various books and accounts of the talks—that the Christian life from start to finish is a battle with the flesh, a struggle against our temptations and the way in which we fall to them. But it can be a victorious struggle, in which we are steadily lifted more and more into the likeness of Christ, or, as Paul put it in the passage we studied yesterday, 'until Christ is formed within you' (4:19).

I remember the story told at this Convention by Stephen Barabas, about a sailor who endured years of drudgery, scrubbing the deck on his hands and knees because the Bosun had taken a dislike to him. And then one day he was summoned to see the Captain, and went full of foreboding that the Bosun had been causing trouble for him yet again. The Captain pointed to some papers. 'Do you know what those are?'

The sailor said, 'No sir, I don't.'

'They are your papers of release,' said the Captain. 'You've served your time. Go and pack your bags.'

The sailor was packing his bags at his bunk and he heard the familiar sound of the Bosun approaching.

'What d'you think you're doing?'

'I'm packing my bags, Bosun,' he said quietly.

'Well get upstairs and scrub the deck!'

'I won't scrub another deck for you, Bosun, or for anybody else. These are my papers of release, Bosun.'

And he walked off the ship and through the gates, and to anybody who tried to stop him he simply said, 'I'm free, I'm free.'

Now, my sisters and my brothers, that's how the Christian life is. Sin has no right over us. Temptation has no right to drag us down. We're free in the Spirit. If I may use my dog Abigail as an illustration—she doesn't like shadows at night and when taken for a night-time walk will pull away from them. So I say to her, as warmly and encouragingly as I can, 'Abigail; it's only a shadow.' One night I thought, that's how it is, this idea that we are somehow obliged to sin. It's a shadow, a myth, a mirage. It's invented by the evil one. The Spirit enables us to have victory.

That's what Paul is expressing here. We'll never be out of the battle, but we certainly don't have to be overcome by it.

The acts of sin (19–21)

Let us move on to verse 19. 'The acts of the sinful nature are obvious . . .', and a list follows. 'Immorality', meaning general immorality, particularly unlawful sexual intercourse; 'impurity', meaning fornication with an emphasis on impurity (it's the word that's also used for rubbish, and especially anything that defiles); 'debauchery', which has the idea of blatant sexual offence. Let me say something in passing about those three together, because they are all predominantly sexual sins. Sometimes people say today that of course there's no substantial discussion of such matters as homosexual practice in the New Testament, that Jesus didn't even mention it, and so on. The same is said about cohabitation before marriage, and similar issues. But I think we have to remind ourselves that these words in Galatians 5 are catch-all words. They are not specific words about a particular activity, they are deliberately general and vague because they include all forms of unlawful sexual activity, all forms of impurity, all forms of blatant sexual activity. They're all incorporated in these words.

'Idolatry' means what you'd expect it to mean, and Romans 1:18ff gives a good list of some of the offences it covers. But it also involves the idea of greed, and I would remind us that anything which is legitimate in itself, which takes precedence over everything else in our lives, has become idolatry. Anything that takes the place of God, or anything that's being used in a way other than God intended, is idolatry; let's not forget that.

The word used for 'witchcraft' is actually the one from which we get the English word 'pharmacy'. I can only assume that means there were drugs involved, though it touches on much modern-day religion, not least the importance accorded to astrology in much of our culture today.

Those are the religious sins. The social ones follow: 'hatred'—hostility of attitude and action; 'discord'—strife or contention; 'jealousy', *zelos*, which can mean 'zeal' which can be a good thing, but here it's meant as an envious activity; 'fits of rage'—angry outbursts; 'selfish ambition'—the idea of disputes, with the aim of securing something for yourself (it's a very rare word); 'dissension'—heated disagreements; 'factions', which refers to sectarianism and exclusive groups; 'envy', which is zeal without any good aspects; then 'drunkenness' and 'orgies', which simply have to do with excess. Finally, 'and the like', just in case the list hasn't included your particular sin.

Now, the point of this list is not that it is meant to be exhaustive. It is not meant to allow you to say, 'Well, if my sins aren't in there I'm all right.' The point of the list is to express the direction in which we are going: are we on the narrow road of Jesus, or the broad road? The Christian who willingly goes down any of these broad roads is a delinquent, one who sins without concern for the consequences. We are entering into delinquency if we behave like this, because we are putting ourselves on the road that leads to destruction. And it makes no sense at all. Not only will we be caught, we are already caught. He knows about our sin, we can't hide it.

Oh! says Paul, why would anybody want to be going down any of those roads? 'I warn you, as I did before, that those who live like this will not inherit the kingdom of God.'

Let me make it clear that 'those who live like this' is a present participle. It is referring to a continuous style of life. And it is those who willingly and deliberately commit themselves to this kind of life who will not inherit the kingdom of God. As we shall see in a moment or two, it is not about the unfortunate slip. It is not about that moment when we longed to do the right thing but did the wrong one. It's about a regular style of life that Paul is speaking.

So we have to stop and reflect that the gospel passes judgement on our society, and that we are meant to be God's example to everybody else about how it could be. We have to face the fact that the way our culture is going is precisely down this broad road. Some of the things in Paul's list could almost be a description of much that goes on in our culture. But in the midst of it all, we have to be aware that we ourselves are split up into sects so that we are not able to do the good work we are meant to do for the kingdom of God. And it means that as we as a culture reap the harvest of the sixties and the seventies, the world desperately needs people who can show how the word of God offers something different.

The fruit of the Spirit (5:22–26)

Verse 22: 'But the fruit of the Spirit is love, joy, peace, patience, kindness, goodness, faithfulness, gentleness and self-control. Against such things there is no law.' I won't go down through the list; you can find out the various meanings if you wish to (incidentally, if you are wondering what book on Galatians to buy, I do most warmly recommend John Stott's *The Message of Galatians* in 'The Bible Speaks Today' series[3]). You can look up the meanings of all these different qualities of the Spirit. You may well be familiar with their meanings already.

I do want to say one thing. Not everybody has all the *gifts* of the Spirit, thank God for that; though each of us has at least a gift, thank God for that! The gifts are diverse and different people among us have different gifts for the building up of the Body. But the *fruit* of the Spirit that is listed in verses 22 and 23—all of the fruit is for everybody. We may have only one gift, but we're meant to have all the fruit. So don't read down that list saying, 'Well I'm all right on two, five and seven', like the university examiner in David Shepperd's story who, asked to read the Old Testament lesson by the Curate found himself reading the Ten Commandments; and having been marking examination papers all week, instead of saying 'Here endeth the lesson', concluded 'Only four of these need be attempted in the allotted time . . .'

That isn't how it is with the fruit of the Spirit. All fruit are meant to be in us. As a matter of fact, that list makes not a bad description of our Lord Jesus Christ Himself. The formation of Christ in us takes place as we, by the grace of God, allow ourselves to be filled with the fruit of the Spirit.

Verse 24—just in case we've missed it—'Those who belong to Christ Jesus have crucified the sinful nature with its passions and desires.' The verb 'have crucified' is an aorist tense, which it means it's done at a particular time and completed then. You and I know when we gave ourselves to Jesus Christ, whether in a moment or over a period of time; and our baptism, whatever form it took, was meant to celebrate this—we gave ourselves to Jesus Christ. We were saying, as we learnt in 2:20, 'I am crucified with Christ.' The selfish life is put behind me. Those who belong to Christ have crucified the sinful nature. Who crucifies it? I do, by recognising that His death gathers me into the drama, and I say to myself, that's an end to that. And those of us who have become Christians look upon all this list of awful things that Paul's been talking about, and we simply say in Christ, 'We're finished with that.' There is a custom in some parts of the world when people are baptised, that they turn from the world and face Christ and say, 'No turning back.'

So, my sisters and my brothers, what's holding up your holiness? What's standing in the way of your Christian development? Is it a relationship, is it a habit, is it a lack of trust in God, is it a demand for something that God doesn't seem to want to give? Is it an unwillingness to do what God is calling you to do? Well, be finished with that. That has been crucified with Christ.

Now learn to walk in the Spirit, says Paul. Verse 25: 'Since we live by the Spirit, let us keep in step with the Spirit.' It's the Spirit who leads us, it is we who do the walking. 'Let us not become conceited, provoking and envying each other.'

Caring for others and being accountable (6:1–7)

So finally to chapter 6, and we have to look at it very quickly.

In verses 1–5 we see how people should be cared for. And this reinforces what I've said before: 'If someone is caught in a sin' can mean trapped in the sense of overtaken, which is what I was talking about earlier. Or it can mean caught in the act. But either way, it's not about the consistent, deliberate doing of sin with which Paul deals in 1 Corinthians 5. Here he is talking about the person who is overtaken in a fault; it just happens to that person. Well, 'You who are spiritual should restore him gently.'

'But watch yourself, or you also may be tempted.' How many times I have the sad task of chairing disciplinary committees against ministers. How often the sexual sin is committed by a male minister, trying to help a female member of the congregation who is in some kind of emotional or marital trouble; getting gradually more and more involved with that person, until the line is crossed from being a minister who cares, to being a person sexually involved. 'Oh,' says Paul, 'you who are spiritual, by all means help other people—but do watch yourself.'

So 'carry each other's burdens'—that is, carry the daily burden of life; that's what love does.

Verse 3: 'If anyone thinks he is something when he is nothing, he deceives himself.' I'm sure that the reference is to the leader of the trouble-makers. Then Paul goes on to talk about accountability: 'Each one should carry his own load.' He's talking about being finally accountable; the 'carrying one another's burdens' he has just talked of is about the daily problems, today, and of course we help one another with those. But 'each one should carry his own burdens' is a forward-looking matter beyond the daily here-and-now. Paul is reminding us: I am accountable for what I do. My words and actions are being recorded on video and tape; it's all recorded; I am accountable for all I have said. And you are accountable for how you have listened. We are all accountable.

In verse 6 we find that lovely comment, 'Anyone who receives instruction in the word must share all good things with his instructor.' I think that's a defence of ministers being paid for! And then in verses 7 and onwards, the lovely agricultural picture. How many of you have said, 'I wonder what the garden will look like when I get back from Keswick?' Why is that? Surely if you're not doing anything to the garden, nothing will happen to it—will it? No! You see, whether you're there or not, something's going on all the time. What we do is co-operate with this incredible power that seems to have the capacity to produce more weeds than flowers if you leave it to itself. 'Exactly!' says Paul. 'That's all I'm asking you to do. There is a spiritual power at work in your life: the Holy Spirit given to you. What I'm asking from you is that you recognise that, and live in conjunction with Him. So let's not have any of these weeds I've been talking to you about. Let's have only fruit growing in this garden; because be sure—whatever you sow you reap.'

Paul's farewell (6:14–18)

I must finish now, and I want to end these studies with Paul's final words. Verse 14, 'May I never boast except in the cross of our Lord Jesus Christ, through which the world has been crucified to me, and I to the world.'

Paul is using the word 'world' in the same way that he used the word 'flesh'. 'Flesh' means the whole of us as susceptible to sin; 'world', in this setting, means the whole of the created universe as capable of going the wrong way. Paul says that just as I am crucified to my own sinful nature that wants to go that way, so I am crucified to anything in the world that takes away from God's grace and goodness.

But what follows from that is, I am alive! I am risen to everything in the world that is for good. It doesn't mean that we are to cut ourselves off from the created universe and from our culture. Quite the opposite, it means that we should be getting in there witnessing to what it's like to be crucified with Christ. 'Neither circumcision nor uncircumcision means anything; what counts is a new creation,' says Paul, and I wish we had time to explore that verse fully. Verses 16–17: 'Peace and mercy to all who follow this rule, even to the Israel of God. Finally, let no-one cause me trouble, for I bear on my body the marks of Jesus.' I could weep at that. Here is Paul travelling the world—look at 2 Corinthians 11 again, that awful list of what they did to him—he's travelling the world, concerned for them all: 'I bear on my body the marks of Jesus.' He doesn't mean cuts and scars, he just means the wear and tear of serving the Lord and living at the foot of the cross.

I have in my study a print of Rembrandt called 'Paul in Prison'. I could weep every time I look at it. He is sitting there, an old man, one slipper on and one slipper off. The manuscript's in front of him, his pen is in his hand. His travelling bags are there, and a sword, and the evidence of journeys. His hair needs washing; it's straggling back from his forehead; his face is lined. And his eyes just look straight through you. He's sitting there looking out into the future —Paul in prison. The eyes are the eyes of heaven. It is such a moving picture: 'I bear in my body the marks of Christ, don't trouble me.'

My sisters and my brothers, that's the call, at the end of the day. The joy, the blessing and the happiness of the faith come through bearing on our bodies the marks of Christ, through being crucified with Christ, and risen to serve with Him. If you go that way, you're free.

So be free!

Notes

1. John Stott, *The Message of Galatians* (see n.3 below), p.146.
2. Charles Price's address 'The Law of Life' had been given at the Convention on the previous Tuesday. It is included in the present volume, p. 168.
3. Stott, John R. W., *The Message of Galatians: Only One Way* (IVP: The Bible Speaks Today series, 1991).

Dare to be Different: Studies in Daniel 1–6

by Rev Alistair Begg

1. Chosen, Called and Faithful (Daniel 1)

Some of us have known the Book of Daniel since our Sunday School days. For others of us, to dip into Daniel is a completely new experience. Down through the years, the Book of Daniel and the message it contains has tended to be obscured by a number of factors.

On one level it has been obscured by what we may call *intellectual contempt*, and those who have read theology will know that the Book of Daniel like other Old Testament books has not been unscathed by critical scholars. I don't intend to get into that, but merely to acknowledge the controversy. Suffice it to say that the crisis of intellectualism has obscured the message of the book, and diminished the desire of some to study. And that's a shame.

Another factor impinging on the study of Daniel has been what we may call *eschatological confusion*. All the best sermons I've heard on Daniel I couldn't actually find in the book when I searched for them later. Some students of Daniel have become so preoccupied with prophetic details and apocalyptic visions that most of us sitting under their instruction are in danger of missing the big picture and even the message of the book itself.

And thirdly, the Book of Daniel has been obscured to some degree by *devotional preaching*, of the kind that pays scant attention to its context and the historicity, preferring to launch immediately into such applications as 'When life is a

furnace', or 'How to deal with your lion's den'. Which is not
to say that those things are wrong, but simply that they may
be dealt with without any consideration of the nature,
historicity and overall theological content of the book.

So let's establish our objective in coming to these studies.
We are not going to engage in some of the critical disputes,
nor shall we be addressing the apocalyptic sections (it's a
brave man who will tackle Daniel after chapter 7; it's not by
chance that I shall be concluding at chapter 6!). Our
objective is simply this: that we might so understand what
God was saying to Daniel and doing with him in Babylon
that we will learn what God wants to say and plans to do with
us in Great Britain, or wherever we may live. Since the very
ethos of this Convention aims at the establishing and
maintaining of lives of practical godliness, we're seeking to
come to a solid experiential grasp of theological truth,
unfolding in the historical events described in these early
chapters.

The events before us, and those within the whole book,
are framed by two points in history. One, with which the
book begins, is the Siege of Jerusalem, the invasion of the
Babylonian forces around 615 BC; at the other end of the
book, a reference point is provided by the existence of Cyrus
King of Persia who was alive in the region of 537 BC. So a
simple mathematical calculation shows that we are talking
about a span of some seventy years. We can therefore
extrapolate that if Daniel was twenty or so when he was
carried as an exile into Babylon, then by the conclusion of
the historical narrative he is somewhere in his nineties. We
pick him up as a young man at the beginning of his life, and
we see him at the end of it.

Now although these events are long ago and far away, the
issues which Daniel and his colleagues were facing are not
unique. They face a fundamental question, that framed by
the psalmist in Psalm 137 as he describes the experience of
the exiles in Babylon and the kind of songs that they were
singing.

> How can we sing the songs of the Lord [Zion]
>   while in a foreign land?' (Psalm 137:4)

That was the great pressing issue. Was it still possible to live in an environment that was totally alien to all that they had known, to be on the receiving end of forces and impulses that would seek to crush their spirit and drive them in a totally different direction, and still remain distinctively committed to the God of their forefathers?

Well, it hardly needs application. For here we live, as the New Testament tells us, as aliens and strangers in this world. We are looking forward to an ultimate destination. Our citizenship is in heaven; we live in an environment that is totally counter to that which the Scriptures teach. And we may find ourselves saying with Daniel and his friends this morning, 'Can we live in such a way, facing the seductive and sometimes hostile environment with its world view that is totally different from the Bible's? Can we proclaim a sovereign Lord over the affairs, not just of individuals, but also of nations? Can we sing the Lord's song in 1993 in Britain?

Well, we can; but do we?

I believe we shall discover in these times together, as God enables us, the ability to re-affirm in a very uncertain generation the truth encapsulated in a great evening hymn, 'The day Thou gavest, Lord, is ended', with its triumphant last verse:

> So be it, Lord; Thy throne shall never,
>   Like earth's proud empires, pass away;
> Thy kingdom stands, and grows for ever,
>   Till all Thy creatures own Thy sway.[1]

As we open up this study we are going to discover simply this, that the great issue of our world today is what God has purposed to do in His people from the very beginning of time; and that He has established them as the key to future history, that His purposes for His kingdom as it reaches into the four corners of our world—His world—is of great significance. Those of us who read in our newspapers only of crushing events, potential hostility and moral decay may be forced to believe that somehow or other our songs should no longer be sung. How can we sing that song in this environment? We need the spirit of Daniel to be engendered once again in our hearts. He was a man who stood out among men. He was able to see what the apostle John states so clearly in the Book of Revelation: 'The kingdom of the world has become the kingdom of our Lord and of his Christ, and he'—in the words immortalised by Handel—'will reign for ever and for ever' (Revelation 11:15). The Lord God omnipotent reigns; it doesn't always seem so, but it is so. And it is this to which we turn in this book.

All that by way of introduction.

An apparent disaster (1–2)

We are told that the prevailing peace in Jerusalem has been shattered by the arrival of a foreign power. As a result the king has surrendered. The extent of the defeat is seen not only in the carrying away of the sacred articles into the temple of the foreign god, but also in the abduction of the cream of the population. In the opening two verses there is something that is vital for us to note; not only does it run through the book, but it runs through the Bible and it runs through all of history. Namely, the juxtaposition of a largely historical statement and an essentially theological statement.

For example, in verse 1 we are told that Nebuchadnezzar came and besieged Jerusalem—a historical fact. In verse 2 we are told that the Lord delivered Jehoiakim into his hands—a theological fact. This is not unique to the book; it runs through history and is aptly summed up in the well-worn saying that 'Man proposes and God disposes'. When we read of the besieging of Jerusalem, on one level we can see it simply in terms of powerful military strategy. Nebuchadnezzar had an expansionist policy and he recognised the strategic location of the people of Judah. So he made his raid on Jerusalem. What of it? It's just another historical event.

Not so, Daniel tells us. Because at a far deeper level we discover that God was at work amongst His people, fulfilling statements that He'd already made through the prophets about what would happen to the people of God if they did not listen to His words of correction and guidance. And here, in the unfolding events that allowed the people to be carried into exile, is the dreadful tale of God's name being discounted and of His glory being disregarded.

Sinclair Ferguson helpfully points out that in the Babylonian siege of Jerusalem we have a microcosm of the conflict that runs throughout world history: that between the people of God and the people of this world. And until we see history in those terms, we will be tempted to allow the pundits and politicians to explain our world for us simply in the machinations of man and in the political endeavours of humanity. And we will be tempted to believe that it is places like Beijing, Washington and London that hold our destiny, that the warring feuds between human beings are the real, ultimate issues of our day.

But the Book of Daniel, concurring with the rest of Scripture, says, 'No; the ultimate conflict is the conflict which began in the garden of Eden, in the fall of man as Satan came and enmity was created.' And that dysfunctional element has permeated the whole of culture and the whole of family life and the whole of humanity ever since. He that has eyes to see, sees that the real issues of the day cannot be explained in a purely secular reading of our newspapers. We need to lift our eyes and look up. We should never forget that this is the meaning of history on both the cosmic and personal scales. A spiritual conflict lies at the heart of every event, however great, however mundane.

Now the circumstances confronting the people of God posed a theological problem: Where is God in this? 'This wasn't what we expected,' they must have said to one another, as they reflected on their immediate history. They thought only in terms of triumph, peace, fulfilment and prosperity. After all, weren't they the people of God? And wasn't God on their side, and hadn't they every right to expect that everything was going to be hunky-dory for all time? Hadn't they the right to expect that the messianic promises would be fulfilled, until one day the Messiah Himself would take His seat upon the throne in Jerusalem and reign there in an uninterrupted, unmitigated fashion?

But they hadn't listened to what God was saying. Now their triumphalist songs were being crushed under the boots of foreign soldiers, their praise meetings were being drowned

out by the cries of hostage children. And the symbols which
exemplified God's power and presence were being carted off
and put in the temple of a foreign god. This wasn't how it
was supposed to be. 'I didn't sign up for this,' they must have
said to one another. How were they to respond?

How do we respond to the apparent disasters in our lives?
How do we respond when our homes, our dreams, our plans
go up in smoke? Some of us face illness that we would like to
be without. Some of us have been confronted by unemploy-
ment, others have faced the dreadful destruction of a
marriage relationship, and some of us are children living lives
that we wish were vastly different. How do we sing the
Lord's song in the midst of that kind of environment? It isn't
helpful either when those in that kind of situation constantly
find themselves on the receiving end of a kind of triumphalist
preaching that tells us that there's always going to be peace
and prosperity, that it's always going to be fun and it's always
going to be fulfilling. We find ourselves saying, 'Then why in
the wide world am I in the condition that I'm in?' And then
people give us those puerile explanations, instead of reading
the Bible and understanding that we may be in the position
in which we are because it is God's appointing for us.

Nebuchadnezzar came and it was devastating, and the
Lord delivered Jehoiakim into his hands. Do you remember
the Sunday School song?

> Twelve men went to spy in Canaan,
> Ten were bad, two were good;
> Some saw giants big and tall,
> Some saw grapes in clusters fall,
> Two saw God was in it all.

Two out of the twelve were at least thinking biblically,
thinking theologically. They didn't intend to join the ranks of
the panic-stricken. They knew what God could do, they
knew who God was, and they said 'Let's go up there and get
them.' And it is exactly the same here in this narrative,
because here is that same remnant of those who still are able
to look on the affairs of time and pronounce God's over-
ruling hand. The reason was that Daniel knew God's word.

We must not miss that. Look at Isaiah 39:5–7. The prophets spoke of these events, and here Isaiah describes them. And Hezekiah (verse 8) replies, 'The word of the Lord you have spoken is good.'

So what we discover in this apparent disaster is that the Lord Himself was involved in the overthrow of His own city and the defeat of His own people. And Daniel understood it. He understood, as it has been said, that in the believer's life nothing is accidental or incidental. And that is a lesson that many of us need to learn afresh as we face the events that are unfolding before us. William Cowper wrote,

> Blind unbelief is sure to err,
> And scan his work in vain;
> God is his own interpreter,
> And he will make it plain.

An obvious dilemma (3–7)

Having been dragged off into exile the question now was how to respond to the situation. We are told (verse 4) that Nebuchadnezzar had chosen the cream of the crop. He had an express reason, he wanted them to 'serve in the king's palace'. And for these individuals, it was all change. What changed? Well let me tell you four things that did. They are all in this chapter.

Their location had changed
They were no longer living in the safe surroundings of Jerusalem that had provided opportunities for worship and the privileges of fellowship. For some, this would have been enough to silence their songs. Some of us are very good at singing when we've got a big group and an orchestra, when the band's playing and there's a crowd marching. It's very different when you're on your own on a cold Tuesday afternoon in an office somewhere. A change of location is enough for some of us to lose the song, to cease to sing. Being taken away from all that represented security to them,

it was now going to be revealed to the exiles how much of
what they had given lip-service to actually went right through
to the core of their being.

That's the test for the youngster when he or she moves
away from home to college or university. That's the test for
the businessman when he goes out of town on a two-and-a-
half-week business trip overseas. Can we change his location
and remove him from the level of committed zeal? If a
change of location is enough to diminish our influence and
silence our tongues, then something's wrong.

They had had their location changed, but it wasn't in
Daniel's case enough to dampen his enthusiasm, to divert his
gaze or diminish his zeal.

Their education had changed
The individual who was appointed over them was given the
responsibility of teaching them in the language and the
literature of the Babylonians (verse 4). It might, of course,
have been nothing more than an orientation course;but I
don't think so. I don't believe that it was neutral. Surely at
the heart of any process of re-education is the desire to
change the way men and women think, because any military
commander knows that if he can take young men—the cream
of the crop—and change the way they think, he will be able
to change the convictions that drive them, the life-style that
marks them. Paul writes about it: 'Therefore ... be
transformed by the renewing of your mind' (Romans 12:1–
2).

And so perhaps what was going on here was a concerted
effort on the part of Nebuchadnezzar and his intelligentsia to
control this group. After all, if he had merely conquered
Jerusalem militarily and left the brightest of them behind,
they would have proved recalcitrant and ingenious enough to
resist and perhaps to seize back what was their own. He
didn't want to run that risk so he took the brightest and the
best away with him. But then he didn't want to have them in
his house causing trouble; so he decided to offer them an
unsurpassed university education, thus seizing the chance to
realign their thinking. He would create in their minds, if he
could, a world view that no longer relied upon the God of

Abraham, Isaac and Jacob. In every dictatorship that has ever risen in history exactly the same thing has been attempted: to get hold of the brightest and the best and to reprogramme their minds so they will become allies in the cause for a subsequent generation. It would be difficult to resist. Probably some of the mums and dads carried off with these youngsters fancied the idea of this kind of education. After all, it sounds quite good on a resumé: 'University of Babylonia'—a well-known, prestigious place. It couldn't really hurt, could it?

We shall see.

Their diet had changed
Verse 5: 'The king assigned them a daily amount of food and wine from the king's table.' This was no transport café meal. It was old-style luxury, with lovely cutlery and the nice cushion seats and a napkin on the gentleman's lap. This was guaranteed to make them feel special. 'I hope you understand that the food that you are receiving is exactly the same food we just served to King Nebuchadnezzar'—that would be enough for some of us, wouldn't it? We like a good tuck-in. After all, nothing could be wrong with what we ate or drank, surely? Could it?

What was going on here? Was it simply that the king was seeking to seduce them by offering them the good life? No more of the rigours of Judah; now they could live in the lap of luxury. That's enough for some of us. Once we get a little taste of the good life it diminishes our zeal, it alters our convictions, we back off a little bit. It could be that. Or was it an attempt (which I think more likely) to break them of their annoying conviction that somehow they were different? One of the ways in which they were always declaring their distinctiveness was in what they ate. Have you noticed how the way we eat creates barriers? Even at the simple level of what kind of food we eat (and the Jewish people have proved this down through the generations), we are made distinctive as people. If Nebuchadnezzar was going to successfully reprogramme their minds and reorientate their vision, he would have to break them of their food habits. And so he offered to them the food from the king's table.

Their names had changed
Verse 7, he incorporated the names of the Babylonian deities. That creates a severe potential for an identity crisis. Did you know that cults give their members new names? It is an important part of the programming. Nebuchadnezzar understood that names matter.

The issue was whether the exiles could be made to think differently, not as the result of blatant demands but of subtle coercion. It is like the illustration of the frog in the kettle full of cold water: if we heat the water very gradually, we can lull the frog so that it never has the sense to get out; but if we were to put the frog into a kettle full of boiling water, it would immediately jump out. We live in an environment where, so to speak, the water is being heated up very slowly. It's not that we're asked to bow down to idols: that would be easy to understand and respond to. It's not that there is some kind of blatant and manipulative process on the part of a totalitarian government; that too would be easy to identify. No; it is the slow, subtle, degenerative, coercive process that is eating into the minds of our children, which is destroying the absolute values that have underpinned so many of the biblical convictions that have given strength not only to the people of God, but have given moral consensus to the whole nation. And only the perceptive can see enough around the corner to understand what the real issue is.

What these young men faced was simply this question: Were they going to be quietly absorbed by this? were they going to be withdrawn from it and live as freedom fighters? or were they going to find a way of co-operating without compromise? For surely there were people of whom we do not read, who when they found themselves in this situation simply said, 'Well, hey! That was Jerusalem, this is Babylon. Don't let's make a fuss. We're a nice little family, and this is a lovely place for you to go to university. You just get on with it and don't worry about a thing.' And eventually by their absorption they were completely neutralised. But others presumably took on the role of freedom fighters and revolutionaries. 'We'll stand against Nebuchadnezzar. We'll make sure he knows what we believe.'

Down through the ages God's people have always tottered between those two extremes. Being absorbed by the culture of our day, so that we have an audience but no message to speak because we've been neutralised; or being withdrawn from the culture of our day, so that we have a message to proclaim but no-one to talk to because we never talk to our contemporaries. Daniel is a wonderful illustration of a man possessing the wisdom of God, interacting with an alien culture in such a way as still to maintain the distinctives of his God. A very necessary lesson for us, I think, at this time.

This was the desire of Jesus, praying for His people in John 17. 'My prayer is not that you take them out of the world but that you protect them from the evil one' (John 17:15). I don't know how it is in Britain, but in America there is a worrying tendency to isolationism among evangelical Christians. Isolated in the world of education, embracing Christian schools, now embracing home schools, now embracing holy huddles. Meanwhile we have a putrefying culture in which, I thought, Jesus said we were to be salt and light in a crooked and perverse generation. It is easy to withdraw, it is easy to be absorbed; it is tough to do what Daniel did. And you know it's tough, because you are in that office, you are in that laboratory, you are in that university, you are on that factory floor. And to be able to live in an environment that is hostile and seducing, in a way that still upholds the principles and power of God, is a unique and timely challenge.

Daniel and his friends faced the challenge of living in a culture that is different, receiving an education that is different, being called by names that are different—and yet never forgetting that *they* were different.

An important decision (8–14)

They decided that they would be outwardly involved in a culture in which they remained inner strangers. They were prepared to accept the university education; it is clear they were prepared to put up with the change of name; but there was, as we see now, a point beyond which they would not go. They were not prepared to shift on this issue of food.

They faced the coercive pressure to conform from the outside, and presumably they faced the pressure to compromise from the inside. That will always be true for the people of God. It will be true for a teenager; if you want to live for Jesus Christ as a teenager in our day, understand this, there will be enough people from outside who will try to neutralise your desire to follow Jesus Christ, and there will be enough of your cronies and friends in the youth group who will try and compromise your commitment to Jesus Christ. So you are confronted by hostility without and by compromise from within, and what are you going to do? You are going to have to be like Daniel.

There are certain things in life that we must lay down as fixed points. There are issues in our Christian experience that we don't need to pray about, we don't need to have a discussion about, and we don't need to go to our pastor about, for the Bible has made it manifestly plain that certain things are in and certain things are out. There are issues over which we refuse to compromise. And Daniel understood that.

His approach is very helpful. In verse 8, notice,

The purpose that he declared

'But Daniel resolved not to defile himself with the royal food . . .' I like the King James version better: 'But Daniel purposed in his heart.' He recognised there was a time when you didn't discuss and you didn't debate. It was in this decision that he set the stage for all that was to follow. Notice this: in an apparently trivial matter, in an issue that would seem insignificant to many, he seized the opportunity to nail his colours to the mast, to declare his allegiance and to define his objectives. And it did not happen in a vacuum. Daniel did not display this kind of principled conviction out of nowhere. He must have had a good mother and father. He must have come from a good family context. He must have been nurtured in the 'Deuteronomy 6' process ('Talk about [these commandments] when you sit at home and when you walk along the road, when you lie down and when you get up.'). Daniel must have heard his dad saying many times, 'Daniel, if you ever get in this situation, don't ever forget this!' And now he is in this situation, and the voice reverberates down through the corridors of time. And what a blessing on the young man's life!

I say to you again, Godly mums and dads, get down on your knees and stay there for those children. Our children are going to go away. It is absolutely certain; they'll be gone. They'll be among people who will want to change their name, change their location, change their diet, change their mind. How in the wide world will they ever be able to stand? It won't happen in a vacuum, and what is happening today in your home, in your television viewing, in the literature you read, in the conversations around your family table, is laying down the foundations for the day when like this young man, they will need to stand and declare their purpose. This is not the same as making Pharisees of our children. Any of us can do that; we can dress them up like little grown-up adults and make them respond like Pavlov's dogs when the right kind of bells ring, and they'll salivate the right kind of Christian information. But it is only the grace of God that can transform their young lives, because every single one of them is a prospective juvenile delinquent, apart from the grace of God. We've all got them in our homes. There is none of them that seek after God, no, not one of them. And if all we seek to do is frame their lives, constrict them and constrain them; and if we are unable to convey from our hearts the depth of the compassion and the mystery of the purposes of God; then on the day they fly the coop, they will be unable to stand as Daniel did. Let it be to us a word of warning.

Daniel himself chose to raise the issue. He declared his intention not to eat the food. He set his own sails—as Derek Prime quotes in an anecdote I love to tell,

> One ship goes east, one ship goes west
> By the self-same winds that blow;
> It's the set of the sails and not the gales
> That determines which way they go.

Daniel's sails were filled by the same winds that blew upon

his contemporaries, and the reason his book is here is because of the set of his sails. How we need such young men today, who can set their sails for purity, for truth, for righteousness! He who has ears to hear, let him hear.

You notice that Daniel wasn't bombastic, obnoxious or obsequious. He was straightforward and he was honest. In the same way, Timothy was given his task—'Guard the good deposit that was entrusted to you'—and also the manner in which to do it—'with faith and love in Christ Jesus' (2 Peter 1:13–14). Faith and love. How many of us who pride ourselves on taking a stand do so in such a horrible way that our stand is neutralised by our obnoxious attitude. But Daniel doesn't do this.

The permission that he sought

He's gracious, he asks for permission. He recognises that food is an issue, it's one of the ways that they will remain separate. The food laws were in some sense an indication of their relationship to God. And he says, 'This is important.' He wasn't sure that abandoning the outward would not result in the loss of the desire to be different. I want you to notice that very carefully: he wasn't sure that if he gave up what was outward he would lose the desire to be different, which came from inward.

Most of us like to say that external things are really not important, that it's what's inside that matters, but in fact what is outside affects what's inside too. Take the issue of the Lord's Day. To abandon that in terms of its external dimensions diminishes internal convictions. The last twenty years in Great Britain and the last fifty in the United States show that to be true. But you will find young men or women who are students, who say 'I don't study on Sundays, it's important to me, it's a conviction.'

Somebody responds, 'That's irrelevant, nobody cares about that any more. Don't you think you're making a fuss about something that is external?'

'No! It is *external*, but it's directly related to something inside me in terms of God and His glory.'

And the interesting thing is that it was faithfulness in the apparently inconsequential matter of food that established

for Daniel the opportunity to be faithful in some of the huge
waves that were about to hit him, as we shall see in these
coming Bible Readings.

The prospect that he anticipated
Our time is fast going, but I do want you to notice that the
purpose he established and the permission he sought were
directly related to the prospect he anticipated. He clearly
anticipated that Ashpenaz (cf verse 3) would be proved
wrong. Ashpenaz was doubtful, for he says, 'Why should [the
king] see you looking worse than the other young men of
your age? [He] would then have my head because of you'
(verse 10). He is not convinced.

Daniel obviously believed that God was going to be
faithful, and so He was. And that's why we come penultima-
tely, and briefly, to,

An amazing display (15–17)

It would have been one thing if they had been able to hold
their ground, would it not? If they hadn't eaten the food, but
looked just as good? In some people's minds that would have
been an outrageous success. Not for Daniel! It would have
been enough for Ashpenaz, because so long as they didn't
look worse, he would keep his head. Looking just as good
would be fine. He didn't reckon on them looking better. But
at the end of the ten days, they looked 'healthier and better
nourished than any of the young men who ate the royal food'.

Why? Because God is no man's debtor. When we commit
ourselves devotedly to God out of principle, no matter how
apparently immaterial, He will ensure that we will live in the
pathway of His blessing. And the reason that many of us have
just never seen amazing displays of God's provision is
because we are not prepared to put ourselves in the realm of
dangerous faith. We will not go with a small group that is
committed. The faith and character of Daniel and his friends
were tested and strengthened, and they were now better
prepared for the challenges that awaited them.

I played golf last week and I shot a 69. That's the good
news. The bad news is I was having a dream. For some of us

that's where the greatest triumphs are in our Christian lives
—in our dreams. We are heroes there. There, we take our
stand in our new school; there, we stand up to our colleagues
in the office; there, we let it be known that we are
unashamed concerning Christ. And then we wake up.

We see in this passage that usefulness in God's service
doesn't begin in a world of dreams. It begins in the context of
life's harsh realities.

An excellent discovery (18–21)

In verse 19 the king makes an excellent discovery. I wish I
could have been there, just to watch the eye contact! We are
given no record of the chief official admitting to him what
had happened. I think it's highly likely he hadn't. Nebuchadnezzar must have been saying to himself, 'You fellows are
looking really good! How come I don't look as good as you?
After all, we've been eating the same food!' Probably
Ashpenaz just looked silently at his shoes at that point and
hoped that conversation would move on to another subject,
because the king found none equal to Daniel and his friends.
Not just in one or two matters, but 'in every matter of
wisdom and understanding about which the king questioned
them, he found them ten times better than all the magicians
and enchanters in his whole kingdom' (verse 20). This
company of deluded wizards, which we shall be meeting
tomorrow, are still around in every generation. But these
fellows were ten times better than all of them. And
consequently they were immediately placed in the king's
service.

Ronald Wallace in his commentary on Daniel[2] imagines
Nebuchadnezzar's bureaucrats and politicians taking their
morning coffee break while these events are going on and
reflecting on how well things were going. One, I imagine,
might have been congratulated for commanding a strategic
military raid: 'Excellent work I see that you did there! Only
someone as strong as you could bring those people from
Judah into captivity here.' But he didn't know what God was
about. Somebody else, perhaps, was commended because he
had become the chancellor at the university, and the fellows

from Judah had come through the university programme, and were so intelligent and such good students. How the politicians must have been preening themselves! And the king, of course, would have wished to say, 'Yes, and I'm sure they've done well by eating my food—I'm glad that we thought of that as well.'

But what they didn't know, and what they don't face very often in meetings in the White House and in 10 Downing Street, is that it is the God of Abraham, Isaac and Jacob who is in sovereign control, who provides unique abilities, who lifts people up and who brings them down. They didn't know that it was on the anvil of experience that these young men were hammering out the implications of faith in God.

So we, like them, will grow in confidence as we rest in the reliability of His word, as we learn that the apparent disasters of our lives, far from being isolated nightmares, are evidences of the unfolding purpose of God as He fashions us according to His design. As William Cowper wrote:

> Deep in unfathomable mines
>   Of never failing skill;
> He treasures up his bright designs,
>   And works his sovereign will ...
> Judge not the Lord by feeble sense,
>   But trust him for his grace;
> Behind a frowning providence
>   He hides a smiling face.[3]

He is the God of Daniel, the God of all who sincerely trust in Him.

Notes

1. 'The day Thou gavest' (1870), by John Ellerton (1826–93).
2. Ronald S. Wallace, *The Lord is King: the Message of Daniel* (IVP: The Bible Speaks Today series, 1979).
3. Quotations from William Cowper are from the hymn 'Light shining out of darkness', contributed to *Olney Hymns* (1779).

2. 'Take Me to the King' (Daniel 2)

Nebuchadnezzar gets agitated (1–13)

'In the second year of his reign, Nebuchadnezzar had dreams; his mind was troubled and he could not sleep.' Why? Presumably he had a lovely bed in which to sleep, presumably he was completely secure within his palace; certainly we know that his military expansionist programme was being resisted to some degree on the fringes of his territories, but it surely wasn't the kind of thing that would cause him to lie awake at night wondering what was going on. Indeed, from all external perspectives this man was a picture of stability and security. And yet we are told in this opening verse that he was continually being destabilised by what we are going to see were divinely appointed nightmares—something that he could neither put his finger on nor explain. His sleeplessness was not due to eating pizza just before bed or something like that. The dreams that he was experiencing were dark and they were ominous.

Things that are sometimes merely problematic to us in the light of day can become absolutely paralysing to us when we wake in the middle of the night. This is what was happening to Nebuchadnezzar. In the darkness of the night as he was woken by these dreadful mental experiences, he was deeply unsettled. The population of Babylon, I am sure, would have found it hard to believe. Here was the one whose word was

92

never questioned, whose directives were never disputed; surely, of all people, Nebuchadnezzar was not the man to be suffering from a deep-rooted, growing sense of insecurity? But he was.

So what was he going to do? When you find your mind troubled, and you can't sleep, and you have these dark disturbing doubts—who are you going to call? Well, in the Babylonian context he decided he was going to call the 'ghostbusters' to whom we are introduced in verse 2. These magicians, enchanters and astrologers were his little group that he kept for times like this. I should think it was a pretty good job most of the time. After all, you sit around if nobody's having many dreams or if there's nothing too perplexing going on; you don't have a lot to do. You talk among yourselves and wait for a call. Of course, when the call comes the stress level of the job rises dramatically. And that's exactly what happens here in verse 2. You can see them all trotting into stand before the king: the enchanters and magicians and astrologers—all these wise men.

He makes his request (verse 3); they make their polite response (verse 4). 'Then the astrologers answered the king in Aramaic, "O king, live for ever!" ' A good start, wouldn't you say? 'Let's try to put him in as good a mood as possible, before we tell him we haven't got a clue what was going on during the night.' A good way to start with your boss in the morning! 'O boss, live for ever! The report won't be coming for another couple of days.'

Some of you will want to know what it says that the astrologers answered the king in Aramaic. It's a question that has gained a number of people PhDs in Old Testament studies! What little I've read about it I've found difficult to understand myself. Let me deal with it as an aside.

Chapters 2–7 of the Book of Daniel are written in Aramaic. Chapter 1 and chapter 8 through to the end are written in Hebrew. The most helpful suggestion I found was one from E. J. Young, a former professor at Westminster Theological Seminary in Philadelphia. He said of this problem that the solution which seems to be most free from difficulty is that Aramaic, being the language of the world, is used in those portions of the book which outline the future history of world empires and their relation to the people of God; and Hebrew is used in those portions which interpret for the Hebrews the meaning of the visions of the world empires. He adds, 'The present writer is fully aware of the difficulties which are entailed in this position and hence has no desire to be dogmatic upon the point.' Basically his conclusion is the same as mine, I suppose! And for those of you who like to send home Bible study groups right up a blind alley with questions like this—stop the nonsense! The main things are the plain things, and the plain things are the main things.

For the real issue here is that the astrologers, one might say, were on a sticky wicket. Their request is intensely practical. 'Tell your servants the dream, and we will interpret it' (verse 4). 'That's fine, King—just let us know what the dream was and we'll go and check in our books, see if we can find similar dreams from the past and give you the explanation.' Apparently, that was what these enchanters and magicians did. They compiled books, a bit like legal tomes, over the years; and just as a lawyer consults books to see if he can find anything remotely related to the question at issue, so these men consulted these books.

In verse 5 it all starts to heat up. The king doesn't only want to know the interpretation, he wants to know the dream itself. Traditionally, we have thought that he didn't know what the dream was. Actually I believe that myself, but the text allows the possibility that he did know what it was. Although there's good reason to believe that he didn't know, it's also possible that he wanted to make sure that these potentially scurrilous characters weren't just going to fob him off with any old kind of explanation, and so he was checking up on his little troupe of magicians. It's possible. But I'm still inclined to believe that Nebuchadnezzar could not anchor his deep-seated anxiety to what had been disturbing him in the night, because he couldn't remember it. So in verses 5 and 6, as we've noted here, he uses the 'good news/bad news' approach. He gives them the bad news first. 'If you don't manage this you'll be cut into pieces and your houses turned into piles of rubble.' That's fairly easy to assimilate; you don't need to be a rocket scientist to know that all is not well.

They must have looked at one another and said, 'Things are not good.' However, if they perform well, he will (verse 6) bestow upon them 'gifts and rewards and great honour'.

'There are the alternatives,' he says, and reiterates his request.

The interesting thing that runs throughout this little encounter is the clear insight it gives into how this man Nebuchadnezzar had risen to a position of power: by creating leverage through who he was, what he owned and the influence he was able to bring to bear. But here in the darkness of his own mind, in the slumbers of his own experience, the things that have given him enough leverage to create a throne do not work any more; namely bribery on one hand—'I will give you all this'—and brutality on the other—'If you don't do this, this is what will happen to you.' These are the things that he's been able to use as coercive influences to bring him to this point, but now they don't work. I don't know how his wife and children must have coped with him as he became increasingly agitated. They must have dreaded breakfast when he showed up. Everyone was afraid to ask, 'Did you have a good night?' A horrible character, morose and paranoid, always looking around, looking over his shoulder. I expect that if they had a tablecloth he picked it up and looked underneath it before he would sit down.

You see, it's hard for Mr and Mrs Successful to discover that in some area of their lives they are no longer able to control their circumstances. They are no longer able to use the usual things that have made them what they are, to answer the deep-seated questions of their lives. This is especially true in a very materialistic, success-driven society, where we seek to share the good news of the gospel with many powerful and influential people. They need to come to an end of themselves. They need, somehow, to dream in the night. They need to realise that they aren't taking care of the most significant business.

In the 1960s Ray Stevens wrote a song which contained the words, 'You'd better take care of business Mr Businessman, before it's too late.' And somehow or other Nebuchadnezzar, sitting on his powerful throne, has lost all ability to take care of the real business that is before him; and gathering this group around him he hopes for success.

In verses 7 and following, they respond, asking again what the dream was. The king says 'I think you're just trying to play for time.' So in verse 10 the astrologers pluck up enough courage to give their boss the bottom line. 'No king, however great and mighty, has ever asked such a thing of any magician or enchanter or astrologer. What the king asks is too difficult.'

The king had thought he was the big bad wolf, but he was actually Humpty Dumpty. He had fallen off his wall, and all his king's horses and all his king's men had to admit that they weren't going to be able to put Humpty together again. I sympathise with their predicament and I admire their courage. They must have weighed the possibilities, reckoned on the outcome and said, 'There's nothing else for it; we'll have to tell him straight. This just can't be done.' Would that some of our modern-day wizards were as quick to realise the limitations of their potions and prescriptions, especially some in the realm of modern psychology! Certainly in the USA, men and women are hastening here and there for every kind of potion and cure from the magicians and enchanters and astrologers of our day. And it would often be a great help if those they consulted were honest enough to say: 'There is not a man on earth can deal with this.'

In verse 11 they are partially correct. 'What the king asks is too difficult. No-one can reveal it to the king except the gods.' If they had said God with a capital 'G' they would have been totally correct, but their polytheism demanded that they said 'the gods'. And consequently their polytheistic approach to life, the absence of revealed truth in their own experience, meant that they were totally inept and totally unable to answer the predicament that was before them. So in verse 12 the king's fury reaches its zenith, and he orders the wholesale slaughter of all the wise men of Babylon. 'Men were sent to look for Daniel and his friends to put them to death' (verse 13), so they were obviously not involved in the initial encounter in verses 1 and 2.

As you mentally fast-forward through the biblical record, do you find yourself thinking of another king who was furious with wise men? And who, as a result of his fury, demanded slaughter? Herod too couldn't cope with the notion that he was not ultimately on the throne of everything, that he could not make demands and have them satisfied. Finding himself in that precarious position he lashed out in fury and ordered the wholesale slaughter of all the innocent children within the sphere of his influence. Nebuchadnezzar and Herod combine to display for us the vicious reaction of human beings in all our pride when we sense that our thrones are not as secure as we had imagined.

Let's transpose this from the sixth century BC and start to bring it here into Great Britain, as we approach the twenty-first century, and into your life and mine. It then becomes very clear, first of all, that Nebuchadnezzar does not stand alone upon the stage of human history. He is, six centuries before Christ, almost a prototype of many who were to follow, many world leaders who like him were going to be marked in their power and influence by a deep-rooted hostility towards God. What really drives him is that he is reminded very clearly of his humanity in the face of divinity. Like Nietzsche who was to come many years later, he is saying, 'If there is a God, how can I bear not to be that God?'

That is what we saw in our first study. It is the conflict that is ultimately at the heart of humanity, the conflict which is the basis of all human history. Was not this what happened in the Garden of Eden, when the evil one came as a tempter to say, 'If you take this you shall be like God?' Human beings cannot cope with not being in total control of the universe.

Reinhold Niebuhr, in *The Nature and Destiny of Man* (1941, 1943) makes the interesting suggestion that this 'anxiety complex' discernible throughout the pages of secular history, is at the root of much modern political tyranny. Mankind's lust for power, he suggests, is fronted by a 'darkly conscious realisation of the insecurity of his existence'. So, in facing the fact of their insecurity, Nebuchadnezzar and others who have followed him seek to make themselves doubly secure. Yet they discover that, to paraphrase Paul Simon, 'The nearer their destination the more they're slip slidin' away.' They just can't get there.

'Well,' somebody says, 'that's also very interesting. I can

see how there is some point of correlation with world leaders, but I'm still not particularly clear as to how this could possibly relate to me.' Let's be honest. Have you ever had dark, disturbing dreams? Have you ever experienced this kind of insecurity and hostility? What about those angry outbursts in your life, those strange irrational cries that your wife or your husband or your children have never fully been able to understand, and when you get in your car to drive to the office you don't understand it yourself? You never planned to explode in that way. You don't know what it is that is deeply unsettling you at the heart of your existence, but you know there's something there. Think about it. When you drive to the office in the morning—from whence cometh all this unbelievable hostility in people's cars? Something happens inadvertently and the driver rolls down his window and lets forth the most unbelievable torrent of profanity and abuse; he tells you all that he's going to do to you if ever he catches you. Five minutes earlier, he just finished his cornflakes. He doesn't understand the riddle of his own existence.

The greatest tragedy is if you are the person giving it out rather than taking it in. From whence cometh our never-satisfied sense of one-upmanship? We too face dark questions. We face the questions of existence. Who am I? Where do I come from? Why do I exist? Where am I going? And in any case, does it all matter? What's it all about, Alfie? Is it just for the moment that we live? You see, at the heart of all that Nebuchadnezzar was facing was the fact that he was facing his existence. He was facing the fact that although he was strong and powerful and mighty and had a whole world under his control, he didn't even know what was happening in his own mind, and he couldn't get to the bottom of it all. Says Ronald Wallace in his commentary,

> Why does there come to me, too, at the very best and highest moments of my life, the strange disturbing thought that even this may be the material of tragedy? Why is so much that is good and beautiful marked so deeply and indelibly with clear signs of instability and frailty? (*The Lord is King*, p. 51)

When they begin the overture they start to end the show. The first time that you say hello begins your last good-bye. The anticipation of the vacation is immediately soured by the fact that once begun, it's going to end. And for a man or woman who walk their days along the life line without any knowledge of God in Christ, this is a perilous way to live.

So it's small wonder that Nebuchadnezzar gets agitated. And what he needed is what we need. He didn't need simply an explanation of his predicament, he needed to be brought face to face with the real nature of his problem. He was surrounded by the best of human wisdom, but his advisors couldn't do it for him. What was required was the wisdom and the word which are from above.

Daniel gets involved (14–27)

Enter Daniel. Verses 13 and 14 set the context. Notice that Daniel speaks to Arioch 'with wisdom and with tact'.

I'd like you to note six points about Daniel's involvement and his approach.

Daniel was tactful

This is in keeping with what we saw in chapter 1. He doesn't over-react, despite the fact that things are not looking particularly hopeful for him and his colleagues. But he does take the initiative. The word has gone out, the king has spoken in his fury. What is Daniel's response as a man of God, in this situation that is far from good? You might imagine he would adopt a kind of Christian fatalism, resigning himself to the fact that they were all going to get their heads chopped off. But he doesn't. His confidence in God doesn't make him indolent. It stirs him into action.

Where did the crazy idea come from that confidence in God always just sits you on your bottom doing nothing? I don't find that in the Bible. Nehemiah was really confident in God. When they came and said, 'We'll knock your wall down', Nehemiah said, 'Let's have a prayer meeting and take these swords.' Nehemiah 4:9—'We prayed to our God and posted a guard.' He worked with a trowel in one hand and a sword in the other, confident in God's purpose for them on the wall, and yet taking the initiative when action was demanded.

But Daniel's was a tactful, wise approach too.

Is there not a lesson here to learn in passing? How many opportunities have we missed by a striking lack of initiative or abused by a blustering heavy-handedness that were nowhere close to wisdom and tact? That kind of approach is not the same as zeal. It is possible to be zealous and silly. Daniel's approach has to do with understanding God's ways, it has to do with a sense of the appropriate, it has to with approaching things in a way that is marked by wisdom and by tactfulness. That's why we all need one another. Some of us tend more to the blustering approach and perhaps God will give us a companion or friend to hold us back when we are about to bluster on. Some of us are very indolent and not prepared to do anything, and God has given us someone to help us in our initiative-taking. For example Martin Luther was a bit of blusterer, and God gave him Melanchthon at his side to temper a lot of his blustering.

Daniel was practical

Having gone into the king and asked for time to interpret the dream, Daniel returned to his house and explained the matter to his friends (verse 17). And he's able to explain his motivation in a phrase: 'So that we don't get executed'.

'We're going to have a prayer meeting,' says Daniel. 'We've got a very straightforward request here. I'm urging you to plead for mercy from the God of heaven, that He will reveal this mystery, and just in case you're in any doubt as to the significance of this prayer meeting, it's in order that we don't get executed with the rest of the wise men in Babylon.' That's the kind of incentive that some of us need to jazz up our prayer meetings! Because they are sadly lacking in most places I go to.

How much self-preservation was involved, and how much concern for God's glory, we cannot say; though we would assume the latter more than the former. But Daniel was practical enough to realise that if he and his friends were dead they wouldn't be making the same kind of impact that was possible if they were alive. And since he believed that

God had put him in the kingdom for such a time as this, he had reason to believe with confidence that God had purposes for him. And therefore he now had something. He had the questions of his mind and he had the convictions of his heart. Was he going to allow the unsettling questions of his mind to over-rule his faith? or was he going to allow his faith to over-rule the questions of his mind? You will see here that practicality and spirituality made good bedfellows.

Daniel was prayerful

The explanation given in verse 17 was a plea for intercession. Somebody has said that we can do more than pray after we've prayed, but not until we've prayed. The implication of verse 19 seems to be that this prayer time was prolonged, because the mystery was revealed to Daniel in a vision 'during the night'. We wouldn't want to make much of that—this is not a proof text for all-night prayer meetings, but it is at least possible that this was more than the kind of 'arrow prayer' that we find in the opening chapter of Nehemiah.

Years ago in our church in Edinburgh, when we used to kneel for prayer before the service, there was an elderly gentleman who paraphrased Shakespeare's Hamlet every Sunday. He used to say, 'Oh Lord, more things are wrought in prayer than ever this world dreams of.' And it has been said too that 'when our prayer is meagre it is because we regard it as supplemental and not fundamental'.

Daniel was thankful

In verses 20–23 we have what is essentially a hymn of praise. Daniel had seen no possible way out; and yet, like others before him, he'd acted in supreme confidence that God would supply all that was necessary. And God had done just that.

I wish we had time to work through these verses. Read them in your own personal study. Ours is a God who changes times and seasons, the One who sets up kings and deposes them. The news networks may explain the fall of the Berlin Wall in terms of socio-political factors; we know differently. He gives wisdom to the wise, He reveals what is deep and hidden, and so, says Daniel, 'I thank and praise you, O God.'

Daniel was purposeful
His prayer didn't remove him from the realm of action. Rather it propelled him into action, for we read in verse 24 that having prayed in this way and heard the result, Daniel went to Arioch. And we are told that his expression of concern was once again straightforward. He says: one, do not execute the wise men of Babylon; two, take me to the king; and three, I will interpret his dream.

There was great potential for him to feel pretty powerful, wouldn't you say? But that's the sixth point.

Daniel was humble
Listen to Arioch in verse 25. 'I have found a man among the exiles from Judah.' (What do you mean, *you* found him?) But Arioch sees this as an opportunity for a bit of promotion, 'I know you couldn't find anyone, king, but *I've* found a man for you; he can tell you what this dream means.' Verse 26, the king asks Daniel whether he can interpret the dream, and Daniel replies 'No wise man, enchanter, magician or diviner can explain to the king the mystery he has asked about, but there is a God in heaven who reveals mysteries' (verse 27). Arioch's pride is set in direct contrast to the humility of Daniel. 'This is the man to whom I will look,' says the Lord, 'he who is humble and contrite in spirit and who trembles at my word.' It's a sobering thought to ponder how our usefulness might be greater, were we only humble at the core of our beings.

The dream gets explained (28–45)

We now discover a profoundly encouraging truth. The people of God had presumably thought that God would only speak through the exclusive relationship He had with them (which incidentally is a characteristic that remains true of our thinking today). But the fact was that God had chosen to use the circumstances and dreams of a pagan king to reveal part of His purpose for the future of the history of the then known world. In the dreams of a pagan Godless ruler, God was unfolding the mysteries of His providence.

That is something that ought to greatly encourage us, as we think about praying for nations in our world and as we think about situations across the world. Think for example about that little island of Cuba and the strange bizarre circumstances there involving Fidel Castro, as he continues to prop up a dreadful atheistic regime. The people live in abject poverty for it is impossible to buy things on the streets. They are held in tyranny and captive. We need to pray, 'Oh God, make him dream in the night; unsettle him in the core of his being, speak into the mind of Castro; and then give to someone the privilege of introducing him to the God in heaven who reveals the deep mysteries of life.'

So Daniel in verses 31–35 explains what it was the king had seen. He describes the great statue from top to bottom. He says it is an unstable, top-heavy structure and it cannot move. Its destruction will come not primarily because of its clay feet but from the impact of a rock not cut with human hands. Steven Spielberg would have a wonderful time creating special effects for verse 34!

And when you read this description, does it not make you think of the first psalm, with its contrast between the man who doesn't walk in the counsel of the ungodly or stand in the way of sinners, who is like a tree planted by the rivers of water, and the wicked who are not so, but like the chaff which the wind blows away? Here Daniel says that is exactly what is going to happen to this image that is emblematic of the kingdoms of the world. The wind simply swept them away and never left a trace. Meanwhile this rock became a huge mountain and filled the whole earth—another tremendous opportunity for the special effects department! Then the crushing impact of the rock; and as the statue is neutralised in dust, this rock now begins to form an all-embracing rock, that begins to encroach and fill up the whole earth.

Let me quote to you what Ronald Wallace says about this:

Daniel was brutally frank in explaining the meaning of the dream to the king. The time remaining to the empire he was building was comparatively short. It would, of course, go through its development in the process of history. It would help to give place and shape to three or four other empires, each in its own way impressive and mighty. But this development itself would ultimately reveal that all the greatness and magnificence of the structure was resting on feet of crumbling clay that could not bear it for long. The end, however, would not come about because there were these feet of clay, but because the whole structure stood in the way and blocked the progress of another kingdom that must come and fill the future. It was because this future kingdom was approaching and because its triumph was inevitable, that Nebuchadnezzar's empire and dynasty would be broken up. (The *Lord is King*, p. 57)

And so in verse 37, speaking somewhat respectfully, Daniel says, 'You, O king, are the king of kings. The God of heaven has given you dominion and power and might and glory ... You are that head of gold.' That is the only point of explanation Daniel gives. He does not then go on to explain the next piece of the statue, the next kingdom. We have to learn from that that the plain things are the main things and the main things are the plain things. What do we know categorically? We know that in this statue Nebuchadnezzar was the head of gold. What do we know beyond that in terms of specific explanation as to these coming kingdoms? Not a lot. He does make clear that these four outstanding different empires will run their course before the kingdom of God, pictured in this rock that is come from hands uncut, will finally with dynamic power become the all-embracing force of human history.

As the Scriptures provide no clear and obvious explanation, we do well to avoid the speculative dogmatism that has traditionally marked these verses. I recall as a boy hearing stirring sermons on the ten toes of the statue. They're never mentioned in the whole chapter! But that didn't seem to unsettle the preacher. If there were toes there must be ten, if there were ten it must be this, and if it was this it must be that ... it's an amazing form of wizardry. The average proletariat hasn't got a clue what's going on and so they simply take it from these prophetic high-priests.

Verse 44 describes how 'in the times of those kings' (clearly in my view a reference to the rulers of the kingdoms he has just mentioned) 'the God of heaven will set up a kingdom that will never be destroyed, nor will it be left to another people'—it's going to be like no other kingdom ever. 'It will crush all those kingdoms and bring them to an end, but it will itself endure for ever.' Some have suggested that this is inevitably a reference to the birth and the death and the resurrection of Jesus in the Roman era. How does this fit? Well, if you want to read it that way, the empires are first the Babylonian empire, followed by the Medo-Persian empire, followed by the Greek empire and then by the Roman empire. And that would seem a fairly natural logical explanation of the events. In this view, what we would see is that the kingdom, says Daniel, is running parallel to all these other kingdoms. In some mysterious way God is working His purpose out as year succeeds to year, working His purpose out in the actual dream life of this pagan king. God is sovereignly in control. He has been in control of the dramatic events of the siege of His people in Jerusalem; it is He who has ultimately brought them into bondage. They don't understand that. That's why they've hung up their harps and why most of them are not singing. But God is working His purpose out. And the definitive, decisive moment in the expansion and the establishment of the kingdom, in this view, in the period of the Roman empire when Christ is born as a baby in Bethlehem and God walks on *terra firma*.

'Well,' you say, 'that's fairly good, but I heard that verse 44 refers to the return of Christ at the end of the ages.' I heard that too. Somebody else told me that verse 44 refers to Antiochus Epiphanes. Maybe you heard that too. So what are we going to do? Well, the main thing which was established in the mind of Nebuchadnezzar, and for the encouragement of God's people, was and remains this: the inevitability of the coming and triumph of the kingdom of God.

That's the all-embracing prevailing message. When kingdoms crumble, when thrones topple, when political parties are in the ascendancy or decline, behind it all and in it all God is at work. And parallel to it all is the all-embracing development of His kingdom. You will notice in verse 44 that it is God's kingdom; that it is an indestructible kingdom; that it is an all-victorious kingdom; and that it is a universal kingdom. And in it all, the stone is clearly Christ. You remember again the words of the psalmist in the second psalm, prophetically anticipating the one who was to come: verses 8–9, 'Ask of me, and I will make the nations your inheritance, the ends of the earth your possession. You will rule them with an iron sceptre; you will dash them to pieces like pottery.'

The message is plain. The way to understand and explain the rise and fall of empires is not ultimately in terms of military might or financial power, but in terms of the moral and spiritual unfolding purposes of God. Every institution that stands against the kingdom of God is destined for destruction. At the name of Jesus every knee will bow, and every tongue confess that Jesus is Lord to the glory of God the Father. That is an absolute certainty. Therefore when we build our business empires, when we build our countries and when we stand against God, we simply draw ourselves up to our supreme height and the bigger we become the greater our fall.

Nebuchadnezzar gets religious (46–47)

The interesting thing, when you read verse 46, is that when you look at chapter 3:1, you will find that King Nebuchadnezzar made an image of gold ninety feet high and nine feet wide. So at the end of chapter 2 we have him emotionally and religiously stirred, and at the beginning of chapter 3 he's back to his old tricks.

What does it tell us? This: that it is very possible for a religious encounter to stimulate an impressive response at a superficial level and yet leave us untouched at the depths of our being. That's what happened to Herod when he listened to John the Baptist preach. Herod liked to listen to John the Baptist (Mark 6:20). In the King James version it says that he 'did many things'. I'm not sure what that means. It may mean that he scurried about, or he tried to reform himself on the outside; but he still had John the Baptist's head on a plate. Let us beware lest the kind of proclamation that we bring is simply that which is content to see powerful people emotionally and religiously stirred yet only at a superficial level; so much so that they are untouched and unchanged at the depths of their being. Nebuchadnezzar got religious. It helped him with his dreams. It superficially changed him in some way. But he wasn't what you would call converted. Says Ronald Wallace,

> It is because men have nothing . . . bigger than themselves and their own world to worship and wonder at, nothing more certain than their own ideas by which to steer their destiny, nothing more inspiring than their own goodness to lead them to repentance, that life grows stale, feverish and frustrated, and bad dreams become a matter of course. (*The Lord is King*, p. 61)

Was it not Hamlet, Prince of Denmark, who reflected,

> How weary, stale, flat, and unprofitable
> Seem to me all the uses of this world . . .
> . . . What is a man,
> If the chief good and market of his time
> Be but to sleep and feed? a beast, no more.
> (*Hamlet*, I.ii, III.iv)

When our friends and our neighbours drive their cars out of their garages and make their way along the thoroughfares of their lives, remember this, believer. God has established eternity in their hearts; all that is necessary for an understanding of God has been revealed to them. But, as Paul says in Romans 1:25, there has been a great exchange. They have exchanged the truth of God for a lie and have given themselves to myths and nonsense. For when a society ceases to believe in God, it doesn't believe in nothing—it believes in everything. And that is where our culture is today. Men and women will believe the most bizarre nonsense. But when we would speak to them of the rationality of the Scriptures and the profundity of the resurrection of Jesus Christ, they reply, 'Oh, you don't possibly expect me to believe that kind of thing, do you? Give me another Shirley Maclaine book would you, I'd like to get down to some reality. Silly!'

'The fool says in his heart, "There is no God." ' (Psalm

14:1, 53:1). And despite the fact that Nebuchadnezzar got religious, he didn't get changed. Maybe there's somebody here today who got religious enough to come to Keswick, religious enough to get involved in the PCC, but you didn't get changed.

But you could.

Daniel gets promoted (48–49)

And finally Daniel gets promoted. Because he was a politician? No. Because he told the king what he wanted to hear? No. Because he brought him coffee at the right time and a couple of extra biscuits from the tin? because he stayed a little later after work? No. It was because he was a young man who purposed in his heart and couldn't be moved. He was really co-operative, but he never compromised. He was really trusting, but he always took action. He was prepared to stand out from the crowd, to stand up for God and to stand still and see God intervene for His glory.

Don't you love that personal touch in verse 49? How many of us would have done as Daniel did? 'Excuse me, King, I've a few friends here as you know. How about them?' He seizes the opportunity to make the improvement of his circumstances an occasion to bring his friends along. By way of an aside—think how many times a promotion in our lives has distanced us from those who've been most helpful in getting us to where we are today. We moved up a floor, got a different key to the bathroom and a different kind of letter on our car, and suddenly we were too big for the boys with whom we'd spent our time.

Daniel was a great guy. Daniel, the man of purpose: 'Take me to the king.' And in his praises I'm sure he came back to his little hymn in verses 20–23. I'm sure he and his friends would sing it to each other: 'Praise be to the name of God for ever and ever; wisdom and power are his. He changes times and seasons; he sets up kings and deposes them.'

It was true six centuries ago BC; it is true on the threshold of the twenty-first century.

3. Ultimate Questions (Daniel 4)

We've jumped chapter 3 because it has to do with Daniel's friends rather than with Daniel, and also because we are on our way, via chapter 4, to Daniel 6, which I think is indispensable to any study in Daniel.

If Nebuchadnezzar had had a personalised number plate, which he probably would have had if he'd been alive today, it would doubtless have been number 1. Or perhaps it would simply have said 'KING'. There was no question but that in his private world and the public world of his time, there was nobody greater than Nebuchadnezzar. He would have sympathised with the person who said 'I am not conceited,' and then quickly added, 'though I have every right to be so', for Nebuchadnezzar was consumed with himself and his own achievements. His little world was bounded on the north and the south and the east and the west by Nebuchadnezzar himself. He had a palace, he had prestige, he had power.

There was probably no finer home in which he could have lived, and yet his home didn't give him security. He would definitely have had posture-springing in his mattress and there probably wasn't a better duvet to be had; yet his bed did not give him uninterrupted sleep. He had everything that people might imagine represented security, and yet as we've seen, this man was far from secure. Had he lived in the sixties he would probably have enjoyed singing along with Simon and Garfunkel: 'I've built walls ... that none may penetrate ... I am a rock, I am an island.' But he would probably have identified with the angst expressed in lines by the same duo: 'As I lie upon my bed in the early evening gloom, impaled upon my wall my eyes dimly see the riddle of my life and the puzzle that is me.' Nebuchadnezzar could not unscramble the strange complexity of who and what he was.

The focus of chapter 4 is simply this: God dealing personally, using his servant Daniel in the life of Nebuchadnezzar to bring him to the place of personal testimony which you find in verse 37—the final verse of the chapter—'Those who walk in pride he is able to humble.' The story of chapter 4 is the account of how God brought Nebuchadnezzar, in all his pride and grandeur, to the place of this personal declaration.

The declaration (1–3)

The chapter begins with declaration and ends with declaration. The author, adopting the style of ancient letter writing, names himself and then those whom he is addressing. Notice,

The people he addresses

'The peoples, nations and men of every language, who live in all the world'. A person's ability to address other people is in some senses directly related to the measure of his or her influence. Any of us could hold a press conference. We could ring the ITN and BBC news desks and tell them that at twelve noon we would be holding a press conference at the Keswick Convention. If you or I were doing it, they wouldn't come. They don't know who we are, and frankly they don't care.

But that's not the case with Nebuchadnezzar. If he had been a twentieth-century man, his words would have been carried simultaneously via the BBC and the CNN all round the world. It is not simply delusions of grandeur that lead him to express himself in this way. God has provided a platform for him, and on this occasion he is about to put it to good use.

The pleasure he expresses

Verse 2 begins, 'It is my pleasure'. Much of Nebuchadnez-zar's life had been marred by the pleasure he derived from magnifying his own achievements. His listeners would have been only too familiar with verse 2, 'It is my pleasure to tell you about . . .' People were growing old listening to Nebuchadnezzar telling other people about all his amazing accomplishments. What they could not have anticipated was what followed: 'It is my pleasure to tell you about the miraculous signs and wonders that the Most High God has performed for me. How great are his signs, how mighty his wonders! His kingdom is an eternal kingdom; his dominion endures from generation to generation.'

By this time news would have spread far and wide of Nebuchadnezzar's bout with depression. Rumours would have abounded about his animal antics in his hanging gardens (cf 4:33). Now it would be common knowledge that Nebuchadnezzar was back to his old self; the word would have been going around the cities and communities that Nebuchadnezzar had come out of this strange malaise in which he had been and he was all right again. And probably people would have said, 'We can doubtless expect more of what had happened before.'

Daniel 4 records for us that Nebuchadnezzar is addressing this issue, wanting to make it clear to people that far from being his old self he is a man made new. And the signs and wonders to which he refers demonstrate the fact that God is the sovereign God who rules over all. It's interesting that we read this little phrase, 'How great are his signs, how mighty his wonders!' As we are going to see in this chapter, Nebuchadnezzar of all men understood this. The signs and wonders of God throughout all human history are simply the clues that He has given in an apparently chaotic world, that He is the One who rules over all things and is the One who will establish His kingdom for ever. Any time we see God breaking in to humanity in a dramatic way, whether in the Old Testament or the New, it is in order that His name might be glorified and in order that people might realise that He is actually in control.

Think of the disciples on the Sea of Galilee, worried because of the storm. They awaken Jesus, who commands the winds and the waves to be still. 'What manner of man is this that even the winds and the waves obey him?' ask the disciples (cf Matthew 8:27). And in that moment once again the incarnate God gives a clue, in this chaotic world, as to where power and authority really lie.

Now it is in this declaration, in these opening verses, that Nebuchadnezzar makes it perfectly clear that he has come to understand that his kingdom and all the other kingdoms to come will eventually crumble, and that it is imperative that men and women—starting with himself—understand the thrice-iterated truth of chapter 4, that the Most High is sovereign. You will find it in verse 17, verse 25 and verse 32. Whenever you find repetition like that you realise that the emphasis is for our instruction and for our encouragement. And you will notice that this declaration with which the chapter begins is actually its coda, as we shall see.

The dream (4–18)

The context of the dream
'I, Nebuchadnezzar, was at home in my palace, contented and prosperous.' Things were going really well. He may not have been dreaming for some time. Some years have passed since the events we have been considering, and here he is expressly in his golden years.

Nebuchadnezzar was enjoying security on his borders and prosperity within the land. Doubtless he could congratulate himself on the success of his military policy. He must have looked around with a measure of great satisfaction as he looked at the grandeur of his architectural and horticultural achievements. All in all, he saw himself to be the master of all that he surveyed. And had he been living in our century, and summoning favourite artistes to give royal command performances, no doubt he would have been very happy to hear a contribution from Frank Sinatra, Ol' Blue Eyes himself: although his reign wasn't over and hopefully his death wasn't imminent, he would have been able to identify with the lyrics with a measure of satisfaction:

'I've lived a life that's full, I've travelled each and every highway,
And more, much more than this—I did it my way.

'Sing it up,' says Nebuchadnezzar, 'I love this part.'

To think I did all that; and may I say, not in a shy way,
Oh no, oh no not me, I did it my way . . .

'Encore! Encore!' he would have cried. 'I love that song!'

And in the moment of his contented prosperity, verse 5, 'I had a dream that freaked me out [that's my translation], that made me afraid.' That little phrase reminds me of King David, in ease and prosperity at the time when kings go out to war. Danger zone! It reminds me of the story Jesus told of the man who, because of his ease and because of his prosperity, was to hear the words, 'You fool, tonight your soul will be required of you.' It is a reminder of the principle that runs throughout the whole of Scripture: 'What will it profit a man if he gains the whole world and loses his own soul? . . . What will a man give in exchange for his soul?'

These were the ultimate questions that Nebuchadnezzar was being brought to face, and God was intervening in his experience by means of a further dream.

Maybe Nebuchadnezzar had deduced from all of his prosperity that he must be being blessed from above. We sometimes fall foul of that mistaken notion, don't we, as we build our little empires. Some of us have empires, though not as grand as Nebuchadnezzar's. Some of us are proud of our little financial empire, our professional empire, our academic empire, or even our ecclesiastical empire. And we come to a Convention like this and we like to take our seat in our usual place, we like to meet the usual people; and all is well with us in our ease and in our prosperity, and we feel that frankly all must be well with our souls; because obviously all is well with our external circumstances.

Yet one telephone call can make us shake in our shoes. One visit to the doctor, when he looks at the radiographer's report and then looks at you with a look you don't like. Just one look, one telephone call, one moment; and all of our ease and prosperity will be seen in an instant for what it is—dust in the wind.

The impact of the dream

Verse 5 tells us that he was terrified by these nightmares. The result is that he turns once again to his deluded wizards (verse 6). You would have thought he would have thrown them out: they've been a pain in the neck from start to finish, and they were causing trouble in chapter 3. But here he is in chapter 4, going back to them again.

Incidentally, he's not the only monarch or world leader to continue to take his chances with clairvoyance and the horoscope pundits, rather than seek out the source of true wisdom. He wasn't the first and he certainly wasn't the last. I wonder, why would he go to them when he knew that if he went elsewhere he would get real wisdom? Perhaps it is because he knows that if he goes there he will not only get what he wants, but also what he doesn't want. 'Men want to come to Christ for the relief He offers,' said C. S. Lewis, 'but decide not to on account of the fact that they cannot have the benefits without having the responsibilities.' And it may be that somewhere in his psyche Nebuchadnezzar recognises that every time that he goes to Daniel a radical change takes place. Perhaps he thought that by means of these characters he had gathered around him he might be able to get an interpretation of the dream. However (verse 7) they are incompetent. And so, once again, he seeks help from Daniel. He calls him by his pagan name, Belteshazzar, and (verse 9) calls him 'chief of the magicians'. Could it be that Nebuchadnezzar is still unwilling to see the events of life in terms of divinity—ultimately, in terms of Daniel's God? Sure, he had been stirred in the past as you know, but he had remained unchanged.

The content of the dream

The content of the dream is described in verses 10–18. It is an interesting and graphic picture. Verse 15 onwards begins to explain it. You will notice that there is a move from the neuter to the personal. 'Let him' (so we know now that the stump is indicative of a person) 'be drenched with the dew of heaven, and let him live with the animals among the plants of the earth. Let his mind be changed from that of a man and let him be given the mind of an animal, till seven times pass by for him.'

Is there some bright spark in your home Bible study group who'll keep you going long into the night on what 'seven times' represents? Seven times may be seven periods of time—maybe seven weeks, months or years; maybe a picture of the perfection of the totality of the time that God intended, since the use of seven in the Bible is so often that of perfection. The answer is, we don't exactly know how long it was, but it was for however long God intended it to be.

The purpose of the predicament

Now the purpose of the predicament is made perfectly clear. The reason (verse 17, and here it comes for the first time) is that the individual has forgotten that his human dependence is to be upon God. The general message could have been lost on Nebuchadnezzar. The messenger (verse 13) had already made it obvious that it is God who reigns, that He sets up kingdoms and that His actions in the course of history focus on the humbling of those who are proud, bringing them to the place where they acknowledge who God truly is. So, verse 18, 'This is the dream that I, King Nebuchadnezzar, had. Now, Belteshazzar, tell me what is means, for none of the wise men in my kingdom can interpret it for me. But you can, because the spirit of the holy gods is in you.'

Once again his polytheism is in him and he still is reluctant to get to the place of genuine conviction concerning Almighty God. And in that respect he is like modern men and women today. I don't know what the British situation is, but in the United States at the present time people have no problem whatsoever with acknowledging God, provided that 'God' is a vacuum into which they can pour whatever notion they choose. God is a cosmic principle, an idea, the sun, Mother Nature ... but the God and Father of our Lord Jesus Christ is an anathema to modern man. The God whom we worship, the God of Scripture, is perfect and plural and powerful and praiseworthy. Nebuchadnezzar was close but not quite close enough. And so this interpretation was vitally important as God unfolds His purposes.

The interpretation (19–27)

When you read verse 19 you discover that now we have two men who are perplexed. Nebuchadnezzar is perplexed because he doesn't fully understand what his dream means, and Daniel is perplexed because he understands perfectly what it means. Is it not somewhat ironic that, at the end of verse 19, we have the king counselling Daniel not to be alarmed about the reason and meaning of the dream? 'Belteshazzar, do not let the dream or the meaning alarm you.' That's an interesting juxtaposition, isn't it?

Listen to his reply. 'My lord, if only the dream applied to your enemies and its meaning to your adversaries!' This wasn't only polite sentiment, it was genuine sensitivity. Because Daniel as the servant of God recognised that the message that he was now about to bring was not good news. It would be so ultimately, but Nebuchadnezzar would never understand the good news until he understood the bad news. And when we endeavour to proclaim the gospel by telling people only good news, we can so readily make them feel that Jesus Christ and the gospel is an addendum that may be hitched on to their lives, like an extra carriage on the train lines of life. Only when the Bible makes clear the bad news of man's condition, does the good news of God's provision have any relevance to the heart of man.

That's why, when we read the stories of the Great Awakenings of the eighteenth century in the United States and of similar things that happened in Britain, we need to see that the kind of proclamation that brought about heart-rending change in the lives of thousands was not some easy call to a better life, to security, or to an answer to loneliness, or to peace in an age of anxiety; it was an understanding that men and women would have to come before God and say,

> Nothing in my hand I bring,
> Simply to Thy cross I cling . . .
> Foul I to the fountain fly,
> Wash me Jesus or I die.'

Nebuchadnezzar says, 'You don't need to be alarmed by this dream,' because he doesn't understand what he's saying. And Daniel, recognising what the implications will be for him of preaching the authoritative word of God, says out loud, 'I only wish that what I am about to say applied to your enemies and to your adversaries, Nebuchadnezzar.' It wasn't just customary courtesy, but it was also indicative of Daniel's sensitive heart.

I suggest that in Daniel's approach we find a wonderful lesson in pastoral counselling.

Daniel was not a professional. This ought to be an encouragement to all of you who are going back to a normal course of work next week. Daniel is not part of the clergy, the religious establishment. He was plucked out of the contemporary mainstream; he was, if you like, a civil servant. But he knew God. He had a thorough grasp of the way God works; he knew his Bible, one might say. And the great preoccupation of modern professionalism owes more to the spirit of the age than to any great imperative.

Daniel cared enough to respond and confront. Verse 20: 'The tree you saw . . . you are that tree.' If we are going to be of use to people as they come to us with their concerns and questions, we need to have a thorough grasp of our Bibles, and we need also to care enough to listen and to care enough to confront.

Daniel identified and addressed the underlying problem in Nebuchadnezzar's life. The king's problem was pride. If we are going to be of use to people in listening to their concerns, interpreting for them, as it were, their experiences, these things need to be in place. Daniel points out very clearly that until this point Nebuchadnezzar had lived in his own way. He had been unprepared to acknowledge that heaven rules; unprepared to accept—just as modern men and women are totally unprepared to accept—that, as Paul says in Ephesians 1:11, God 'works out everything in conformity with the purpose of his will'; that this is the great scheme of events which is true cosmically and personally. It is true of churches, it is true of nations, it is true of families. God is working everything out in conformity with the purpose of His will.

And Nebuchadnezzar could see no further than his own will, his own design, his own creations. For him, Daniel's words were an unpalatable truth. He didn't suffer from the twentieth-century problem of low self-esteem. He had so much esteem that he probably had to have special entrances in his palace to get his head in. William Temple said, 'The essence of sin is that I make myself, in a host of ways, the centre of the universe'. The Bible says that irrespective of modern theories, the problem that men and women and young people have created for themselves is that they have made themselves the centre of the universe. And the predicaments of our age and the dreadful elements in our culture can directly be related to it.

Nebuchadnezzar, in essence, is too big for his boots. And the illness which is about to befall him is, says Daniel, an indication of God's judgement (verses 23–26). Notice the command in verse 23, 'Leave the stump.' It means, 'God still is weaving His mercy in your life; nevertheless, here's the deal.'

How would you like to have preached that sermon? You go to the most powerful man in the then known world, you are called in, all the magicians have disappeared either by design or by direction; and you know what the dream was, and you explain it to the king. And it is your responsibility to tell him: 'Listen: this is God's judgement on you, Nebuchadnezzar. This is what happens to a mind that feeds continually on itself.'

I don't want to delve into areas that I've no business to, but I do wonder how many of the dreadful psychological predicaments that men and women face might be better addressed by bowing down and acknowledging God as sovereign over human affairs. There's no non-directive counselling here by Daniel; no suggestion that Nebuchadnezzar's problem was that he was a victim of his background or his circumstances. That would be how he'd be treated in America. I'm not belittling investigations that need, in certain cases, to be conducted, but of that which bypasses the clear instruction of Scripture.

And Nebuchadnezzar was confronted by a Daniel who

didn't beat about the bush; he didn't talk in vague generalities that would probably have got him invited back to a couple of Hanging Garden parties but would accomplish nothing definite or lasting. Someone has said, Daniel knew that only words of brutal frankness could have the strength to avert the coming calamity. There could be no cheap and ready comfort for Nebuchadnezzar, and no impression must be left on him that such was possible.

Men and women need to be aware of the critical position they are in before God. If that is true in personal encounter, then surely it must be true in public proclamation. If we see Daniel not only in the personal dimension of a one-on-one encounter with Nebuchadnezzar, instructing us how we ought to be brave, gracious and sensitive in pastoral counselling; if we step back from that and hear him stand on the platforms of our world and speak his word to larger groups, it gives to us a reminder of the nature of his proclamation. How easy it is for people who stand in pulpits to capitulate to a desire for public affirmation! It happens almost imperceptibly, usually over a period of time. People who have been called to authoritative proclamation of the word of God slide into vague general applications. The good news is that the vague applications never offend anyone; the bad news is that they never help anyone. And consequently people sit and wonder why they are wasting their time.

We are living in a generation of wafflers, of story-tellers, of pseudo-psychological gurus. And the question remains: where are the prophetic voices in our nation and in our Western world day? Where are those God has raised up who are prepared to speak as Nathan did to David when he said, 'You are that man.'? That's forthright; that's not going to get you invited to coffee afterwards. It is devastating in its impact. Speaking like that is the role of the prophet.

What did Paul think about, when he was summoned from prison to stand before Felix and Drusilla? I don't know. We'll ask him in heaven. But they'd said to each other that evening (Acts 24), 'There's not much else on this evening—why don't we bring that fellow Paul up? We could talk to him.' What would be going through Paul's mind? 'This is a good chance to secure my release, I'd better butter these people up . . . They're only seekers, I'll make it a kind of seekers' service, I'll build some bridges, I'll really start to work on them next time . . . Maybe I'll just make friends with them, because it'll be really handy to have a couple of friends like that when I get out; having their telephone number will be a real boon to me as an evangelist . . .'

Well, it's futile to speculate what he may have thought, but I know what he said when he got up there. He preached a three-point sermon. One, righteousness. Two, self-control. Three, the coming judgement. And this to a couple who had the power to have him beheaded!

Felix was a rascal of the highest order. He had stolen Drusilla from her husband by the help of a Cypriot magician. They were sitting in an adulterous relationship and the mighty apostle Paul preached a three-point sermon, to an almighty king and his adulterously joined wife, on righteousness, self-control and the coming judgements. When is the last time you heard a sermon along those lines? 'Oh,' you might say to me, 'are you stepping back from what you said yesterday and the day before? Are you only now getting warmed up? Weren't you talking about wisdom and tact?' Yes, I was. Our words are to be full of grace and are to be seasoned with salt. But spinelessness cannot be equated with sensitivity any more than holy boldness can be equated with blustering arrogance. And preaching, according to the New Testament, is not simply a religious professional standing behind a box stimulating the minds of men and women. Not every talk that is given from behind one of these platforms, no matter how emotionally charged or however theologically accurate, can be equated with the New Testament pattern of proclamation. I believe we must pray to God as we pass some of the little churches and pulpits that once reverberated with the sound of the gospel, that He will put back into those pulpits preachers with the character and spirit of Daniel.

So in confronting Nebuchadnezzar with his dream Daniel points out to him firstly (verses 22 and 25) the urgency of his problem, and secondly (verse 27) the necessity of change. He's obviously not suggesting in verse 27 the king can save himself by good deeds, but that by changing his way of life he will be demonstrating his acceptance of the truth of Daniel's words. He reminds him of the possibility of a reprieve. When you read on from verse 28 you can see that the king was given a full twelve months to change his attitude from his heart, to do what Daniel said was necessary, to acknowledge that the Most High is sovereign over the affairs of men.

The great need in his life was not to focus on himself and his condition, but to focus on God and His glory. And he failed to do so.

The actualisation (28–33)

Nebuchadnezzar did not respond to the opportunity for reprieve. His response was to presume upon God's kindness. God had sent to him a great opportunity, given him time to repent, sent dreams to disturb him, and Daniel to instruct him.

Now we find him on his palace roof. Consider what he said, verse 30. 'Is this not the great Babylon I have built as the royal residence, by my mighty power and for the glory of my majesty?' It sounds like 'I', 'me', 'mine'. Then in verse 31, 'The words were still on his lips when a voice came from heaven'—the voice of judgement, the enactment of the decree. That which a few months before had been a disturbing possibility was now a dreadful reality. The judgement of God had struck suddenly—while the words were still on his lips.

Do you remember Jesus' parable with that chilling conclusion, 'The master of that servant will come on a day when he is not looking for him and at an hour when he is not aware.'? The judgement of God as described for us in Scripture always comes suddenly. 'In the last days scoffers will come,' says Peter, 'scoffing and following their own evil desires. They will say, "Where is this 'coming' he promised?" . . . Everything goes on as it has' (2 Peter 3:3–4). History, they say, is cyclical not linear. We're not moving towards any destination. So, says Peter, 'Do not forget this one thing . . . The Lord is not slow in keeping his promise, as some understand slowness. He is patient with you, not wanting anyone to perish, but everyone to come to repentance. But the day of the Lord will come like a thief. The heavens will disappear with a roar; the elements will be destroyed by fire, and the earth and everything in it will be laid bare' (3:8–10).

As Nebuchadnezzar congratulates himself, he finds the decree enacted before the words have even died upon his lips. Consider what he said: 'I, me, mine'. Consider what he heard: 'It's here'. Consider what he experienced: read in verse 33 those dreadful, comic, tragic words. What had been said about him was fulfilled immediately. He was struck with the symptoms of what I believe is known in medical terms as lycanthropy, from the Greek words for wolf and man. Suddenly he's not up on the palace balustrade listening to his music. He's down in the fields. The servants are saying to themselves, 'What in the wide world has got into Nebuchadnezzar? He's doing the strangest things. Just this morning I passed him in the Hanging Gardens and he barked at me. And you know what, he's actually changing in his physical appearance.' This is not mythology, this is history.

Let me quote to you M. G. Barker, a consultant psychiatrist, who comments:

> As far as Nebuchadnezzar's illness is concerned the features are of the fairly acute onset of insanity with the apparent delusional idea that he was an animal. The length of time that he was unwell is unclear, but he also seems to have had a spontaneous remission and returned to sanity and changed his way of life subsequently. This kind of history is much more typical of depressive illness with relatively acute onset of delusional beliefs of a morbid nature. And in the days before drugs and ECT most such illnesses had a spontaneous remission within a period of one, two and occasionally more years. The person who recovered would recover complete insight, as did Nebuchadnezzar, apparently.

That's a description in psychiatric terms and I think it's quite helpful. But look again at verse 33. He who has refused to give God glory is now deprived of any glory of his own. He who refused to share with the poor has now become poorer than the poorest in his land. He who had had a beastly attitude of heart now finds that his outside matches his inside.

Man cannot reject God without consequence. Surely the

verses our day needs to hear are Romans 1:18 ff. Surely we ought to be bold enough to say, 'Yes, I believe there is a direct cause-and-effect in the fact that man is engaged in this great exchange and has turned his back upon God. Surely I believe that the wrath of God is being revealed from heaven against all the Godlessness and wickedness of men who suppress the truth by their wickedness.' And not only do they do these things, says Paul, but they encourage others to do them also.

You see this in Galatians, which those of you who were here last week will have studied. Galatians 6:7—'Do not be deceived: God cannot be mocked. A man reaps what he sows.' The linkage between the physical, psychological, moral and spiritual elements in Nebuchadnezzar's condition is complex, and is material for further discussion and for lively conversation.

The restoration (34–37)

I think that Nebuchadnezzar would have sung with great passion those lines,

> With mercy and with judgement
> My web of time He wove.

For in the restoration described in these verses, we have just such a display of the merciful dealings of Almighty God. What Nebuchadnezzar in no sense deserved, he received. This is the wonder of the gospel; it is the wonder of the atonement, that He took upon Himself that which we alone deserved, in order that we might enter into the benefits due to Him alone. God's judgement was tempered with mercy. Even in the explanation of the problem back in verse 32, Daniel had given a hint of this: 'You will be driven away from people and will live with the wild animals; you will eat grass like cattle ... Seven times will pass by for you until ...' Notice that little word 'until'.

Sinclair Ferguson argues (in contrast to the view of the eminent psychiatrist quoted above) that Nebuchadnezzar did not experience spontaneous remission. No-one ever does, he says. 'The term is a convenient description of a cause-and-effect sequence for which there is no explanation in terms of our ordinary expectations.' What we discover from this story is that the words of Scripture, that God gives and God takes away, are true here. God was as much in charge of Nebuchadnezzar's remission as He was in charge of his affliction. And the chain of cause-and-effect is expressed in the first sentence of verse 34: 'At the end of that time, I, Nebuchadnezzar, raised my eyes towards heaven.'

You see, Nebuchadnezzar's problem lay in the fact that he had never raised his eyes towards heaven. He had never raised his eyes much above his own ramparts and balustrades and architectural genius. He had completely lost perspective on life. He was the archetypal 'Nowhere Man' of whom the Beatles sang. And suddenly Nebuchadnezzar says, like the psalmist of old, 'I lift eyes to the hills.' Like the young man in the story Jesus told, he came to his senses. That is what we need to pray for our leaders, our friends, our empire builders and not least of all for ourselves, that we might come to our senses.

I've got one last quote for you: in 1965, Nebuchadnezzar would have been singing along with this one as well:

> When I was younger, so much younger than today,
> I never needed anybody's help in any way ...
> Help me get my feet back on the ground.
> Won't you please, please help me.'

In an interview in *Rolling Stone* magazine twelve months before his brutal killing in New York, John Lennon said, 'When I wrote "Help" in 1965 it was hailed as just another advance in rock music. What nobody understood was that it was the cry of my heart which no-one came to answer.' Some of us are so busy singing our songs and marching that we cannot hear the genuine cries of those who, confronted with an end of themselves, are ready to cry out to God for mercy.

'I raised my eyes towards heaven, and my sanity was restored. Then I praised the Most High.' The little hymn with which the chapter ends should be put to music. Nebuchadnezzar expresses the power of God and the place of man. Notice the amazing thing in verse 36, 'My advisers and nobles sought me out.' Usually he sent for them. But something's happened now. His advisers and his nobles are seeking him out. There's been a change in Nebuchadnezzar.

'And I was restored to my throne.' It would have been enough for him simply to have been restored to sanity, simply to get a good hair-cut, a shower and a new set of clothes. That would have been an amazing display of God's grace. But what a mighty God we serve! He takes him into a new place. He causes him to see his great need, and lifts his eyes to the place of victory and authority, and causes him to be restored, turned the right way up with his feet on the ground, and causes him to sing with Reginald Heber,

> Holy, Holy, Holy! Lord God Almighty!
> Early in the morning our song shall rise to Thee.

And he is replaced on his throne so that he can call the press conference that we discovered in the first three verses, to which all the nations and peoples of the world would pay attention. God moves in a mysterious way, His wonders to perform.

Nebuchadnezzar is not unique. He had to face what others have to face, the question 'What are you doing with all your feverish activities and scurrying around?' Some years ago I conducted the funeral of a very distinguished trial attorney in Cleveland. He was a man who had had all the rewards of success, plenty of money and a wonderful family. One day he went to hear a talk by a doctor who gave this illustration: 'There was a man who climbed the ladder of success, and everybody knew he'd reached the top. But when he looked at the ladder he discovered that it had been propped against the wrong wall.'

He came to me and said, 'What do I do?', and I had the privilege of sharing Christ with him.

I arranged to meet him for breakfast some weeks later. In the meantime he had been diagnosed as having a cancerous tumour. Within nine months he was in glory.

Do you have friends like that? So have I. Their ladder's up against the wrong wall. And they're not here at this Convention.

You didn't come here simply to increase your knowledge, did you? You came to ask God to change your life, to stir you up, to make you zealous in evangelism, to take good news to a bad news world, to be unashamed, ready, prepared. Let's go!

4. Servant of the Living God (Daniel 6)

It's been said that few great men or women finish well. That certainly wasn't true of Daniel. When we come to the sixth chapter, arguably one of the best-known stories in the whole of the Old Testament, we need to bear in mind that many years have passed since the passage we began with on Monday morning. It's a long time now since Daniel was snatched from the security of his home in Jerusalem. By this time he would have been fairly well absorbed into the culture. His accent would probably have been indistinguishable from those around him. His family would have blended into the society, his loyalty to his adopted country was not in question, because as we know now he had served these various rulers with consistency over many years. We've seen him with Nebuchadnezzar; chapter 5 tackles his activities with Belshazzar; and now in chapter 6 we come to Darius (whose historical identity, incidentally, has been the cause of much spilt ink).

By the beginning of Daniel 6, Daniel was probably somewhere between seventy and eighty years old. Interestingly, we don't find him living in retirement at the palace gate house. We might have imagined that by now he would be merely a memory, somebody pointed out to tourists on guided tours of the capital as a great man of the past. But not at all; he is still in the thick of things.

No retirement for Daniel. The temptation to compromise

and capitulate seems never to have entered his life. What had confronted him in his youth as he was carried away into captivity was the temptation to compromise convictions and to capitulate to his surroundings. We often make the mistake of assuming that the greatest tests of our Christian lives are going to come in our earliest years, in the first flush of our enthusiasm, and that if somehow or other we overcome that initial battle, we'll be fine from then on. But when we read the lives of the people who have served God both in biblical times and in church history, we see that it isn't true.

It certainly wasn't true of Daniel, who was here facing a magnificent test in the latter stages of his life. It's a reminder to us that the evil one wages a war of attrition, knowing that it will be a great gain if he neutralises the impact of God's servants in the final laps of their life, thereby calling into question all that has gone before so that people will come to speculate whether he or she was really living the Christian life all the way through—for how in the world could somebody possibly end in that way?

How we run the final laps is, it seems to me, of great importance. Those of us who are now in our middle years know that God is able to keep us in our teenage years, that He is able to sustain us through the early days of marriage or the development of a single purpose in life. What we are not sure of experientially is whether God will keep us all the way to the very end. We know His word teaches it. We want to believe it. But we're looking for examples, we're looking for models. We're looking ahead, round the corner, to see those who have gone before us, to make sure that they finish well. When Eric Liddell was asked the secret of his success in running the 400 metres, he replied: 'The secret of my success is that I run the first 200 as fast as I can and then for the second 200, with God's help, I run harder.' And when the *Edinburgh Evening News* reported his victory in the 1924 Paris Olympics, they said, 'It was the last 50 metres that meant the making or the breaking of Eric Liddell.' Let me say to those of you who are potentially in the last 50 metres of life, it is often those final metres that drive home to the watching world, and assures the soul, the gracious way in which God sustains His children.

Daniel was distinguished (1–3)

The structure of government is given to us in verses 1–2. Darius has chosen to rule his kingdom by means of 120 satraps. Their responsibilities extended to various parts of the empire, and they in turn were brought under the jurisdiction, we are told, of three administrators of which one was Daniel. He had distinguished himself to the degree that the king was planning to see him appointed as his prime minister. The job of the satraps was to ensure that the king didn't 'suffer loss' (verse 2), presumably the loss of revenue due to internal corruption or the loss of territory as a result of external civil unrest. The story tells us that Daniel had something that the others lacked, an 'x factor' that put him above the others, so much so that he was in line to become the premier. What were his distinguishing characteristics? I'll just point out two.

The quality factor
Verse 3 shows that Daniel was exceptional. From what we've seen in the earlier stories, we know that he had an extraordinary capacity for facing and overcoming difficulties. We know that he had frequently come to the fore in explaining the dreams that his colleagues had been unable to tackle. We know that he had incredible wisdom which he brought to bear upon situations, and was able to make shrewd practical judgements. He was an excellent fellow; there was a quality about him that even his colleagues understood.

The integrity factor
The kind of position which he now held and those he had been privileged to enjoy in the past were always susceptible to all kinds of graft and dishonesty. And yet in all of this, Daniel had remained blameless, as we shall see. Indeed we are told (verse 4) that he wasn't negligent, and that they could find no corruption in him; he was absolutely trustworthy. There was, in short, no gap between his public administrative duties and his personal private life. He didn't cheat in the office and he didn't cheat when he played with his grandchildren. His 'yes' was 'yes' in public and his 'yes'

was 'yes' in private. There was none of that modern-day nonsense of holding public positions of morality while privately abusing them in one's own life-style. Not for Daniel.

He was in some senses the embodiment of that of which the prophet speaks in Micah 6:8, 'He has showed you, O man, what is good. And what does the LORD require of you? To act justly and to love mercy and to walk humbly with your God.' His life could have been summed up like this: 'Daniel is that kind of man.' He is a man of integrity in a shady world. He is a man of purity in a dirty world. He is a man of stability in a shaky world. Such individuals will always rise to the top, and there's no surprise that he becomes the king's choice for this key position.

We might therefore assume that somebody like that would have been loved and admired by everybody, but it wasn't so. And so we go on to notice that not only was Daniel distinguished but,

Daniel was despised (4–9)

The quality of Daniel's life was more than matched by the jealousy of his colleagues. They disliked him; he was in line for the top job. So they tried to discredit him for his management of government (verse 4), looking first at his day-to-day procedures. But they couldn't catch him out. Daniel displayed the characteristics of Godliness in his job, the kind of things that mark men and women out—punctuality, respect, attention to detail, kindliness, honesty and so on. So when his colleagues scrutinised his nine-to-five routine, as it were, they could level no charge against him.

What a challenge! Could someone walk in on our nine-to-five routine, and find that God permeates *our* work? Or do people just know us in the office because we are kind of crazy, we wear big badges on our labels with 'Christian messages', and all we seem to be to our friends is a genuine Christian mess. Is it the case, perhaps, that we're such a mess that they don't even get the message, our life speaks so loudly that they never hear our words, we are unlikely to gain promotion because of the quality of our work? If we are too busy being Christians to be good in our jobs, that is not right. 'Let your life so shine before men,' we might paraphrase Jesus, 'that they may see how good you are at your work and glorify your Father who is in heaven' (cf Matthew 5:16). There is no gap between the secular and the spiritual. We don't work just so that we can then go off and glorify God. We glorify God in the way that we work.

Daniel understood that. Godliness permeated his life. He wasn't relying on some badge in his lapel. 'They could find no corruption in him, because he was trustworthy and neither corrupt nor negligent.' And they recognised that the only possibility of success will be if they can catch him out on some matter relating to his commitment to God and specifically to the law of God.

So in verses 6–9 we read how these characters hatch a plot and go to the king together. They persuade him to issue an edict—short enough for them to be able to cope with, and long enough in its enactment to give them time to trap Daniel. Thus they will be able to achieve their objective; to successfully prevent him from rising to the position of influence planned for him by the king. They went 'as a group'; there is always safety in numbers when you're up to this kind of nonsense. Assured solidarity presumably helped.

They were less than honest in their use of the little word 'all'. Telling lies is not simply walking in and saying 'It was so' when it wasn't. The way in which we tell lies is much more subtle. My mother always used to tell me that God was concerned that I would not become 'one who maketh and telleth a lie'. I wasn't sure what it meant but I thought it was fairly comprehensive. And it covers this present dishonesty. There were 120 satraps and three placed above them, and one of those top three had nothing to do with it at all. And if Darius hadn't have been half-asleep, he would have said 'Is Daniel involved in this?' He would have looked around and said, 'I don't see Daniel here.' That was the big question in the Iran Contra scandal: Did Ollie North know or did President Reagan know? The Press Corps in the early days of the Reagan administration kept going to the press conferences and saying to him, 'You know, Mr Reagan, you're out of touch.' Mr Reagan would often reply, 'No you're wrong, fellers. I'm in charge.' As soon as the Iran Contra scandal broke out, they went to the press briefings and they said to him, 'Mr Reagan, you're in charge.' To which he replied, 'No, no, I'm out of touch' . . .

And somehow or other Darius was out of touch here. He was out of touch and manipulated. They manipulated him by appealing to his pride (verse 7). In effect, they said, 'We'll have thirty days of absolute devotion to Darius. Don't you think that would be good for the community, Darius? Don't you think it would be good for people to rally behind you? Wouldn't it unite the nation and the people? It's a great idea! All you have to do is issue the edict, put it in writing.'

So Darius agreed.

His manipulators were cool, calculated and spiteful; their hatred and their jealousy was deep-seated. Ronald Wallace points out that there was however no question of their doing the deed each with his own dagger, as did the Roman senators to Caesar. 'Their guileful intention was to wrap themselves in ostensible innocence and to lay the death of Daniel at the door of the innocent king' (p. 111). So the laws were changed and the penalties were set. The trap was laid. That which they would be horrified to do for themselves, they were going to trust the system to take care of for them. After all, these were honourable men who only cared about their king and their country.

Now think with me, what was the basis for this spite and hatred? Do you think you would have liked Daniel if you had met him? Do you think the average person would have enjoyed the company of Daniel without question? So why did they hate him?

It wasn't that Daniel had trampled on them on the way to the top. There is nothing in the whole record of Daniel's dealings to suggest that he was somehow grasping after position and was prepared to do whatever it took to get there. Indeed, they might have forgiven him that, for that was the game of politics and they could identify with it. One man's ceiling is another man's floor. But what they couldn't forgive him for, and what a secular person cannot forgive a true believer for, was his unswerving commitment to his God. That rankled badly. 'Why, when he's such a nice chap, does he have to keep this God-of-Abraham-Isaac-and-Jacob stuff going? If only he wouldn't be so forthright about it! Otherwise, he's a fine chap; we really like Daniel, you know.'

It wasn't that they themselves were irreligious. They had their gods with a small 'g', but people who only have gods with a small 'g' cannot stand individuals who profess to know God with a capital 'G' and by doing so proclaim that all other gods are mere idols, as the prophets said. That was what was happening here with Daniel. You see when Daniel got down on his knees—as we are about to see—and turned his face towards Jerusalem, he wasn't simply going through some kind of external religious exercise. In those moments he was affirming in his own heart his convictions that the God of Abraham, Isaac and Jacob was the final truth and that all else were pretenders to His throne. And every day, as he bowed in prayer, as he thought of from whence he had come and of how God had led him, and as he pondered his traditions, he realised the wonder of God.

In the musical *Fiddler on the Roof* Topol says 'Tradition? Tradition teaches who we are and what God expects of us.' Daniel's tradition had affirmed him in his identity, he wasn't in any doubt as to who he was. Sixty years of pluralism and syncretism could not swerve him from his conviction concerning the God who had watched over him, and when he knelt in prayer he affirmed that. And his friends couldn't tolerate it.

Well—that's long ago, and far away. Is it? No it's not. This posture remains equally unacceptable in our day. Our social climate is pluralistic: lots of opportunities, lots of ways, all roads lead to heaven. It is pluralistic and it is syncretistic, the amalgamation of those various roads to create a great amorphous mass of religious cluelessness. And that, added to a kind open-mindedness, holds the lives of men and women at the moment. The issue is no longer truth, it is tolerance. And when we seek to stand for truth we break the one commandment that remains in our culture, 'Thou shalt not be intolerant'. If we proclaim Christ as Lord and Saviour, we are accused of arrogance. If it is not true we *are* arrogant. If it is true, we are merely obedient. And Daniel lived it out. Jesus said, 'Blessed are you when people insult you, persecute you and falsely say all kinds of evil against you because of me. Rejoice and be glad, because great is your reward in heaven, for in the same way they persecuted the prophets who were before you' (Matthew 5:11–12).

If you and I, centuries on, were prepared to do what Daniel did, which is to remain true to the truth of the Bible; if we were prepared to proclaim that Jesus is the Good Shepherd and all the rest are, as Jesus said, thieves and robbers; that Jesus is alone the truth and the light—in short, that there is salvation in no one else 'for there is no other name under heaven given to men by which we must be saved' (Acts 4:12), then I say: Look out, look out! And I believe there will be a very clear realigning of convictions in the Western world. The truth will out, and God's people will be forced to take a stand—not simply on political and social issues but ultimately on issues of theological truth. It happens in small measure at the moment, it is yet to be seen what will happen.

Surely, just as Daniel was framed, some will be framed in the coming days. They hated him, they plotted against him, not because he was a bad fellow but because he stood for truth. He loved what God loved and he lived it out. The hatred that is described here is presumably what Paul is talking about in 2 Thessalonians 2:7: 'the secret power of lawlessness'; the kind of hatred that was displayed between Cain and Abel, the hatred of Joseph's brothers for Joseph, the hatred that permeates humanity, the hatred that vented itself at Christ. It is that amazing lawlessness which pervades our world.

Sociologists have no answer for this. With the coming of the twentieth century they were going to educate us and give us a good social system and make good hospitals for us and give everybody a nice house and a roof over their head. And when we had all this accomplished we would all settle down and be able to sing, 'You got to admit, it's getting better all the time.' But in fact it seems to be getting at least a little worse all the time. And instead of bowing down on their faces before Almighty God and crying out for help, human beings stumble and plot their journey along their days.

Daniel received a charade of justice, the same kind of mockery that took place in the courts of Pilate when Jesus stood before a hypocritical, fraudulent, illegal assembly that was propped up by corruption and weak-willed men. And the fulfilment of the prophecy was manifest in His life. 'He was despised and rejected of men, a man of sorrows, and familiar with suffering. Like one from whom men hide their faces . . .' Wherever did we get this strange recent triumphalism, this notion of unassailable victory, of inviolable triumph and majesty? No doubt there is a balance that needs to be restored in some of our morbid fretfulness. But let us not, in endeavouring to see the pendulum come to a biblical centre, push out to some other strange and alien extreme. We don't want to go out and seek contempt, but we might ponder whether our desire and designs for acceptance are signs of victory or evidences of cowardice.

Do you want to be liked so much in your office that you are prepared to smile at your colleagues' dirty jokes, laugh at their dishonesty and share in their degeneracy? This Daniel stuff is dangerous faith.

Daniel was disciplined (10–11)

Now we look at a characteristic over which Daniel had control. Discipline was something that he did; the two previous characteristics were something he received. Indeed, it was this discipline that provided the foundation of the satraps' plot. The one thing they knew they could count on was that Daniel would be consistent, and the only way their plot would work was if he remained so. It depended on his commitment not being spasmodic in the way some of our lives are, with our initial bursts of enthusiasm followed by periods of chronic inertia.

That wasn't true of Daniel. When they went into his house ('as a group' again, verse 11: safety in numbers again) they went not to see if he was praying but because they knew he would be praying. They were in no doubt about what they would find.

They caught Daniel and went back to the king (verse 12). And now they catch the king. They persuade him to verbalise what he has written down, and then tell him of the dissident.

'Didn't you publish a decree?'
'Quite right; can't be repealed.'

They must have exchanged triumphant looks as the king spoke. They deliver their news. 'Daniel, who is one of the exiles from Judah,'—a rather belittling description after all this time, is it not? After all, he was in line to be prime minister—'pays no attention to you, O king.'

It wasn't true, and Darius knew it wasn't. Presumably the very reason he was going to make Daniel his prime minister was because the reverse was true. Of all men in his kingdom Daniel paid attention to him. His loyalty was exceptional, it was greater than people who had been bred in that arena. And it was on account of his loyalty and his attentiveness that Daniel was in line for the top job.

But what *was* true was that he was praying three times a day. Do any of us think that Daniel's attention to prayer was somehow prompted by the king's edict? I must confess that for quite a time I thought it was an overt act of defiance on Daniel's part; that until then his prayer life had a relative importance but that as soon as he was told he couldn't pray he was determined to do it at all costs. We have a similar situation in the United States, over prayer in public (state) schools, where people who never attend prayer meetings in their church and have no personal devotional life are going screaming mad down the corridors of power in Washington to attempt to secure a sixty-second moment of silence in secular high schools all across America.

But it wasn't a display of defiance from Daniel. It was a display of discipline. It would have been one option to say, 'I'll continue to pray, but briefly and quietly.' But he continued to pray with the windows open, and he did so three times a day. Notice the key word in verse 13. 'He *still* prays.'

'He was doing it before; then the edict was issued; and he's still doing it.' You see, the only way they could catch him was because he was always praying before. The disciplined lifestyle he had manifested gave them the grounds for this little plot. The race of the life for Daniel was a cross-country run. It wasn't a few hundred-yard dashes, it was a steady disciplined commitment; a classic example, it seems, in the whole of the Old Testament of the formation and the priority of holy habits. It was his unswerving witness and discipline that made it possible for his colleagues to catch him in the act. Loyal as he was to the empire, nobody could be in any doubt as to his allegiance to the kingdom of God. And in his daily régime of prayer with his face towards Jerusalem, he displayed to all who knew him where he believed the truth was to be found, where he believed all men and women everywhere must look for their salvation. That's what was happening. For after all, if his prayer was some kind of triviality both to him and to his immediate group of colleagues, then no-one would have cared about it. His prayer was symbolic of the deep-rooted conviction of his life concerning God and his desire to serve God. It prompts the question, how symbolic is my prayer life of that kind of conviction?

How do you imagine Daniel's window? A big bay window somewhere on the first or second floor, so that everybody coming down the street would be able to say, 'Oh, there's old holy Daniel praying again'? I don't think so. From what we know of domestic windows at that time in the Middle East, they were small and high up, to give protection from the heat and from thieves. Therefore the picture is probably not one of public display so much as one of personal intrusion by the other satraps. His praying at the window was not blatantly evident to everybody, but everybody knew of his conviction concerning prayer and his commitment to God; so when they invaded the privacy of his own home and went upstairs to his own room, they found him acting according to his own testimony.

He didn't just talk about prayer and about God in his work, you see. He didn't just live out a lifestyle that was not backed up by the devotional impact of his walk with Christ. He understood what somebody has said: that what a person is on his knees before God, that is what they are and nothing else. And that, loved ones, is what you are too. All of our public affectations do not, and cannot, conceal the absence of a core-level commitment that is unassailable to God in Christ.

When they entered his house they found him there. Did the crisis create a prayer-life? Or did the crisis reveal a disciplined life? The latter. When crisis hits your life and mine—be it the loss of a job, bereavement, the falling apart of a relationship—there is a sense in which it does something to us and forges character for the future. But it reveals more than it creates. And the crisis of Darius's edict did not make Daniel a man of prayer. It revealed him a man of prayer. Do you have a crisis in your life just now? If so, it's revealing where you are.

Daniel had made the habit of prayer such an integral part of his life that probably the very momentum of it would have been enough to keep him faithful, with or without any sense of inspiration. I have observed that when men and women learn to pray, the very momentum of a disciplined prayer-life will be enough to sustain them, whether or not they feel inspired or excited by prayer. But if you persistently decide not to pray, for whatever reasons, you will eventually experience spiritual sterility. Daniel prayed three times a day because he prayed three times a day. Some days he got blessed, other days maybe he got a little bored; but he always prayed three times a day. It was his custom.

And the Lord Jesus went up to the synagogue on the sabbath, 'as was his custom' (Luke 4:16). An interesting phrase. Jesus established holy habits. I go to the evening service because it is my custom. Somehow in my early days I decided that if the Lord's Day is the Lord's Day, it's the Lord's Day and it's not the Lord's Hour. Suppose I play golf on a Saturday. If I play eighteen holes in the morning and somebody buys me lunch I'm ready to play in the afternoon. If you buy me my tea, I'll play with you again in the evening. I love golf. I'm poor at it and I'd like to get better at it. And when I worship with God's people in the morning I can't wait to go again in the evening. Why? Because God is present, His word is proclaimed, fellowship is vital and there is a great battle raging.

'Oh no,' someone will object. 'You see, Daniel was a legalist.' He was? How come when you are doing physical exercises it's liberation, and when you are doing spiritual exercises it's legalism? If we play that kind of game with ourselves, we're in a perilous state.

We must move on to the conclusion. Daniel could probably have rationalised about the crisis, arguing that he would soon be home. In later chapters of this book such as chapter 9 you will see that his perception of the prophecies of Jeremiah were such that Daniel had a very clear anticipation that this alien experience was about to be ended and that his people were going to be liberated from captivity.

'I'm going to get back to Jerusalem,' he could have said to himself. 'I'm sure I'm going to live long enough. Now this edict decrees that if I pray I get thrown to the lions. I didn't stay here for sixty-five years holding the line, just to get eaten by lions three weeks before the train leaves for Jerusalem. That's ridiculous! God surely doesn't want me to do that.'

Or he could have said, 'It's only thirty days. What's thirty days in the space of eighty years of faithfulness? God isn't going worry about a month, is He? I can give it up for a month.'

But he didn't do either. Why not? Discipline.

Let's not miss the obvious challenge before we move on. We are inspired here by Daniel's courage, we are inspired by his moral stability, by his spiritual vigour. But let us understand this, that what drove Daniel was a concern for God and His glory, not a hope that Daniel would get a blessing. Do you notice that distinction? What drove Daniel from the inside of his being was that the God of Abraham, Isaac and Jacob was being maligned and dragged down in that syncretistic, pluralistic environment, and not for thirty minutes would he cease to pray for God and for His glory, even if his life should end prematurely.

Listen. Living in a culture that constantly holds out the prospect of immediate gratification, we can find ourselves always assessing situations on the basis of 'What's in it for me?' That becomes the criterion. We have a call from the word of God to purity, and we say, 'What's in it for me and my girlfriend?' Never mind what it will mean for you. Do it, that's what God's word says. And I can tell you it will mean blessing for you. Daniel was not saying, 'Feel good about yourself: pray.' He was saying, 'God and His glory are at stake.' To cultivate habits of private prayer and devotion which hold us in times of crisis will demand that our over-arching objective is something larger and greater than our own personal preoccupations in our longings for self-fulfilment. Meet anyone who has prayed consistently and you will find that to be true.

There was a Crusader leader in Northern Ireland called T. S. Moony. He went to heaven a few years ago. He was leader of the Londonderry Crusader Class for fifty years. He said, 'I want every boy in my Crusader class to have a Bible in his hand, a Saviour in his heart, and a purpose in his life.'

'T. S.' was a man of prayer. His house in Londonderry was like a rogues' gallery. Photographs of boys between the ages of seven and nine, once members of his Crusader class and now scattered all round the world, covered his walls. It was a great discovery to find a small photograph of myself among them!

He was a great talker, and could talk you late into the night. But he was always up before you in the morning. Why? Well, he never talked about it, but in the little old Bible that he always carried with him he kept sheets of paper which were his prayer lists. All the names were scribbled down. He used to write to me and say, 'I remember you daily at the best place.' On the day that he went to heaven they found him in his rooms; his house-keeper had come in to see how he was, and had received no reply. She opened the door and found him kneeling at his bedside. When they lifted his body up, they found he had fallen face down on his open Bible and the prayer lists.

Never mind tomorrow; let's consider our lives up to today. What possibility is there of us being found face down on our bed, fully clothed, early in the morning with an open Bible and a prayer list? You see, what T. S. was when he was 83 was established when he was 18. And what we'll be when we are 83 is simply an extension of what we are today, according to God's grace.

Daniel was dumped (12–19)

The king gave the order reluctantly, trapped by his own piece of legislation. He was 'greatly distressed' (verse 14). His attempts to devise a last-minute legal and constitutional escape clause failed. He ended up having to enact the edict.

Verse 16 tells us that he was 'thrown' into the lions' den. Commentators say there was probably a ramp for the animals and a hole for the victims. When I read that it made me reflect that every putrefying culture will take more concern for its animals than it does for its people. We have campaigns for animals, campaigns for the whales, campaigns for the dolphins: and we have a horrible hole down which we flush aborted foetuses and babies.

From a human perspective the decision was irreversible (verse 17). The stone was brought and placed over the mouth of the den and the king sealed it with his own signet ring, jointly with the rings of his nobles; none of them could wriggle out of the edict. The king had no appetite that night (verse 18). The king didn't eat, the lions didn't eat.

There was more agitation in the palace than there was in the den. There will always be more agitation for the wicked. They are like the waves of the sea, they are tossed and they roar and they stumble. He passed a restless night. Then (verse 19) dawn creeps in and Darius creeps in, down to the den. Can you imagine going down there? He had signed the edict. Daniel had been his choice for prime minister. The satraps had trapped him. He didn't want to do it. He'd had to do it. He'd done it. And now what was he going to find?

Daniel was delivered (20–28)

In verse 20 he calls out, in 'an anguished voice'; and in verse 21 the answer comes: 'O king, live for ever.' The familiar royal greeting must have made him feel wonderful! Then in verse 22, Daniel explains. 'My God sent his angel . . .' Notice, there is nothing of Daniel in this. Who does he mention first? God. Is that a surprise? No. Daniel is concerned for God and for His glory. This wasn't him going on Christian television to explain himself and what a wonderful person he was. No. 'My God sent his angel, and he shut the mouths of the lions. They have not hurt me.' Why? 'Because I was found innocent in his sight.'

Daniel was delivered (verse 23) 'because he had trusted in his God'. Down through the years God has sent His angels to shut the mouths of all kinds of lions, manifesting the innocence of His servants and trust in Him.

Does this give a feeling of anticipation? Verse 17: 'a stone was brought'. What does that make you think of? Golgotha! And verse 19, 'at the first light of dawn'—what does that make you think of? It makes you think of the ladies coming to the tomb, doesn't it? There's a wonderful foreshadowing here. The Old Testament church and the New Testament believer would read Daniel 6 and they would anticipate the wonder of what God was about to do. A fore-shadowing of Calvary. Daniel was despised and rejected: so was Christ. Daniel was convicted on trumped-up charges: so was Christ. Christ was left in a sealed den: so was Daniel. And in the dawn of the morning he was proclaimed alive. He's alive! It foreshadows, too, the day when the lion will sit down and eat straw like the ox. Here in this moment six centuries BC, the powers of the world to come break in in anticipation of what it will be like when the king comes to reign.

The end of the chapter is glorious. We've got Darius the king of Persia singing, 'Sing me the king who is coming to reign.' That's what he's singing: verse 26, this God lives; verse 26b, this God reigns; verse 27, this God rescues. This is the great message, and it comes from the tongue of a pagan king. Why? Because of the impact of one solitary life, one who could not be bought, who would not waffle, who was prepared to stand purposefully though all hell broke against him, though he ended with his very life shredded, gnashed in the teeth of lions.

It was this spirit of conviction, loved ones, which fanned into a great flame. It was what was struck in the heart of Luther, what fuelled the Reformation in Scotland, what gave Tyndale the zeal which allowed us our Scriptures to today. And we will not, under God, sustain for a coming generation and days to come all that God intends for His glory—unless we are prepared by His great grace to stand up and say: 'God helping me, I am only one, but I am one. I cannot do everything, but I can do something. What I can do I ought to do, and what I ought to do, by God's grace I will do.'

Daniel: the impact of one solitary life, given over to God and used to the praise of His glory. May God raise up more and more in our days, of such a spirit that the world might know that He reigns.

THE ADDRESSES

'COMING AND GOING'

by Rev Dr Donald English

Mark 3:13–19

The call

'Jesus went up on a mountainside and called to him those he wanted, and they came' (verse 13).

I wonder why you're here at Keswick?

Was a group coming from your church? Did you hear about a Keswick house party and think it would be a good thing to come to? Was there, perhaps, a friend who has been inviting you for years to come, and you thought you'd finally agree to come? A mention in a magazine article, maybe? Perhaps you've wanted to come for years, and for you, as for my wife, this year is your first opportunity. Or are you one of the regulars, the connoisseurs? Did you hear Graham Scroggie preach here? I'm sure there are lots of reasons. And however you got here, I think God called you.

After all, Matthew was called during an ordinary day at the office. Peter was called as he went to work. Jesus keeps meeting you where you happen to be. It becomes a call. And sometimes you don't realise it's a call until you find out what the meaning is.

The place

The place is important. He went up a mountain. Those who know their Old Testament will know a little bit about that. Mount Moriah—Abraham, offering his son Isaac; Mount Sinai—Moses given the charge of delivering the Ten Commandments; Elijah—'What are you doing on this mountain?'; Jesus, transfigured on a mountain, and Moses and Elijah talked with Him. He called those He wanted from a mountain, because a mountain is redolent with the presence of God.

Well, you don't have to go far from this tent to find mountains. But whether you are on them or just looking at them, this is a holy place. I wonder how many missionaries have gone round the world on the strength of what has happened at Keswick? How many people have been called into the full-time ministry? How many have come tired and depressed and have found here a new way of being a Christian? How many have laid to rest here things that were destroying their Christian lives? And how many have taken up things that made all the difference in the world?

You see, God was saying to Abraham, 'Abraham, would you—if I asked you? Abraham, how far would you go?' He was saying to Moses, up a mountain, 'I'm only asking you this, and I'm only asking you once; will you take My word to that rabble, My people?' He was saying to Elijah, 'It's not in the lightning, it's not in the fire; it's in the still small voice. Elijah, if you will just listen—I'm with you.' And to Jesus, the heavenly Father was saying, 'My Son—you know who Moses is, don't you. You know who Elijah is, don't you. They say to you that the whole of divine history is leading you on to your exodus.' Oh, a mountain place with Jesus can be a very dangerous place to be, because wonderful things happen when Jesus calls you, and you go.

The setting

But the setting was important, too. Not just the mountain, but the time too. Abraham changed the course of history. Moses was so significant in the history of the people of Israel that they could barely get themselves free from being too dominated by him, as we shall see in the Bible studies on Galatians. Elijah wasn't having a private, personal, spiritual holiday—he was taking on the kings of the day. Jesus was about the kingdom of God.

You can't have a private spiritual journey in God's world. You can't come to something like this as if nothing was going on outside, as though somehow we shut the world off. God calls us to be with Jesus among the mountains. But 250 handicapped children were abandoned in Bosnia last week. People are being shot in Somalia. South Africa teeters on the brink of either some great breakthrough or the most awful killing we have yet known. And Northern Ireland goes on being a place where people are being shot.

The world around us cannot be kept out of our Convention. For it's God's world. And in any case, some of the old questions take on new shapes. The question of how a Christian should respond to war has never been the same since atomic fission was discovered. All the arguments about Just War were largely nonsense in relation to what we did to Iraq. And euthanasia isn't the same either, now that we can keep people breathing long after the rest of them seems to have died. Questions about birth are not the same, as we consider how geneticists could help us to choose what kind of baby to have. We can't come into this tent day by day as though those things weren't happening, because Jesus said, 'I have other sheep that are not of this sheep pen' (John 10:16). It was Jesus who said, 'It's wonderful that they're all here, but let's go to other towns and cities, I've got to tell the good news there also' (cf Mark 1:38). It was Jesus who would keep on about the kingdom of God, about God's rule needing to be everywhere, all through the world. So there's no way that you and I can come here this week and switch off the news, get all holy by forgetting the world, when it's God's world.

My wife and I listened to the radio programme *Any Questions* on our way here: the question of homosexuality was raised. Then we listened to *Any Answers*. There wasn't a single attempt to come to terms with any of the Christian attitudes to sexuality. It raises the question of creation, of humanity, of grace, of holiness, of relationships, of God's will—not a single word was said. How can we come away and hide in this lovely tent and talk about holiness, if we're not willing to ask, 'Lord, what does holiness have to do with all of that?'

I wonder how many in this country have the slightest idea what the New Testament contains. My wife and I have a relative, a headmistress in a senior large inner-city school. She read the story of the Good Samaritan to a sixth-form class. Not one of them had ever even heard it before. That's Britain! And those who do know Bible stories, how much do they understand?

Our Lord did not narrow the gospel down to a purely individualistic thing. Everything He said was full of the sense of the world belonging to His heavenly Father, and His having come to claim it back. So, we say to ourselves: in that setting, with all the things that were going wrong around, what was it our Lord was trying to do with these men?

The commission

'That he might send them out to preach and to have authority to drive out demons' (verses 14–15).

The commission to explain

The trouble with the word 'preach', which is how the NIV translates *kerusso*, is that we have fixed it in a first-century setting and then given it our twentieth-century shape. So we think of 'preach' as something that people do in pulpits, or the brave in the open air. But if you look at the Acts of the Apostles, that wasn't how the preaching happened at all. Acts 2: why did Peter preach? Because something happened to the Christians that they were barely ready for; and suddenly they were all speaking in strange tongues, but everybody understood, and everybody said, 'What's going on?' And Peter said, 'I'll tell you; this is what Joel said. It's happened!'

That wasn't 'How many hymns shall we have on Sunday, Mr Preacher?' Something had happened, and it needed explaining. And the preaching was taking the gospel and giving meaning to something that was happening. Acts 3: the Beautiful Gate. Suddenly the man says 'Will you give me money?' And Peter says 'We haven't got any money. But what we have I will give you—in the name of Jesus Christ of Nazareth, get up and walk.' Now nobody records who was the most surprised when he leaped to his feet. But Peter said 'Isn't it wonderful?' He never doubted after that. When you do the works of Jesus, when you proclaim the words of Jesus, the power of Jesus is present.

But that wasn't 'Which readings do you want on Sunday,

Mr Preacher?' Things happened, they were drawn into events, and Peter said, 'If you want an explanation, I'll give you one.'

In Acts 4 they were taken before the court. Now in a legal setting Peter explains what was going on. The whole of Acts was written like that. They didn't go to formal worship and 'preach'—they moved around the world. People said, 'What's going on?' And one or other of them told them. The jail gates burst open in Philippi—you can see the headlines; the poor old jailer was ready to kill himself; Paul said 'There's no need to get drastic about it! We're all here.'

The jailer says, 'But why are you here?'

'Aha!' says Peter. 'I'll tell you . . .'

Do you hear what I'm saying? They walked through the world. They didn't hide away in tents. And as things happened around them and people said 'Whatever are we going to do, whatever are we going to do?', one or other of them said, 'I'll tell you.'

Around us today, people are saying, 'Why are the young so unruly? Why are they turning to drugs? Why is there so much lawbreaking? Why are people being so cruel to each other? Why do blocs of countries fall apart? Why can't the white live with the black? Why can't the rich care for the poor? Why can't the employed work shorter hours so that the unemployed can have a job?' The questions are bursting out all over. And we, you and I, are there. Your workmate says, 'I don't know what it's all coming to. Do you?' That's the moment to 'preach'. The answer isn't 'Oh, we've got a wonderful vicar, you ought to hear him preach.' They don't want to hear that. They want to know why you and why I are still Christians.

We read the same papers as they do. We see the same news, listen to the same radio. And what they want to know is not 'How does your preacher preach?' but 'How do *you* make sense of it? What does it mean to be a Christian today, with all of this going on? How can you believe in a God of love?'

Jesus sent them out to preach. But that's what it includes. As well as the 'preaching', it includes the daily attempting to make sense of life's problems in the light of the gospel, which is the privilege of every Christian.

The commission to embody the gospel

He sent them out with authority to cast out demons. There's been a great deal made in many Christian circles in the last twenty or thirty years, of signs and wonders. I believe that that movement has given an insight into one part of the teaching of Jesus that had been greatly neglected. I don't think, however, that we should limit signs and wonders to the particular things we see happening in the New Testament. Signs and wonders are moments when God does something through his people that causes the rest to say, 'What's the explanation of that?'

It might be something very drastic like the casting out of a demon. And it might be when somebody is wonderfully healed. And it might be when a community is transformed under the power of the gospel. But it's a lot of other things as well. I visited a young minister and his wife in the Midlands, in a little estate where I, to be frank, couldn't live. If anybody was thrown out of the youth club, the youth club leader would be attacked going home. Bricks are thrown through the window—by the members of the youth club. The minister and his wife are staying there. That's a sign and a wonder. And on the Sunday I went, the weekly drama spot in the church included a reading from the Book of Nehemiah by a young woman. Afterwards the minister told me, 'She has never read in public before; and when I came, she could neither read nor write.' The minister had taught her; that was the first fruits. And if that's not a sign and a wonder, I've never seen one.

In Lancashire I went down to the rooms below a great hall where I was conducting worship up above, but below, the dregs of the city were gathering. And sitting in the centre was a huge man in an old pullover, loving them for Jesus' sake; the people of the streets coming in. And I thought, Why am I going upstairs to lead worship? Where would Jesus be? I think He would have sent a substitute upstairs and stayed below, because that's where the sign and the wonder were going on. And you could tell me again and again the signs and the wonders that are taking place in the life of the Christian church.

But we need more! We need such a situation in this land that those who find themselves at their wits' end say 'Let's go to the Christians.' A woman was once brought to my study door by a Samaritans worker. The woman's name was Mary. She'd made an unsuccessful suicide attempt. It was par for the course for her; she'd failed at everything she'd attempted. We talked and prayed, and she started to attend our fellowship. I rang the Samaritans lady later and asked her why she had brought Mary. 'Well,' came the answer, 'she said to me that if you couldn't help, she was going to commit suicide.'

'But why me?' I asked.

'Because everybody in this area knows that if they're in need, they go to *your* church.'

That's nothing at all to do with me, but to do with a church that was a sign and a wonder.

Now, my sisters and my brothers, we've got to be absolutely clear about this. It's no good talking about the failure of evangelism and about needing different leadership and more training courses, if we ourselves are not willing to be the explainers of meaning, as Jesus sent His first disciples, and if we are not willing to be signs and wonders for the world. An American Methodist woman minister said to me, 'In our down-town church we feed hundreds of people every day. And I say to my workers, "You are only here to feed them. Don't preach at them. But you *are* allowed to listen for the golden question."'

'What is the golden question?' her workers asked.

' "Why do you people do this?" ', she replied. 'And when they say that, you don't say "Aw, shucks!" or "The minister told us to." You say, "We do this because the Lord who loves us loves you also." *Then* tell them the gospel.'

That was the commission. Explain what it means in the setting, and be yourselves embodiments of it.

The call to be with Him

Now, those of you who are following the text will see that I have missed something out. 'He called them to be with him.' He called them so that He might send them out, that He might give them authority. He called them to be with Him not to have a conference, nor to form a committee, nor to have a study of the situation (all of which are excellent things to do). He called them to be with Him.

This is where what we are doing here becomes essential to us. The reason why the only answer to the problems I'm setting out is to be found here, is that we have come here to be with Jesus. And He is the only answer to these problems. You see, Jesus in the New Testament is not first and foremost described as our personal Saviour. I hope that isn't too shocking: He is my personal Saviour, thank God; what would I have been without Him?—but He's not first and foremost that in the New Testament, nor is He first and foremost the Head of the church which is the body of Christ, though thank God He is that too.

He is first and foremost in the New Testament the secret of everything.

'In the beginning was the Word, and the Word was with God, and the Word was God. The same was in the beginning with God. All things were made through him; and without him was not anything made that was made' (John 1:1–3, AV). Isn't that beautiful? The heart-beat of the entire created universe is being described. It's as though John is saying, 'God the Father put the living Word at the centre and built the universe around His heart-beat.' Isn't that beautiful. 'And the Word became flesh, and dwelt among us, (and we beheld his glory, the glory as of the only begotten Son of the Father,) full of grace and truth' (John 1:14). He means Jesus! Jesus is the Word of creation. He's the one at the heart of the entire created universe.

That's what John says, and it's not just his idea. Paul says in Colossians, 'All things were made through him and for him and in him they all hold up' (cf Colossians 1:15–17). Jesus is the living Word who holds the world in being, who holds the stars in space. And the writer to the Hebrews says, 'Through his Son he brought the ages into being' (cf Colossians 1)—the world rolling forwards all depends on Jesus. Can you worship a Saviour like that, and narrow religion down? How can you worship a Lord who is the Lord of the universe, and pretend that what happens in Bosnia is none of our business? Or even that coming to Him to have a holy life would somehow not relate to that?

He's the Lord of it all, and He gathered all that His Heavenly Father had written into the universe, in Himself. And that's why when He wanted to explain about His death and resurrection, when the disciples didn't understand, He put it another way: 'You know when you put a grain of wheat into the ground it's to all intents and purposes gone. But you get a crop. Well, that's how it is. That's how it's going to be with Me. As My Father has built death and resurrection into the universe, so I will take that death and resurrection and make it the secret of the salvation of the entire world' (cf John 12:23–26).

That's an offer! The Lord of the universe is the Christ of the cross, is the Lord of the empty tomb, is the risen ascended Lord who sits on the right hand of the Father and will come again in glory. That's Jesus Christ who calls us to be with Him. So if we are inclined to be overwhelmed by the problems of the world, let's remember who we're dealing with.

I've told this story here before, but it seems so relevant. It's said that Lewis's store in Birmingham wanted to extend their building but the Friends' Meeting House was in the way. The directors wrote to them. 'We want to extend our premises and your building is in the way. Please name a price and we will buy your premises and get on with the business.'

The reply came by return: 'We have been here longer than Lewis's, and in order to stay where we are we would be glad to buy Lewis's. Please name a price and we'll get on with the business. Signed . . . Cadbury.'

You see, it's not how big the building is, it's who signs the letters. Who is signing your letters when you listen to the news? As people say, 'What's your God doing about this then?' When people say, 'Has the church anything to say about genetic engineering . . . about homosexuality . . . about what's happening to the children and the poor?' We say 'Oh, well, I mean—I'm just . . .'

Who signs our letters—we the church, who have among us all the people we need to answer all the questions I'm talking about? If the church was concerned enough, why of course we could do it.

So we come to here and now. What shall we do this week?

Jesus did preach. You'll hear His voice this week, thank God, again and again and again. Jesus did move among the crowds. Look out, He'll be among us. Jesus went to the poor and the needy. Are there any in Keswick, I wonder?

Jesus was open to answering questions. My wife and I recently stood for an hour on the Mount of the Beatitudes. I could almost see them walking up that hill, and hear one of the disciples saying: 'Master, who are the happy people?' And I could hear Jesus say, 'Well, happy are the poor in spirit.' Ask Him this week, as He walks with you; ask Him. He could also tell people where they were going wrong; ask Him. He could also tell people how their lives should be lived; ask Him. I'm inviting you by the grace of God this week, to walk with Jesus.

Not a Jesus created in your own image, I mean the real Jesus. I mean the secret of the entire created universe. I mean the Lord who died on the cross for us. I mean the one who lives with us now and in us through the Holy Spirit. I'm inviting you to walk with Jesus and to open your whole life to Him this week. Let nothing be kept back. Bring the world with you. It's His, lift it to Him and say, 'Lord, what could I do? And what kind of person do I need to be to do anything?'

I encourage you to do this, because many years ago Keswick became hallowed in my own life. I came as a young undergraduate in a position of leadership far beyond what I deserved because I knew very little. And I was troubled about holiness teaching, and particularly about 'second-blessing' teaching and I really didn't know where I was. I came to the IVF camp here in search of something to help me out of my difficulty. And in the same day three separate people, none of whom knew either of the others, said the same thing to me: 'Donald,' they said, 'whatever else holiness is about it's about giving the whole of yourself to Jesus, that He might wholly take and use you.'

After the last conversation, over a cup of coffee somewhere in Keswick, I came into my tent. Everybody else was fast asleep. I knelt and I said, 'Lord, I don't understand all these theories of holiness, but I do understand what it means to say: Whatever and whoever I am I give myself to You, and I ask You to fill me.'

The next day two of us hitch-hiked home. We hadn't got very far down the road when we were dropped and we went for a cup of tea. There was a man of the road there on the next table and he was swearing and cursing. And I saw myself get up and walk over to him and say, 'Hello.'

He said 'Hello.'

I said, 'Jesus *loves* you.'

And he just burst into tears. And I was there I don't know how long, sharing with him the good news of Jesus. I wouldn't advise *anybody* to use that method; it's not in any of the text books. But there was some link between what happened the night before and what happened that day that I will never forget.

So Keswick to me is very precious. Not because I learned a great new theory of holiness, but because I learned actually what Keswick is about, which is that our Lord offers Himself wholly to us. He who made it all and died for us and rose and is ascended, He who sent His Spirit among us offers Himself wholly to us. And the invitation is, 'Why don't you give yourself wholly to Me?'

He called them and they came. And He sent them. What power in this tent for this week, if we'll genuinely walk with Him!

'OUT OF THE DEPTHS'

by Mr Nigel Lee

Psalm 130

Psalm 130 is one of a group of psalms, from 120–134, known as the Songs of Ascents; literally, 'the songs of the going-up'. Three times a year every Jew who could manage it was expected to appear before God in Jerusalem. It wasn't just a habit and wasn't just a pattern of the rhythm of national life. This was something that God commanded of them, it was their duty, it was a calling to appear. They would set out on their long journeys from the far corners of their land, streaming in from all over Israel, gradually converging on Jerusalem to climb the hill of the Lord to His holy temple. And these songs of ascents were to be sung or perhaps meditated upon during that journey, depending upon how far they had come, maybe one or two a day. They were not written in an ordered sequence and they were written by a number of different people—four by David, one by Solomon, the rest perhaps by different authors. Some have suggested Hezekiah as an author. But when they were being put together, it was discovered what the Holy Spirit had given in these different psalms. Pilgrims used to sing them, ponder them, allow them to shape their attitudes and prepare their hearts as they were travelling, ready to ascend the hill of the Lord in Jerusalem.

I guess it's true of most of us that during a week like this we have more time for the reflective chewing on the word of God than is the case normally in our lives. And I guess some of us who come from very busy lives find, as we come to a week like this, that our own sense of regular daily Bible reading is frayed at the edges and is sometimes in tatters. Perhaps some of us have got a little bit adrift in our reading. I want to suggest to you, during this time at Keswick; if you don't know where to start again, why not begin with these songs of ascents and follow with the Jewish pilgrims as they prepared to come before God? As they allowed these psalms, one after the other, to direct and move their attitude of hearts—the first, for example, Psalm 120; as they set out from their homes, longing for their real spiritual home when they will appear before God. Perhaps they made that journey after a year of living among those who were not lovers of God but lovers of self, people who with their antagonisms and their words made life uncomfortable.

Psalm 120 sets out on that journey. In Psalm 121, the pilgrim is pondering on the ways of God in his own life over the past year: 'I will lift up my eyes to the hills . . .' Where has my help been coming from? My help comes from the Lord. He watches over you, over your life, over your coming and going. In the next, Psalm 123, the pilgrim thinks about the end of the journey, the Jerusalem that he will come to and all its turbulent history: God's hand has been upon that city and upon its testimony all these centuries. In Psalm 133, which we looked at briefly in this morning's Bible reading, they are now very close to the end of the journey. Pilgrims who never meet each other at other times of the year are beginning to stream in together. 'How good, how pleasant it is, when brothers dwell together in unity, for there the Lord commanded the blessing' (AV). And as those who came down from the north saw those coming up from the south and the people from beyond Jordan, I guess it wasn't very easy for them to live together in unity. They would ponder the psalm as they moved closer to the Lord's home.

Read them this week. You can work out yourselves the stages of that spiritual journey. You will come at the end to Psalm 134: 'Praise the Lord, all you servants of the Lord who minister by night in the house of the Lord. Lift up your hands in the sanctuary and praise the Lord.' That's where that journey ends.

Tonight we are going to be looking in close detail at Psalm

130 on that journey. Where is this particular pilgrim coming from?

Well, he doesn't say, except that he has been in the depths. Psalm 130, a song of ascents, out of the depths. 'Lord I've been facing discouragements ... Lord I've been facing near-despair ... Lord I feel really down.' How honest the Scriptures are! Here is a man on his way to worship God with the great congregation, to take his own part with the crowd in one of the national celebrations of God's people in the house of God, and he feels empty. There's nothing there. Yes, he's on the journey day by day, walking along. 'Lord, I'm in the depths and I need to meet with you and hear you.'

You can be walking along through your own journey of life actually carrying your depths with you. Each day a day's journey closer to home, and they come with you. Boris Becker, two years after becoming the youngest tennis player ever to win Wimbledon, was in utter despair contemplating suicide. He was only nineteen and he said: 'I was on dead-end street.' It was the old story of stars who have everything and yet are the most unhappy people in the world. The man was exhausted. Outwardly he was the star, and inwardly a human being at the end of his rope. What depths!

Some years ago I was staying over night in the University of Cambridge, taking some meetings there. While I was asleep the young man in the room above me took his own life, leaving simply a two-word note: 'Nobody cares'. There are hundreds of people in hospitals and prisons, in nursing homes, who are sleeping homeless on the streets of our big cities, and who are in our churches; and they feel that 'Nobody cares.' Sometimes the depths can be very, very low. Maybe some of you are sitting here and every day it comes back to you that the partner or the friend who was with you last year is not with you today. Or you come grieving over your children, who as they have grown up have grown up away from the Lord and from you. You sit longing for comfort out of the depths.

With this particular psalmist the problem is not exhaustion or loneliness. It's not that life has taken one of its funny turns. It seems rather to be a growing consciousness of sin as he takes each step. Every step and every day takes him nearer to a God he doesn't really want to face. Maybe it was a sense of national sin; maybe it was a concern for God's people in his own area that caused him to write this. But I suspect that it was more probably his own guilty conscience about the way he himself has been living. And as he's coming to that occasion when people gather from all over the country, when he knows he's going to hear the word of God read, when he knows he's going to have to sing the praises of God and be exposed to the things of God, the light begins to intensify; and there are things in his own heart, conflict in his own family life, areas of selfishness in his own life this past year, that the Lord has been speaking to him about and he knows he's been disobedient. There's something between him and the Lord that will have to be dealt with before he gets to the end of the journey.

Maybe this happens to us also. Sin stops us running, as the psalmist puts it, 'in the way of your commands' (Psalm 119:32). That is a great thing isn't it, to get up in the morning and say, 'I want to run, Lord, in the way of Your commands.' Sin hinders, so easily entangles us (cf Hebrews 12); and the Lord brings us to these points in our lives where we must face it.

I had an uncle who lived in this area who was a sheep farmer. It was my delight to go and work with him whenever I possibly could, and to go out on some of these nearby hills with his sheep-dogs, Panda and Rock. High on the hills, looking down at the dogs gently bringing the sheep back to my uncle, was an experience that reminds me of the thought in Psalm 23 that the Lord's two sheepdogs, Goodness and Mercy, will follow me all the days of my life. The Lord, with His goodness and His mercy, sheep-dogs us to these points where we have to face the reality, and not be anaesthetised any longer to our sensitivity of where we have offended the Lord and hurt Him.

Martin Luther was once asked at table which in his opinion were the greatest of the psalms. He thought for a moment or two and then said, '32, 51, 130 and 143.' When asked why, he explained, 'Those are all psalms of deep repentance and glorious forgiveness.' You'll see he included the psalm we are reading tonight.

What does the psalmist do? Two things, which divide the psalm into two parts.

I cry to you, O Lord (verse 1)

Notice that he has decided to cry to the Lord even before he's arrived. Maybe he would tiptoe away from the crowd and just stand silently and cry out to the God whom he was going to meet at the end of that long pilgrimage. 'I cry to you, O Lord.' And God heard him. Friends, it does not matter what depths of circumstances and sin you are in; it does not matter so long as you still have breath in your body to cry. Spurgeon used to say, 'Deep places beget deep devotion. He that prays in the depths will not sink out of his depth.' And that was the testimony of Daniel in his lion pit, Jeremiah in his dungeon, Jonah in the belly of the fish, and that un-named tax collector standing at the back who wouldn't even look up to heaven, crying out, 'Lord have mercy on me, a sinner.'

Notice that the psalmist is crying out loud. He's not simply thinking these things over in his mind, he's expressing them audibly, he's crying out loud. In the Revised Version it puts it like this, 'Lord, hear my voice: let thine ears be attentive to the voice of my supplications.' I think it's a great thing when we can pray out loud. I work a lot at home, and sometimes the only way to get free is to go out and pray. I have certain walks—a short prayer walk and a long prayer walk. The long one is round the golf course. I like to pray as I walk; I sometimes lift my arms up and wave. I've disturbed many golfers! It's a good thing to be able to pray out loud. Don't be afraid to pray and let your voice be heard; make it definite with the Lord.

Notice, too, that he's crying for mercy. You hear Christians pray a lot for strength. They pray for wisdom, they pray for guidance. I spend a lot of time in prayer meetings, and I have to say, I rarely hear people crying to the Lord for mercy. The psalmist senses that he's been wrong, he's been disobedient, he needs God's mercy. There are things he's done that he should not have done, there are things that he's not done this past year. Perhaps last time he was up in Jerusalem or at a great Convention, he promised he would do things, and now he's back. 'O Lord, I need mercy.'

And as he begins to cry he makes two discoveries. First,

With you there is forgiveness (verse 4a)
If God kept a record of sins, not one of us in this room could stand. 'But with you there is forgiveness', because He's willing to take that record and tear it up. No-one in the history of the world has ever come to God in heart-felt repentance and found God gruff or hard to deal with.

That was what the Old Testament declared. In Exodus 34:6, 'He passed in front of Moses, proclaiming, "The Lord, the Lord, the compassionate and gracious God, slow to anger, abounding in love and faithfulness, maintaining love to thousands, and forgiving wickedness, rebellion and sin." '

With me, sin; with the Lord, forgiveness. I guess many of you have grasped that and lived in the light of it for years and years. You come back to it over and over again, it's the anchor of your life. And there are others here tonight with a needle-sharp awareness that things have gone wrong, that sin stains your heart and your mind.

I love preaching to students in my work with UCCF. It's such a joy and privilege to gather a roomful of pagan godless British students. The New Age movement creeps around them like a poisonous fog; and the result is the thinking that is so prevalent among our young people: 'Yes, I believe that probably there's a God out there; at least, you can believe if you wish; and I have my own god.' But that god they believe in is speechless, he's nameless, he's powerless, he has no personality. What it is to preach this God who has the name Jesus, who forgives sin! Students are human beings, they have guilty consciences, and the stuff they pick up from the newspapers and television somehow destroys for them the sense that there is a God who cares and loves them and can forgive them. And so they've got no-one left to cry to.

After I've talked about this God, I love to be able to tell them, 'You could write down every single thing that you know about your own life that is an offence to God. Then call in your friends, get them to add to the list. And then you could go for hypnotherapy and more things could be dragged out. And then, if you like, the Angel Gabriel could arrive fresh from heaven with a hot, glowing further list. Then, when you've got the whole list and hardly enough paper to contain it, I would want to read to you Colossians 2:13. Christ forgives us all our sins. God forgave us all our sin because of Christ. He doesn't keep the record.'

If He doesn't keep the record, what does He keep in heaven? He keeps His wounds—'Those wounds yet visible above, in beauty glorified'[1]. And He knows why they are there; they are there so that you and I might be there. Will the Lord Jesus Christ have forgotten in heaven that you and I are sinners? Imagine you were strolling down the streets of heaven and there was the Lord Himself. 'O Lord Jesus,' you say. 'I've been meaning to ask you—these holes in Your hands, where did you get them?' Would the Lord say, 'What holes? I never noticed them before. How strange you should draw My attention to them!' Is that a likely reply? The Lamb that was slain is the very subject of praise in heaven right now. He knows exactly why the wounds are there, and so do you. Yet He will not keep the record, He will not hold it against us. 'With you there is forgiveness.'

And then the second thing that's discovered,

Therefore you are feared (verse 4b)

What an interesting thing to put into this Old Testament psalm! It's God's grace that causes people to fear Him. Some will tell you that you need to preach the law and preach it strong and hot to folks, to get them to learn to fear God. I think, how foolish. We only have to look into our own hearts. What is it that has made your heart run after the Lord Jesus? Was it the law? Surely it was Calvary, surely it was seeing for yourself the grace and the kindness of a God who would do that for you.

> Soften my heart Lord, soften my heart,
> From all indifference set me apart,
> Bring me to Calvary.

And the converse is also true. As Christian men and women,

what is that causes our hearts to gradually harden up and to become cold? It's because it's been a long time since we were last asking personally out loud for real forgiveness.

I wait for the Lord (verse 5)

'Whatever my circumstances, whatever's happening, I wait for the Lord.' Notice, it's personal. He's not waiting for correct doctrine or a good meeting; he's not even saying that he's going to wait for forgiveness; it's much more personal than that. 'I am waiting for the Lord.'

The answer is never 'it', it's always 'Him'. The psalmist says, 'I am going to wait for the Lord, my soul waits . . .' My soul is engaged; I am not going to be passive in my dealings with God. The innermost core of my being is going to hunger for God and wait upon Him, and I am going to wait for His coming. He is coming ultimately, yes, when the heavens are going to be unzipped and the Lord will come through with the angels—that will be great! But those other comings, the kind the Lord talked about when He said in John 14: 'If you love me and keep My commandments, My Father will love you, and I will love you and I will show Myself to you' (cf John 14:21).

'I am going to wait' says the psalmist, 'for those manifestations of the Lord to my own soul. I am going to wait more than watchmen wait for the morning—more than for the sunrise.' I suppose you can say two things about the sunrise. You can't hurry it; and it will come. 'I am going to wait'—wait as the West Indian slaves waited on the last night of July in 1830, knowing that the next day they would be declared free: I don't think anybody slept. They gathered in their places of worship and began to sing. Waiting for those first streaks of dawn which would see their freedom arrive, they would send some of their young men onto the hilltops to watch to catch an even earlier glimpse and send the message down into the valley. How eagerly those slaves must have watched and waited!

I am old enough to have something of a sense for the changing fashions and trends in preaching. Is it just my wrong impression that we hear less of the return of the Lord

Jesus than we used to? We don't often talk about the return of the Lord in a way that makes people want to live in holiness, to wait for the dawning of that coming day.

'My soul waits,' says the psalmist, 'my soul waits more than watchmen wait for the morning.' And he makes two more discoveries.

With the Lord is unfailing love (verse 7)

Isn't it tragic to see marriages breaking up? I imagine that some here have watched weddings in which vows were made before God, and then seen even in a short time those promises forgotten and the marriage broken, and the love that was promised unconditionally turn out to be a very short-term thing. But 'with the Lord is unfailing love'.

There was a father in the Old Testament whose son had been involved in a murder within the family. He then tried to foment a rebellion and steal the crown from his father David. There was a civil war and an army went out to fight young Absalom; and David sat waiting. Eventually the message came back to say that Absalom had lost his life fleeing from the battle, caught with his long wavy hair and thrust through the heart with an arrow. The rebellion was over, the rebel was dead and David went sobbing to his room. 'Oh my son Absalom! My son, my son Absalom! If only I had died instead of you . . .' (2 Samuel 18:33). A father's love—and yet greater is the love of God for us. With him is full redemption ('plenteous redemption', says the Authorised Version).

The psalmist started off in the depths, he began to pray, he found relief in God's unconditional forgiveness, he began to hope that the Lord would visit him, his hope grew to expectancy because of the Lord's character—His love, His redemption—and now, what's happened?

O Israel, put your hope in the Lord (verse 7)

He Himself will redeem Israel from all their sin. The focus has gone from the sin to the Saviour, from the depths to having the heart of an evangelist. And brothers and sisters, I want to tell you that the one thing that gets many evangelists back into the depths is that they are so often criticised and unsupported. Of all the giftings in the New Testament, it seems that sometimes the evangelist is the one who gets it in the neck most often.

Billy Graham?—but of course, Billy Graham's made one or two false moves, hasn't he, with regard to Catholics . . . Luis Palau?—well, he's not quite as good as Billy Graham . . . And the same with Eric Delve and J John and all the rest. It amazes me how somebody can be mentioned, and then a little criticism slipped almost within microseconds.

Friends, if we are to have contact with the living word of God, it's going to put a living word in our own mouths. The heart of an evangelist begins to grow up at the end of this psalm. The man who set off on his pilgrimage in the depths and struggling along, now finds that he's got something that he wants to share with the other pilgrims. 'I want to tell them that God's heart is brimming over with love and forgiveness and acceptance.'

For many of us opportunities for full-time missionary service are limited. But you can pray, you can get behind those who go out calling other folks out of the depths. Just think of the potential. Four thousand people in this tent. Just think of the power of an army like this, really getting behind the evangelism that goes on in this country alone, let alone others.

I wish that you could sometimes see some hurting students with whom we work. I was in a mission just a few months ago. A knock came on the door at midnight. It was a young student, come to talk with somebody on the mission team. He had only that day been diagnosed as having AIDS. His life was all broken up. To be able to share the gospel with such folk, to know that there are thousands who are going to get involved and play their part in seeing others brought out of these depths!

To share the gospel we discover, that which we express back to God as we raise our voices and say, 'Lord, I need forgiveness for the selfish use of money, for the wrong use of time, for persisting in that silly quarrel with that other person in the church.' And then, as you discover that He is just full of love and forgiveness and mercy, we fall silent.

The end of the psalm: you cannot avoid it; let the two

sheep dogs Goodness and Mercy bring you to it—*He has a word for the others all around.*

Let us who are redeemed get behind those who have opportunities and gifts to see the work of evangelism go forward in this country as we move towards the end of this century, and forward beyond this country.

God is working. People are queuing up in Albania to start churches—unbelievable! A little OM team goes in and does a bit of work, and next thing they know they've got a church to run—bigger, I guess, than some of the churches we come from here. God is working, and it's exciting: to be involved, to move from those depths to see that God wants to draw us not merely into being sorted out and going home and chewing over what we learned one week in July for another year until we come back; but to be part of that great army that the Lord is putting together; to go out onto those streets where dark forces are waiting.

'The one I regard,' says the Lord, 'is the one who is humble and contrite in spirit and who trembles at My word.'

May the Lord give us soft hearts. May the Lord bring us from wherever He finds us today back to the cross, and then open our mouths, even if only in passionate prayer. But why should I say 'even'? Pray that there might come that pouring out of God's Spirit upon us and a manifestation of the Lord Himself in our midst these days.

Note

1. Matthew Bridges, 'Crown Him With Many Crowns'.

'THE LAW OF LIFE'

by Mr Charles Price

Romans 7:21–8:8

I want to talk about something that will concern every person here tonight who really means business with God, whether you've been a Christian for a year or a month or fifty years.

Most of us are aware that we have a problem perhaps deeper than that of our sins being forgiven, and it's this: 'How do I deal with my self, which is the cause of my sins?' You've probably heard it said that a person is not a sinner because they commit sins, they commit sins because they are a sinner. You know that a plum seedling will eventually produce plums, not because you are a prophet but because you know that if it came from a plum seed that's all it can produce.

Coming to the cross for the forgiveness of our sins is wonderful, and it's part of the necessary discipline of the Christian life. But the Bible has something to say about the fact that in addition to the things that I do, there is a reason why I do them, which Jesus Christ came to do something about.

You've probably heard of the Four Spiritual Laws; but Paul described Three Spiritual Laws in the passage we have before us, and I want to base what I am going to say upon them.

The law that reveals the character of God (7:22)

Let's first talk about what Paul calls 'God's law', the moral law that God gave to Moses on Mount Sinai but which ever since has only ever caused problems. For it demanded a totally impracticable quality of living, and you and I know that no man, woman or young person in this tent tonight or anywhere has ever kept the law of God.

Why then did God give the law? It seems rather unfair to give laws that nobody can keep. If you make such rules you are asking for trouble. And yet God in giving the law on Mount Sinai gave to Moses a set of demands that from that day on only ever brought failure into the story of the history of Israel. You can write that word 'failure' across the whole Old Testament from Sinai onwards. The historical books record its details, the poetic books weep about it, the prophetic books preach about it. In 7:10 Paul says about that law, in effect, 'It did not do me any good. It only brought me harm. It brought me death.'

So why did God give it? What criterion caused God to determine what the law should be, when He called Moses at Mount Sinai? Was it an arbitrary set of rules trimmed to fit two stone tablets? Or was there some objective criterion? I think there was. And I think it is important to what I want to say to you.

To discover what that criterion is, let me compare two verses in the New Testament which describe sin.

The mark we miss

'Everyone who sins breaks the law; in fact it is lawlessness' (1 John 3:4). Sin means 'to miss the mark'. It's a word that comes from archery. Miss the bulls-eye by half an inch, and it's called sin. Miss it by six inches, that's called sin too. The degree of failure is irrelevant. For sin is not a measurement of how bad we are. It's a measurement of how good we are not. You heard in the morning Bible studies that you cannot appeal to a cricket umpire on the grounds that you did not miss the ball by very much.

Now if sin means to miss the mark, then sin itself is not an absolute. The absolute is the mark that we miss. John says in 1 John 3:4 that every time somebody sins, no matter what sin it may be, we know that they have broken the law of God. Because, he is saying, the law of God represents the target we miss every time we sin.

That doesn't tell us *why* the law is the standard. We might ask, 'Why didn't God make the law a little bit lower, a little bit easier, a little more encouraging?' Let's turn to our second verse.

The glory of God

You probably know this verse by heart. 'All have sinned and fall short of the glory of God'—whatever that is, and we'll come to that in a moment. Put the two verses together. The glory of God is the target that we miss when we sin; all have sinned and fall short of the glory of God. Thus, the law of God and the glory of God are the same thing. So to answer the question 'Why is the law what it is?', we must ask another: 'What is the glory of God?'

In Scripture the word 'glory' occurs with slight variations of meaning depending on its context. But essentially, the glory of God is the character of God. For instance, when John wrote in his Gospel about the Lord Jesus, he said, 'The Word became flesh and made his dwelling among us. We have seen his glory, the glory of the one and only [Son], who came from the Father, full of grace and truth' (1:14). What did they see when they saw His glory? A halo over Jesus's head? Of course not. I suggest that John is saying: 'We saw in Jesus Christ the moral character of God, so that those of us who were boys in Nazareth with Jesus, we saw in the way He played and the way He treated His friends, in the way He talked to His mother—we saw what God is like. When He began to work in His father's carpenter's shop, we saw in the way He went about His business, the way He paid His bills on time, the way He treated His colleagues—we saw what God was like. When He began His public ministry, when He went across the road to talk to a dirty woman with whom everyone else was embarrassed to be seen—we saw what God was like. When we saw Jesus meeting a man who rang a bell crying "Unclean, don't anyone come close", and we saw Jesus take the man's bell and throw it away and touch the man and say, "You're whole, go home and kiss your wife for the first time since you were diagnosed. Play with your kids, rest on the floor, there's nothing to catch any more"—we saw what God was like. Because the glory of God is the character of God.

Now this was not only intended to be true of Jesus. It was intended also to be true of Adam. When God created him, He said, 'Let us make man in our image.' Whatever that means, it means that when you look at Adam you'll be reminded of God. And so I suggest that primarily the image of God in Adam was His moral image. It was not a physical image, because God is not a physical being. But had we been there when He created Adam and Eve and placed them in the Garden of Eden, we would have seen what God was like. The way they handled the animals, the way they patted the dog, stroked the cat—we would have seen what God was like. You look at the image and you see what God is like. But man sinned and came short of the glory of God, and he no longer showed you what God was like.

So the first baby ever to be born grew up to be a murderer. In Genesis we see greed, theft, rape, cheating, scheming and manipulation. And when God gave the law to Moses, He gave a law that revealed His own character, for the law equals the glory of God. He said 'You shall not steal', not because stealing isn't nice but because God is not a thief and human beings are made in His image. He said 'You shall not commit adultery', because God is totally faithful. He said 'You shall not covet', because God is not greedy. He said 'You shall not bear false witness', because God never ever tells lies. He said 'Six days shall you labour and on the seventh day do not work' because God rested on the seventh day. He said 'Children, honour your father and mother', because within the Trinity the Son says, 'I do those things that please the Father'.

And human beings are made in God's image. So do, and be, the same.

The law, I suggest, was given not as an arbitrary guide to behaviour, but to reveal the character of God so that human beings could discover what they are supposed to be like, being created in His image.

That's why this first law, which Paul speaks of as 'God's law', is an absolute law. It is holy, righteous and good. It reveals the character of God. That's why it is absolute, that's why in 7:12 it says 'The law is holy, and the commandment is holy, righteous and good.' Jesus said, there's none good but God alone. What makes good good is that it is equal to what God is. And therefore the law was given in order to reveal the character of God.

The law that resists the character of God (7:23)

We need to understand that, in order to understand what Paul says next in verse 23, about the law which resists the character of God, the law of sin which Paul describes as holding him down and fighting against the demands of the law of God.

In verse 14–21 Paul has been saying, 'There are certain things that the law demands that are good. I agree they are good and I resolve to do them, but I don't. There are things that the law declares are bad and I agree that they are bad and I resolve never to do them again, but I do.' Anybody here got that problem? Yes!

Some of you know that there is a debate about Romans 7:14ff. Is the speaker an unregenerate (non-Christian) person, or a regenerate person? Most of you obviously agree with me that it is a Christian speaking, for you indicated that you share these experiences as do I. There are significant aspects of the description. Verse 18: 'I have the desire to do what is good.' Romans 3 tells us that no-one seeks after God and no-one seeks after righteousness, but this person does. Verse 22: 'I delight in God's law.' Verse 25, 'So then, I myself in my mind am a slave to God's law, but in the sinful nature a slave to the law of sin.' So Paul, the great apostle, is saying, 'This is the real me. This will tell you what goes on in my heart. I know what is right and I want to do it, I know what is wrong and I don't want to do what is wrong, but somehow there is this pull in me and I find I can't do what is right and I do do what is wrong.'

In verse 20 he says, 'Now if I do what I do not want to do, it is no longer I who do it, but it is sin living in me that does it.' My, what a convenient cop-out! It is very interesting, I didn't notice it until this morning in the Bible reading that in Galatians 2 Paul says, 'It is no longer I but Christ living in me,' and in Romans 7 he says, 'It is no longer I but sin living within me.' What does he mean? Well, in verse 23 he speaks of it as the law of sin. It's a bit like the law of gravity. If I hold my pen in the air and let it go, it's going to fall; not because I give it a push, but because there is a physical law that says what goes up must come down. And Paul says, 'There's a natural law in me called the law of sin which pulls me down. We'll never know what it is to appropriate what Jesus Christ accomplished upon the cross by His resurrection, until we accept this diagnosis about myself, that the natural "me" loves sin.'

That's why temptation is a problem. Every temptation is to something I like to do, otherwise it wouldn't be temptation. By definition, it's attractive, it appeals to what I want. Every sin I commit I may regret thirty seconds later, but I did it because I wanted to. Don't kid yourself! 'There's a natural law in me pulling me down,' and this man that Paul describes in Romans 7 is a man who loves the law of God, who is zealous for the law of God, who really wants to do what is right—but has discovered he is bankrupt: 'I can't do it.'

Thirty-eight times in verses 15–25 Paul uses the words 'I', 'me', 'my'. This 'I' is hungering to do right, and is not enjoying falling into the mess and muck of his sin. And in verse 24 he comes to this conclusion: 'What a wretched man I am! Who will rescue me from this body of death?' He has come to the depths of the psalmist in Psalm 130: 'Out of the depths I cry to you, O Lord . . .', 'My soul waits for the Lord . . .' And Paul in Romans 7 has come to that point. 'Who will rescue me?'

And the question is not 'What will rescue me? Is there a method, programme, technique or experience that will set me free?', but 'Who will rescue me? Is there someone?' And verse 25 responds, 'Thanks be to God, through Jesus Christ our Lord!'

The law that restores the character of God (8:2)

'Through Christ Jesus the law of the Spirit of life set me free from the law of sin and death.'

Is there a way out? Yes, says Paul, there is. It is the life of
Jesus Christ lived in me by the Holy Spirit who empowers
me and enables me to be Godly in a Godless world. Let me
illustrate this. Three years ago I was speaking in Cape Town
on the fact that the Christian life is the consequence of the
life of Christ in the Christian. Jesus is not the patron or guru
of our Christianity. He is Himself the very content of it, for
Scripture says God has given us eternal life and this life is in
His Son. A young man in his thirties objected that it all
sounded very impracticable. 'You've been saying that it is the
Spirit of Jesus Christ living in me who is the source of
deliverance and power over the old natural self.' I said, 'Yes'.
He countered, 'But you haven't told me what I have to do to
make it work.'

I said, 'Maybe you're asking the wrong question. Not
'What do I have to do?' but 'Who has to do it?''

He replied, 'I'm not a zombie. I don't want to sit back and
say "Well, it's not me, it's Christ" and hope something will
happen.'

He worked as a helicopter charter pilot, and one of his
jobs involved flying round Cape Town on a Friday afternoon
observing traffic patterns. He suggested I accompany him, so
that we could continue the discussion.

So that Friday I found myself getting into a tiny helicopter
and feeling quite nervous. 'How does it work?' I asked. He
showed me the rotor above me. 'The blades are slightly
angled. When the rotor begins to rotate, they push down the
air which creates a vacuum which causes a lift.'

I said, 'What's that called?'

He said, 'That's what we call the law of aerodynamics.'

'What does it do?'

'Well, it lifts the helicopter off the ground.'

'What happens to gravity?'

'What do you mean?'

'Well—I'm secure with gravity, I'm used to being on the
ground. I don't like this idea of floating in the air.'

'You'll be safe,' he reassured me, and we took off.

I said, 'What do I have to do though to make sure that it's
going to work? Do I have to flap my arms at all?'

He laughed, but I continued: 'We were talking about the

fact that the source of Christian living is Christ Himself, and that as we live in dependency upon the life of Jesus Christ in us, it is He who enables us to live a Godly life. You're telling me now that this helicopter, when you begin to rotate its blades, begins to bring into force the law of aerodynamics which is more powerful than, and sets the helicopter free from, the law of gravity.' And I read him Romans 8:2. 'That's what I'm telling you about Jesus Christ. When we got into this helicopter, I said to you "What do I have to do?"; and you said, "Put your seatbelt on and relax." Don't you see, you've been illustrating what I've been preaching, that there's a more powerful law than the law of gravity, the law of aerodynamics? There's a more powerful law than the law of sin, which otherwise will pull you to the ground.' I hadn't been preaching about the law of sin but the principle is the same, it's the Spirit of Jesus Christ which sets us free.

He said, 'I think I've got it. Are you saying that as I trusted Jesus Christ to set me free from my sins, as I trusted Christ who enabled me to become a Christian, I equally trust Christ everyday to enable me to be the Christian I've become?' I said, 'You've got it.'

And that's exactly what these verses say. Just as it took Jesus Christ to save me from the penalty of my sin, so it takes Jesus Christ to do for me what I cannot do for myself to set me free. Look at verses 3–4: Paul is saying, 'The law left me aware of what God demanded but hopelessly inadequate to bring it about in accordance with it. What the law could not do, God did, by sending Jesus as a sin-offering, where He condemned sin in sinful man.'

As John Murray says in his commentary on Romans, 'That is not simply that He condemned my sins, but He broke the power of sin in me when He died and rose again from the dead.' Romans 5 says, we are reconciled by death to be saved by His life (cf Romans 5:10). He died for me, and rose again from death, so that having cleansed me from my guilt through His death on the cross, He can now, in me, by the presence of His Spirit, as a result of what He did on the cross, break the power of sin.

It doesn't mean that you no longer are tempted, of course

not; any more than the law of gravity gave up. It didn't give up for one moment. We took off and flew, but the law of gravity was still in operation. If half an hour after being in the air I had said to my friend, 'Listen, I'm really getting confident now, we've broken the law of gravity for the last forty-five minutes. I'm really feeling confident. I'd like to see if I could manage this on my own'—the moment I stepped outside the helicopter what would happen? Gravity would be waiting for me and I would become a lump of strawberry jam on the top of Table Mountain.

The law of sin in your life and mine will be there till the day we die. The flesh will war against the spirit, the spirit war against the flesh: that is a never-ending civil war that takes place in your soul, and will until you die. But the marvellous thing is that, although the law reveals the character of God and my natural instincts are to resist the character of God, it is the presence of the Spirit of God living in me—the life of Jesus Christ, says Paul—who sets me free. God did what the law could never do.

The law could tell me what was demanded, but it could never make it happen. But it's the Spirit of Jesus Christ, through the death of Jesus paying for my guilt and on the cross dealing the death-blow to the power of sin; and then by His resurrection imparting in me power, strength, and ability.

One last thing. My friend was totally right in his question, 'What do I have to do?' You see, we are not teaching some kind of pietism or pacifism, in which you sit back in some neutral position and say 'It's all over to God' and simply sit here. That is not what the New Testament teaches.

Look at Romans 8:5. 'Those who live according to the sinful nature have their minds set on what that nature desires; but those who live in accordance with the Spirit have their minds set on what the Spirit desires.' What is the difference in that verse between the one who ends up doing what the sinful nature desires—that is, pulled by the law of sin—and one who lives in accordance with the Spirit and fulfils the requirements of the Spirit? It lies in the words 'have their minds set'. If you want an interesting study sometime, read what the New Testament says about the mind.

Read what Romans says: 'Count yourselves ... reckon yourselves ... be transformed by renewing your mind.' It's not a psychological process to enable us to be Godly. Paul is saying that the person whose mind is set on the things of the flesh, the old nature, will live that way; but those whose minds are set upon the things of the Spirit of God will live that way. In Proverbs 23:7 we are told that as somebody thinks in their heart, so they are. I remember seeing a slogan once that said, 'You are not what you think you are: but what you think, you are.'

They say you are what you eat. But even more important, you are what you think. That's why in the Psalm 119 David asks, 'How can a young man keep his way pure?' That's a good question; here's his answer, 'By guarding it according to thy word' (verse 9, RSV). And he says, 'I have hidden your word in my heart that I might not sin against you.' As I say, not because God in us is a psychological process; it is the Spirit of God that makes us Godly. But we know the Spirit of God through the word of God. How do you keep your way pure? Guard it according to Your word. We must never detach the Spirit of God from the word of God. If we do, one will create mysticism, the other create legalism. But as through the written word we get to know the living Word, the Lord Jesus Christ and the Spirit who is there to inhabit our hearts—as we get to know Him through the word of God, as our minds are set on truth, our minds are set on those things that are good and Godly, then He reproduces in us His own character and goodness and likeness.

You see when Jesus died on the cross He dealt with our sins; he also dealt with our selves. I am crucified with Christ. I live, but not I, but Christ who lives in me.

And what began in Romans 7 was, 'It's not I but sin living within me'—the man who has allowed the law of sin to dominate. As we turn in repentance (you will know that the word repentance literally means 'to change your mind', *metanoia*) and so become a Christian in an attitude of repentance, we turn from our selves and from that which would naturally appeal to the old self and pull us down, and turn our minds to the things of the Spirit, to Christ and His word. And as we get to know Him, allowing Him by His Holy Spirit to accomplish in us that for which He died when He gave Himself on the cross.

From one degree of glory to another we are being changed, 2 Corinthians 3 says, into His image. It's a process to be completed one day in heaven when we are glorified. In the meantime, the process. The old nature will always be there. You face the temptation, you will fall. We say we have no sin; we deceive ourselves. But we can go up into every new day and say, 'Lord Jesus, thank You. You live in me today and I trust You. I trust You to impart to me the wisdom, the strength, to be my strength, to be my light, to be my power, to enable me in a dirty world to live a life that's clean in a godless world—to live a life that speaks of God.'

'DO YOU LOVE ME MORE . . .?'

by Rev Bob Key

John 21:15

It's very important, though often forgotten, that John 21 comes after John 20. Sometimes we imagine that the passages on which we preach dropped out from the sky, but it's not the case. So I want to dwell for a few minutes on the word 'afterwards' in John 21:1. You see, John 20:31 reads like the end of the story. So some commentaries tell us that John 21 was an afterthought—'Oh look—PS—I did remember this story as well.' The same commentaries will often tell you that John 1:1–14 was a piece of literature that John found after he'd written his Gospel and thought 'That would make a lovely introduction—I'll get my spiritual Blutac out and stick it in front of my Gospel.'

It's not true. There are no Greek manuscripts of John's Gospel that lack either chapter 1 or chapter 21. It's the whole thing, or nothing at all. And when we get to John 20, John wants to say to us at the end of the chapter, 'You've now got the message, but you haven't yet learned what to do with it.' In those first few verses of chapter 1, he begins to set out the themes like the overture to a great opera. He sets out the theme that he's going to develop in the rest of those twenty chapters, that will show us his glorious good news of Jesus Christ. And he lets us know, when he's finished, that the aim of those twenty chapters is to bring us to a personal saving eternal faith in Jesus as the Christ of the Old Testament and the Lord for the Gentiles.

Now, I want to run the risk of giving you a five minute high-

speed tour of John's Gospel. Don't worry, I haven't forgotten
that John 21:15—'Do you love me more?'—is waiting for us,
but I want to have twenty chapters of John's Gospel behind
me so that you will know it's not just Key, it really is John we
are considering.

Come back with me then to the prologue, John 1. You
really need a Bible open as we go. Here are the themes.

The person of Jesus (verses 1–5). Throughout the Gospel,
John is going to introduce us to Jesus who is first and
foremost Almighty God. He started by making a parallel with
Genesis 1. But he's going to go on, in all those glorious 'I
am' sayings, to make sure that we understand that Jesus
claimed not to be slightly underneath God, nor to be a good
man, nor to be an ethical teacher, nor to be a wonderful
prophet, but to be the great 'I am'. That's why, of course, in
the middle of the Gospel they picked up stones to stone
Him. That was the punishment for blasphemy; and when
Jesus said, 'Before Abraham was I am,' they all recognised
the Exodus quotation and out came the stones.

But John also wants to show us that Jesus who is truly
incarnate, when he sees the bereavement of Martha and
Mary, weeps; that Jesus, who when He is nailed to the cross,
is not somehow removed from the agony of that horrific and
tortuous death but says, 'I am thirsty'.

The testimony to Christ (verses 6–9). 'There was a man who
was sent from God; his name was John. He came as a
witness to testify to that light . . . that all men might believe.'
Here's a bit of homework for you. Read John's Gospel and
look at every other character other than Jesus. Most of them
spend most of the time pointing you to Him.

Let me show you one, just by way of example. Come with
me to the end of chapter 1. There's that lovely bigot
Nathanael—he really loves Nazareth doesn't he? 'Jesus from
Nazareth! Can anything good come from there?' And Jesus
said to him, 'You're a true Israelite, aren't you? What does a
true Israelite do?'

'Rabbi, you are the Son of God; you are the king of Israel'
(cf 1:43–50). John is showing us that any Jew who thinks,
after Jesus, that Judaism is the way to God doesn't know
what it means to be a true Israelite. So to those churchmen

who say we mustn't evangelise God's historic people—tell
Nathanael about it! For John uses Nathanael to point us to
Jesus.

Even Caiaphas; who, at the moment that he gives his
official high-priestly blessing to the plot to have Jesus killed,
says 'It's expedient that one man should die for the people.'
And John, if I can paraphrase it says, 'He didn't know what
he was saying but he never spoke a truer word' (cf 11:45–
53). Even the enemies of Jesus point to Jesus.

Jesus is rejected (verses 10–11). He came to His own home
and they didn't recognise Him or receive Him. And the
rejection slowly builds up. By chapter 6 Jesus tells His large
group of followers then that they must eat His flesh and
drink His blood. We read that from that time onwards many
no longer followed Him. They loved the miracles, they
thought the teaching was wonderful—but that sort of
commitment? So the rejection continues, until in chapter 18
there is a great crescendo, when you see everybody rejecting
Him—the Jewish authorities, Judas, the disciples, Pilot, the
crowds—and He's nailed to the cross.

The mission of Christ (verse 12). You really are left with
absolutely no doubt what this is about. Who, having read
John's Gospel, could really think that Jesus came to teach us
ethics, that He came simply to be one great religious leader
on the supermarket shelf of world religions? Not a bit of it!
He comes as the one and only way, truth and life, so that
every other philosophy and religion is seen as a cul-de-sac.
They are not equal trails up the mountain, they are dead
ends going nowhere. Jesus is the Way that makes you
children of God.

The glory of Christ (verse 14). The Word became flesh, and
dwelt among us. And we've seen His glory. Where did we
see it? Certainly when He turned water into wine and we are
told He 'revealed his glory' (2:11). But above all, on the
cross. Jesus has prayed 'Father ... glorify your Son' (17:1).
And God responds in allowing Him to be crucified for the
sin of the world. For in John's Gospel the tree of agony is the
throne of the king of the universe, so that by the time you get
to chapter 20 and you've had the glory of the resurrection,
you really do have the one great message. It is the only

message that can change man's nature, the only message that can change man's destiny, the only message that can change society, the only message that makes us right with God.

Now, come back with me to chapter 21, and look with me at the disciples' reaction.

You've just had the resurrection. So what do you do? You go fishing. Does verse 21 amaze you? You've got the only message that can change man's eternal destiny. Never mind; let's go fishing. And in case you think this is simply John's view, it's exactly the same with other New Testament writers. Take Luke. Do you remember how the Acts of the Apostles begins? They've had those wonderful weeks with Jesus after the resurrection, and He's been opening their minds to understand the Scriptures. Wouldn't you have loved to have been there? All those questions about those tricky Old Testament prophets you've always wanted to ask! What do they say to Him, as He's about to ascend into glory and send the Holy Spirit? They ask 'Is this the moment we get rid of the Romans?' (cf Acts 1:6). Isn't that what it means? 'Do we get our country back now, please?' The penny still hasn't dropped, has it?

Take Paul, writing in his wonderful systematic way to the Romans. He's going to say to us, 'Offer your body as a living sacrifice'. He spends eleven chapters spelling out the gospel, before he can give the Roman Christians that life-changing challenge. You have to have a firm grasp of the message, but even that, without a commitment to the commission, won't make you serve Jesus as Lord. You can have the most correct theological grasp of the gospel, you can have been to Convention after Convention, you can know all our sermons better than we do, but it doesn't guarantee that you will be committed to the mission of Jesus. And unless you are committed to the mission, you are not serving Jesus as Lord.

That will be our focus as we consider the rest of John 21.

Look over John's shoulder with me, as we look at these challenges that face Simon Peter and the rest of the disciples. For it's this chapter that meant life would never be the same again for them.

Here's the first choice.

My life—or Christ's call?

I wonder why they went fishing. Can you read between the lines? Seven of them went. Peter had the bright idea, but then he was always the first one into action. He's the first one to act; John is usually the first one to understand. But they all agreed to do it. Was it financial necessity, do you think? Or was it simply that being unsure what to do, they stuck to the familiar. That sounds to me like the truth. What do you do as a church if you are not sure of the way forward? Stick to the familiar. And so they went fishing. It was familiar, but it was utterly futile. They thought they were still fishermen. They'd forgot He'd made them fishers of men. Which comes first? My life or Christ's call?

What are you? When somebody asks you, 'And what do you do?', what do you say? I guess many of us immediately think of what we spend our working lives doing. What makes me who I am? 'Well I'm a plumber . . . I'm a doctor . . . I'm a housewife . . . I'm retired . . . I'm a granny'. Maybe we think of our spare time activity: 'Well, actually I'm a squash-player', or 'I'm captain of the bowls club'. Maybe it's more religious than that. Maybe we say, 'I'm a church warden . . . I'm an elder . . . I'm a deacon . . . I'm a church secretary . . . I'm the head steward . . . I'm a Sunday School teacher.' So that we think we get our self-worth by what we do. This passage shows that it's who we are that comes first. They were to be His fishermen.

Tell me, friends, are you a Christian first, who happens to be a lawyer, or a housewife, or a teacher, or a student, or retired? Or are you someone who's any of those things, who just happens—in a spare-time sort of way, when it's not too inconvenient or too risky—to be a Christian? Do you see the choice? Because I've got to tell you, my friends, that there are so many Christians in our country for whom being a Christian is something that's adopted when it's convenient, when it fits in, when it won't cost, when it won't make me stick out like a sore thumb. And it's so easy to take the secure route rather than the risky road to the cross of Jesus.

There are two applications here. Let me spell them out for you. First of all,

Jesus is much better at whatever you do than you are. Just imagine it. He repeats the lesson He first taught them in chapter 5. Now there it really does stick out: there is Jesus who is a carpenter from Nazareth, which is not a lakeside town. You would expect Jesus to be the expert in woodwork, wouldn't you? You want a table and chairs, get Jesus in. Peter, James, John, Andrew, they were the fishermen. So who would you expect to know where the fish were? You don't go to your local Texas D-I-Y Store to find out about fish.

But who knew where the fish were in John 5? Jesus did. And who in John 21 knows where the fish are? Jesus does.

So often we are not prepared to trust Jesus with the Lordship of those particular areas that we imagine are our specialities. What's the thing you are best at, on which you really pride yourself? Jesus is better at it than you are. Jesus can run that area of your life a hundred times better than you can. Students, you are doing your finals, finishing your DPhil thesis or whatever it may be. Do you pray before you do it? 'But I'm not reading theology, I'm reading engineering.' Jesus is a much better engineer than you'll ever be.

'Well, I'm brilliant at bringing up the children.' But is that something you really pray over? 'It's my marriage I really think I'm good at, I think our home's a wonderful place.' But is Jesus the head of it?

But you know, friends, for some of us there is another application. Some of us may already have responded to it. Others may be trying very hard to imagine that the phone call from the Lord is for somebody else. And that was,

Although they were brilliant fishermen, He called them to be something else. It is possible to live a life that is wonderful and fulfilling and makes a great contribution to the church of Jesus—and is second best. If God is calling you to be a Christian accountant, God bless you. If you are a Christian accountant whom God is calling to the mission field or the ordained ministry, it's time you closed your books and sold your calculator. John and Peter and the rest had gone back to the second best. Is that you? Are you going down a route that for you is not God's number-one call? My life—or Christ's call?

Secondly,

Self-reliance—or Christ's provision?

Don't you love it when the Bible says odd things? Have you
noticed verse 7? 'Then the disciple whom Jesus loved said to
Peter,'—I said it is always John who understands first—'"It
is the Lord!" As soon as Simon Peter heard him say, "It is
the Lord," he wrapped his outer garment around him (for he
had taken it off) and jumped into the water.' How do you go
swimming? When I go swimming I take my coat off and put
my trunks on. Peter said, 'Pass my overcoat, I want to go
swimming.' Did that ever strike you before?

The reason he does it is because he's a good Jew. To greet
someone if you were a Jew was a religious act, and you
couldn't do a religious act in a state of undress. So you didn't
greet other in the public baths, because you weren't dressed
properly. So he feels that if he's going to be able to greet
Jesus, he's got to put his overcoat on. He still wants to rely
on himself, not necessarily to be right with God but to be
able to be useful for Jesus. I don't want to build a great big
mountain of application on this small verse, but I'm sure
John puts it here for a reason. How many of us feel that we
can only be useful to God if our gifts match those of some
Christian idol, someone we really admire. You say, 'I really
feel that God may want me on the mission field. But I simply
couldn't be like the folks on the platform. They are much
holier, much more other-worldly than I am' ... 'I really
think that God could be calling me to full-time Christian
ministry; but I can't preach like Charles or Philip or
Mark—how could I possibly do that?' Don't put your
overcoat on to go swimming!

Jesus wanted Peter; not with his tacky self-righteousness,
not with all the things he thought he was good at, but simply
all of Peter: failures, scars, regrets, everything—everything,
brought to His feet.

Notice that Jesus doesn't need their fish. They have a
whole net-full, 153 of the jolly things. They drag it to land,
but Jesus has already got the barbecue going and He's got
bread and fish on it. He doesn't need theirs, but He
graciously uses them. 'Bring some of the fish you've just

caught.' This is the Christ who fed five thousand with a few loaves and fish.

Does He need their 153 fish? No, but He's going to use that which they've caught, even though they shouldn't have been fishing in the first place. How's that for grace? Christian, do you think you might be in the wrong place? Do you think maybe you've made some decision that has mucked things up for you? 'God can't use me now because I've moved to the wrong town, I may have married the wrong person, I'm in the wrong church, I've read the wrong degree?' Bring it all to Jesus. He'll graciously use even the mistakes. That's the lesson of this verse, isn't it? Our God of great grace is even able to use the times we muck things up. If I didn't believe that, let me tell you, I'd never preach another sermon.

The banquet is a mixture of Jesus's provision and the things that the disciples have caught. Won't that be what heaven's like? Jesus has provided the gospel (John 1–20) and He sends us out to catch the men.

My reluctance—and Christ's commission

It seems to be the in thing this year for Keswick speakers to talk about their dogs. Well, our family is looking forward to taking delivery of a dog on Tuesday. He's five years old and he's pure bred. He's a little short-legged scruffy thing from France. We are going to call him Bernie. I say that, not just to prove that I like dogs as much as Donald English does, but also to point out that our scruffy little thing has both a formal title and a name, Bernie. And now Simon Peter has a title: 'You are Peter the rock and on this rock I will build My church' (cf Matthew 16:18). And what does Jesus call him? 'Simon'.

'You think you can hide behind your title?' says Jesus. Those of you with Greek Testaments, the Reverends and the Doctors—you can't hide behind your titles. Jesus sees you as Bill, Mary, Fred, Bob. So please, with me, let's drop our masks, our pretences, our titles and the jobs that we do, our respectability and our Christian track record and how many hundreds of times we've come to Keswick; and let Jesus speak to us with all the love that shines from the Master's face. Because if you were a managing director and you had an employee like Peter, you would have sacked him.

But Jesus is going wonderfully to reinstate him. How many denials? Three. How many questions to Peter? Three. How many assurances and new commissions? Three. There is a wonderful pastoral love in the Lord Jesus Christ that meets Peter's deepest need. But only when Peter lets him deal with him as Simon. When he's got his jacket and he's being the Jew hiding behind his religiosity, or he's being Peter hiding behind his title, nothing can happen. But after breakfast, in the silence of the lake, as Jesus and Peter go for a walk on the beach, wonderful things happen. Verse 15: ' "Simon son of John, do you truly love me more than these?" '

I could spend five minutes pussy-footing about whether He means 'more than these men' or 'more than these fishing boats'. Let me cut the argument and come straight to the point. I don't believe it's 'more than these other disciples'; that's a claim that is made in Mark. And Mark tells us that they all said the same thing anyway, so why single poor Peter out?

The Greek could be either masculine or feminine. It could be 'these men'. But what's Peter just gone back to? Fishing. And it's the crunch question. 'Peter, which is now going to come first? Salmon or sermons? Which is going to have the priority? The gospel or Galilee? Which is it going to be, Simon? Do you truly love Me—or is it back to the boats? Which is it going to be? All the things in which you find security and familiarity, all the things in which you feel you are the acknowledged expert? Or, Simon, will you follow Me to the ends of the earth, wherever I call you, learning new skills, learning to trust Me and taking great risks, being beaten for Me? Eventually, being killed for Me? Do you really love Me like that Simon, more than you love all the things that spell security and a quiet life? Which is it going to be, Simon?'

'Yes, Lord, you know I am Your friend,' he responds.

And so the second question. The NIV translates it, 'Do you truly love me?' And it's the verb form of *agape*—that little

word that was virtually redundant in Greek usage and was
rescued by the Christians: 'We will use this for the way in
which God loves us. Not the cheap love of the diagonal cross
at the end of a love letter, but the priceless vertical cross of
Calvary.' And Peter is asked, 'Simon, do you love Me like
that? Simon, do you love Me as I love you? Am I going to
come absolutely first, Simon?'

And Simon won't use that word. He just says, 'Lord, You
know I am Your friend.'

So the third question comes, 'Are you My friend, Simon?'

John records that the word changes. If the conversation
was in Aramaic, we must assume that John is giving the
Greek equivalent. But Simon Peter and Jesus would both
have spoken good Greek, so maybe that's the language it
took place in. We don't know.

'But are you My friend? Is there a real relationship here,
Simon? Not simply will you act for Me—but will you love
Me, friend to friend? Not simply will you be a professional,
the one who preaches the Pentecost sermon, be the one who
gives your life for Me—but in the darkness, when the
bedroom door's shut and there's nobody else there, will we
be friends, Peter? Is there going to be that relationship at the
heart of your life which gives meaning to everything else? Am
I going to be not simply Lord on the outside, Peter, but Lord
on the inside?'

And Peter says, 'Lord, you see everything. You know I'm
Your friend.'

If you are with Simon Peter on the answers to those
questions, then as we close, will you hear the Lord's commission afresh to you and to me? 'Care for My sheep. Feed
My lambs.' 'Feed'—how can I translate this Greek word? It's
a diminutive, it means almost 'feed my sheepikins'; that's the
nearest I can get to it. It means, not simply 'feed those who
are small', but 'feed those who are precious to Me'.

'Simon Peter, make sure you build and pastor and
evangelise the church for the older ones, the sheep. Make
sure you don't forget the younger ones, the lambs. And
Peter, don't you ever simply be professional about it. Make
sure you love them as I love them. They are My dear ones,
whom I bought with My very blood.'

Is that the mission of the Lord Jesus Christ in which you want to share? Because that's what it means to live with Jesus as Lord. You can't simply sit in the tent and say, 'Yes, Jesus is Lord, but I don't think I want to get my hands dirty. I don't think I want to restructure my life so I'm a Christian first and everything else is second. I don't think I want to be prepared to think about full-time Christian service.' To say that is to say, 'No, Lord, actually I don't want to be Your friend. Can we just call ourselves acquaintances?'

There has to be a readiness for sacrifice. 'Peter, when you're older they are going to carry you where you don't want to go.' My friends, martyrdom is not something for the history books. And it has to be single-minded. Peter is so easily distracted, that's why I think I like him so much. He looks sideways for a moment and sees John following. And he says, 'Lord what about him?' And Jesus says, 'What does it matter if it's My will that he stays alive till I come? Peter, how does it challenge My commission to you if John lives to be two, three, four, how ever many thousand years there are, till the Lord returns? Follow Me.'

The call of Jesus to you does not come to the person next to you. The Lord speaks directly to you, I believe, in this passage. It is to you singularly that He addresses the questions. It is you singularly that have to make your choices. And it is to you singularly that He promises His presence and the overflowing power of His Holy Spirit.

'BODY TALK'

by Rev Mark Ashton

1 Corinthians 12

We come tonight to the ministry of the Holy Spirit in the life of the believer. And we are going to look together at the whole of 1 Corinthians chapter 12.[1]

If we are to understand what Paul's letter to the Corinthians means for us today, we have to start by understanding what it meant when he first wrote it; if we are going to apply it to twentieth-century Keswick, we must go first via first-century Corinth. So let's remind ourselves. Paul loved this young church. He had founded it himself. The sheer vitality of its Christianity was a delight to him and a rebuke to us. But he also had problems with them. We know from 5:9 that he had written at least once to them already, and from 7:1 we know they had written back to him. And we are breaking into the middle of an argument Paul is having with the Corinthians—an argument of which we can only hear one side, Paul's.

According to him, the Corinthians had a problem with spiritual pride, spiritual one-upmanship. They were specialists in spiritual superiority and presumption. He loves them; but he is saying, 'You dear Corinthians, you are so vain.' But you know, if Paul were here this evening he might just turn that back on us: 'You are so vain, you probably think this letter isn't about you.'

Since the beginning of chapter 7, Paul has been answering their letter. In that chapter he started dealing with sexual relations; at the beginning of chapter 8 he started dealing with their questions about food sacrificed to idols; now we get to 12:1, and he says, 'Now about spiritual gifts . . .'. That must have been one of the things about which they had written to him. The topic is going to carry right through chapters 12 to 14. We cannot understand Paul's answers without seeing them in their entirety; but tonight we only have time for chapter 12. So I want to encourage you to have the Scriptures open in front of you as we look at this together, and if I say things that puzzle you, please go back and read chapters 12–14 and check whether I am teaching the Bible faithfully; for what I am going to say is drawn from the complete context of those chapters.

Now chapter 12 develops the analogy of the body, chapter 13 is that very famous passage about love, and chapter 14 is a lengthy discussion of prophecy and speaking in tongues. Read all three chapters right through and it is clear that the problem for Paul about the Corinthian church was its over-use of the gift of speaking in tongues. That is, speaking to or about God in a language that the speaker, him or herself, does not understand.

There are seven lists of spiritual gifts in these three chapters. Tongues is the only gift that appears in every one of them. Except for once, it is always named either first or last in the list. Paul is not against speaking in tongues, but he wants the Corinthians to get the gift in its proper perspective and not to miss out on the other gifts. And so he is writing to them about their spiritual gifts because of their over-use of one particular gift. His whole purpose is corrective, directed at a wrong emphasis in this church. Unless we understand that, we won't understand why these chapters do not answer clearly some other questions that we might want to ask, such as: Can you give a precise list of the spiritual gifts with definitions, so that we can decide which our gift is?

He begins with the basic nature of Christian spirituality. Let's look first at the first three verses of chapter 12. And my first heading is a very simple Christian truth.

The Spirit exalts Jesus (verses 1–3)

'Now concerning spiritual gifts brothers and sisters, I do not want you to be uninformed' (verse 1) writes Paul. That word he uses—'spiritual gifts'—could it be 'spiritual people'? For in fact what Paul is saying here could be put in a general way as 'concerning Christian spirituality, what it is to be a spiritual person.'

Paul says, 'I don't want you ignorant' (NIV). 'When you were pagans, you were enticed and led astray to idols that could not speak' (verse 2). But the Spirit of God does cause us to speak, and say certain things: verse 3, 'I want you to understand that no one speaking by the Spirit of God ever says, "Let Jesus be cursed!" and no one can say "Jesus is Lord" except by the Holy Spirit.' That verse is nonsense unless you understand that it's a verse about the Spirit and what the Spirit causes us to do.

Clearly it is possible for any sort of person just to say the three words 'Jesus is Lord'. What Paul is talking about here is that the Spirit will not do Jesus down; He will exalt Jesus. The issue is, who is the truly spiritual person? Paul's answer is: 'Everyone who makes the basic Christian affirmation that Jesus is Lord.' What is it to be spiritual? It is to exalt Jesus. How do we exalt Him? We acknowledge Him as Lord, King, Ruler, the one and only God. The truly spiritual are not people who speak in tongues or exercise some other special spiritual gift. The truly spiritual are 'all Christians', because all make the basic affirmation 'Jesus is Lord' by the one Spirit.

The greatest miracle God's Spirit works on earth is conversion, leading a person to say from the heart, 'Jesus is Lord.' If you are a converted person, then God's Spirit worked the greatest miracle inside you when He brought you to realise that: that Jesus is Lord. If you are unconverted, then you need to pray for that miracle, that God's spirit will open your eyes and lead you to make that affirmation: 'Jesus is Lord'. No one can say Jesus is Lord except by the Holy Spirit. It is the Spirit who converts. He leads us to Christ. It isn't the other way round. The terminus is Jesus, and it's the Spirit who always points to Him, who has a burning desire to glorify the Lord Jesus. And so we have here a sure test for true Christian spirituality. Does it exalt Jesus?

According to Paul, every true Christian who makes that basic Christian affirmation is a spiritual person. So these chapters are not about the hyper-keen, they are not about special super-saints, they are about the converted. I trust that is you and me this evening.

But, Paul goes on, that does not mean there are no distinctions to be made in the work of the Spirit. So to my second heading, and the main thrust of this first half of the chapter.

Only diversity can reveal true unity (verses 4–11)

Remember the background. The Corinthians were over-exercising the gift of speaking in tongues to the exclusion of other gifts. They were saying, 'This is the one thing we must all do. We must all speak in tongues.' And Paul is concerned they should exercise a variety of gifts. His concern is not actually for their unity, it is for their diversity. But in teaching them about that, he also teaches us the nature of true unity.

First, he says,

Diversity within unity belongs to the character of God Himself (verses 4–6)
Diversity has its roots in God. He loves variety and diversity. What does God do when He freezes water? He makes snowflakes, every single one of them different. What do we human beings do when we freeze water? We make ice cubes, every one the same. He makes every one of us quite different in our mothers' wombs, and having made us He breaks the mould: 'I'm not going to make that one again, I'm going to make a different one next time.'

So we start as different people by nature, and then the Spirit of God makes us even more different as Christians. It's not the Spirit's work to clone us. He delights in variety, but also in teaching us to get on with each other across our differences. When you find a Christian gathering of like-minded people all from the same background, there is very little evidence of unity. Uniformity, yes; but that is not what the Spirit is about. True unity calls for a gathering where the people are obviously *different*. We want those who love the Authorised Version of the Bible and ladies who like to wear hats in church, and those who like to clap and wave their hands and vigorously participate in what's going on. Here the wealthy, there the poor; here the poorly-educated, there the well-educated. If the church is going to show the unity of God it must show that sort of diversity, so that what we see is a true spiritual unity bringing these people together.

Those groups of people have not come together out of a common temperament, psychological type or educational and social background. It is the Spirit of the living God who has brought them together. That's spiritual unity. When you and I have nothing in common except Jesus Christ, then our fellowship begins to become really deep. The trouble with many of our churches is that we have so many other things in common that we never get to share Jesus. Different sorts of people are the evidence of unity. Diversity, not uniformity, is essential for a healthy church; because the church must be like God, and diversity has its roots in God Himself.

How does God's Spirit make us more diverse than we already are? Here is Paul's second point:

The Spirit gives us different gifts (verse 7ff)
'To each is given the manifestation of the Spirit for the common good.' This is a key verse to which we shall refer several times. But for now, notice three things. First, a gift is called a 'manifestation of the Spirit', a glimpse of God's Spirit at work; that's what a gift is in anybody's life. Second, 'to each one'—every Christian is given a gift. Third, 'for the common good'. That's a foundational truth to which we will return. The gifts are not for my benefit, they are for everybody else's.

Paul then lists some gifts, in verses 8–10. As I have said, there are six other lists in these three chapters. None of them match. A comparison with other lists of spiritual gifts in the New Testament in Romans 12, Ephesians 4, or 1 Peter 4 makes it clear that none of these lists is exhaustive, that there is no great significance in the order and that there is no clear distinction between what we might call natural endowments and supernatural endowments.

Look on to verse 28, where you'll see moral attributes and miraculous things put side by side. Paul refuses to define spiritual gifts narrowly. If we try to make him do so we miss the point of what he's saying. So I hope you won't be disappointed if I do not analyse each of the gifts. The point is this. When we Christians meet together, the Holy Spirit goes to work among us to meet our many needs in a huge variety of different ways. And it is all at the initiative, and under the sovereignty, of God (verse 11). Every one of us has a part to play: every one of us, that is, who calls Jesus Lord, because God has so ordained it.

A famous conductor once stopped a full symphony orchestra in full flight saying, 'Stop, I can't hear the piccolo.' God is like that. He has called us into His orchestra and He wants to hear us. Are we audible, or are we so loud that we are drowning others? If Paul is right, then we are here to minister to one another. What attitude did you come here with? 'What will I take home with me?', or 'What can I bring to the meeting to give to others?' God's Spirit is gifting you for our benefit, and He means you supremely to express that when the church gathers. Every assembling of the church ought to amount to a supernatural encounter. It has been said that a church should be like a battleship, and each of us a crew member with a part to play. But all too often they are like buses instead: one man driving, everyone else sitting there watching him—except for the one who comes around and collects the fares. But when we meet under the word of God, we have a job to do.

The body of Christ: the answer to hierarchies (verses 12–13)

The problem with this diversity which is essential in the body of Christ is that we try to create spiritual hierarchies and pecking-orders. We all do it; I don't think I've ever met a Christian who didn't. The Corinthians did it, and that's what Paul has problems with. We do it, it's only human nature. The diversity is God-given, but human sin twists it. And we start to arrange pecking orders.

Samuel Johnson said: 'No two people shall be half an hour together but one shall gain an evident superiority over the other.' It was a typical exaggeration, but there's a shrewd

grain of truth in it. We are very competitive. In so many
different subtle ways, we gently vie with one another. We
compete through our careers or those of our spouses,
through our backgrounds, our personalities, our children,
our looks, our intellects, our achievements, our possessions,
our homes. There is a deep human need to feel just a little
superior. Perhaps it's a twisted facet of our need for security
as human beings.

Paul's answer to this pervasive human tendency to one-
upmanship is his teaching about the body. Verse 12: 'For just
as the body is one and has many members, and all the
members of the body, though many, are one body, so it is
with Christ.' Do you remember how Paul first encountered
Jesus Christ? As he hurried to Damascus to imprison
Christians, that light shone and he fell to the ground and a
voice spoke.

> 'Saul, Saul, why do you persecute me?'
> 'Who are you, Lord?'
> 'I am Jesus, whom you are persecuting' (Acts 9:4–5).

Paul's first living encounter with Jesus Christ identified Jesus
with His followers on earth. Paul is not just saying that the
church operates like a body, he is saying it is a body. It is
Jesus's body on earth now. When He came to die for the sins
of the world, He had a body made of flesh and blood which
men took and nailed to a cross. Now Jesus reigns from the
right hand of God in heaven, but He still has a body on
earth, a body made up of living human beings.

It is the Spirit who makes the body one. Verse 13: 'For in
the one Spirit we were all baptized into one body—Jews or
Greeks, slaves or free—and we were all made to drink of one
Spirit.' There is only one way into the body of Christ, and
that is by being baptised by, or with, or in, the Spirit, and by
being given the one Spirit to drink, or by being drenched in
the Spirit, or by being flooded by the Spirit—the Greek can
mean all those different things. We only get converted one
way, when the Spirit causes us to realise and makes us
declare that Jesus is Lord, as we saw in verse 3. And because
there is only that one way into the Christian life, we all

belong together from that moment on. The church cannot exist without the Spirit. A hundred religious people knit together by good administration do not make a church any more than eleven dead men together in a coffin make a football team. It is the Spirit of Christ who converts us and brings us to new life, it is the Spirit who brings us into the body, it is the Spirit who gives life to the body. If we are not Spirit-baptised we are not Christians: if we are Christians we are Spirit-baptised.

Images of the body (14–26)

The concept of the body is a powerful and rich idea. So rich, in fact, that Paul spends the rest of the chapter developing it and applying it.

We must be careful that our applications do not overstep his. It's possible to go too far. One curate preaching on 1 Corinthians 12 got rather carried away; he started identifying members of his congregation with different parts of the anatomy. 'Some of you are the hands, you are the ones who do all the work that needs doing around the church. Some of you are the knees, you are the pray-ers. Some of you are the heart, you are the ones who comfort others. Some of you are the tonsils, we'd really be better off without you. Some of you are the false teeth, now in, now out. Some of you are the appendix we never knew we had till you gave us trouble . . .'!

Paul's applications are all encouraging. And his first is that because of verse 14, there can be *no inferiority*. It's the first point of the paragraph. Verses 15–16 illustrate it. We are not to look at one another and then at ourselves, and be filled with self-pity because our gifting appears to us to be inferior or with resentment because somebody else's gift appears superior.

Secondly, *no cloning* (verses 17–20). A body that was all one organ—a massive toenail, say, or a giant eyeball—would be grotesque. It would not be a body but a monstrosity: 'For the body does not consist of one member but of many.' It is not a case of our being different and the Holy Spirit trying to cobble us together into some semblance of unity. God has specifically arranged things in this way: verse 18, 'But as it is,

God arranged the members in the body, each one of them, as he chose.' It is His initiative.

Thirdly *no superiority*, (verses 21–26). Paul is not saying that all parts of the body are to be counted the same; it is their very differences that make them indispensable to each other. But he is saying that they are all of equal value to God. They are all put there by God. They all fulfil God's purposes. No inferiority, no cloning, no superiority.

The case at Corinth (27–31)

In his final paragraph, Paul brings these applications right home to Corinth.

Notice, first, his general drift in these verses. Those questions in verses 29–30 all presuppose the answer 'No'. Do all do these things? No. 'So,' says Paul to the Corinthians, 'stop expecting everyone to speak in tongues. Do not make one gift a measure of spirituality for everyone. And start exercising a much wider diversity of gifts.' Now I do not think it is the problem of the Keswick Convention that we are expecting everyone to speak in tongues. Therefore we need to listen to the other side of that truth: 'Start exercising a much wide diversity of gifts'.

'But,' adds Paul in verse 31, 'eagerly desire the greater gifts'. We end our passage half-way through verse 31. He's going to go on to explain what the 'greater gifts' are in chapter 14: they are the gifts that build up the church. But he hasn't told us about them in chapter 12. In fact he's been at pains to stress no inferiority, no superiority within the body. It's true that in verse 28 he does rank the first three gifts he lists there—'And God has appointed in the church first apostles, second prophets, third teachers.' These are the people who planted the early churches, and that ranking is as much chronological as it is to do with status.

Secondly, after those first three Paul switches from people to ministries, and he ceases to allocate rank. The next two gifts are miracles and gifts of healings—both what we would call supernatural gifts. Then follow very general abilities—literally, helps and guidances, neither of which expressions come anywhere else in the New Testament and both of which appear extremely vague and extremely general. Once again Paul is determinedly ducking the question we want to ask him: 'Which is my gift?'

It seems a perfectly reasonable question to ask. But Paul is determined not to answer it. He's not interested in doing so. Why not? I suggest it's because my desire to know all about my own gifts may well conceal a desire to know my status in the church. Where do I come in the pecking order? Once I know my gifts clearly I am likely to put myself above some and below others. Both are wrong. Looking up to the platform, looking down to those in the church you don't think much of; inferiority, superiority and cloning. All of them have already been ruled out by this chapter.

Do you find yourself sometimes asking the question, 'How important am I in the church?' I think we often do when we assemble on a Sunday morning. Perhaps not at the top of our minds, but just underneath, there is that feeling, 'How important am I in this group?' It is an illegitimate question. We should not ask it. I am important because Christ died for me. That makes me infinitely important, and any other question about importance has no place in the Christian life. God does not range people in ranks in His church. And God has brought me into His church through His Spirit.

'But hang on a moment, Mark,' you may be saying. 'How can I possibly exercise my gift or gifts in the church if I don't know what they are?' Well, I think we can. In fact, I think that is exactly what this passage is teaching us: to adopt the attitude, 'If I set myself to serve other people, God will equip me for service.' He will gift me for it, but the gift is His. In one sense it never becomes mine. I don't own it, and I may not even be aware of it. I would go so far as to say that some of the people who are most gifted in building up the church are the least aware of their gifts. I don't know if my liver is aware of being a liver, but its self-consciousness or otherwise doesn't affect my health.

The gifting is God's own business.

Look again at verses 11, 18 and 24. Do you get the sense that this is a matter in which God will not let us have the initiative? The gifting is His business, and He never gets it wrong. You know how hard it is to buy presents for people at

Christmas time? God does not have that problem. He knows me better than I know myself.

So our challenge from this chapter is not to discover what our gifts are. That is God's business. Our challenge is to be prepared to exercise them for other people, to lay down our lives for one another. That's the difficult thing which our sin stops us doing. You may be saying to yourselves, 'If only I knew my gifts, I'd love to serve other people.' No, no, no —that's not what God's word tells us. He says the question of gifts is His job, He'll do that.

My problem is with my own selfishness and sin, my reluctance to lay down my life for other people within the church. In 1 Corinthians 7, marriage and singleness (celibacy) are listed as gifts. Have you ever heard a talk on the gifts of the Spirit that included marriage and celibacy? They don't normally come in the lists, do they? But what does that mean about your state at the moment, and mine? I am married to Fiona, she was given to me in Christian marriage for your benefit. Oh yes, she's for my benefit and I hope I'm for her benefit, but we have been given to each other in Christian marriage for your benefit. It's a gift for the church. The state of every one of us at the moment is either single or married, whatever our circumstances may be. And both are for the benefit of other people.

You see how this teaching turns round the way you and I think about ourselves? God's Spirit is taking us out of selfishness into love. That's what holiness is. It's to start living our lives for other people and saying, 'All these things I've got, they're for you, they're not for me, they're not to build my own little world round myself.' We will never guard ourselves against spiritual one-upmanship if we become more interested in identifying our gifts than in exercising them. The question 'How important am I?' is illegitimate. I am important, everyone of us is; and everyone of us has a part to play.

My prayer is that we will take that back with us to the fellowships from which we came. Keswick exists for the local church, I hope you are aware of that. I hope Keswick never has the effect of making you less happy with your local fellowship. I know there are stacks of problems in local fellowships, but the purpose of Keswick is to equip us for life in the body, the laying down of our lives for one another. And my prayer is that we will take that back with us into our fellowships and there pour out our lives for one another. That attitude is the Spirit's way of glorifying Jesus by building up His body on earth and reaching the nations. It is the holiness that God wants to bring into our lives. 'By this,' said Jesus, 'shall all men know that you are my disciples, if you have love for one another.'

Notes

1. Mr Ashton is using the New Revised Standard Version of the Bible.

'SPIRITUAL DECEPTION'

by Mr Dick Dowsett

Acts 5:1–11, 8:9–25, 19:13–20

I want to expound to you tonight three dangerous stories from the Book of Acts. They are the word of God and you can trust them completely, which isn't remotely true about my preaching. So if you are a serious Christian, you will keep your Bible open and check up on me. If you see it there, do as you are told. It's God's word, and it is no risk, because God always underwrites His word with His power.

The key words in those three stories are in Acts 5:11, 'Great fear seized the whole church', and 19:17, 'They were all seized with fear, and the name of the Lord Jesus was held in high honour.' What do you know, what does your home church know about an awesome sense of the fear of the Lord that says, 'We can't muck around any longer'? There's lots of talk in our churches these days about acceptance, tolerance, self-fulfilment, happiness and peace. Where's the fear? We are told the fear of the Lord, not the fun, is the beginning of wisdom. When you've got that right you begin to think straight and act right. We are told that our God is a consuming fire, so we don't play games and have fun worshipping. We come with awe and reverence. We call Him 'Abba', not 'Mate' or 'Buddy'. He is God.

And the stories I've chosen for us to think about tonight are three stories that I need to take seriously, and which I believe in the church we all need to take seriously: stories that show us that our God hates Christian sin. And that's what we need to grapple with.

Ananias and Sapphira (Acts 5:1–11)

First, that terrible story of Ananias and Sapphira. At the time things were really happening in the church. You can read all about it at the end of chapter 4. There was growth in the church, the church was learning to share (4:32–37). As the Spirit of God moved, people stopped just looking after number one. They sold their property if anybody was in need, so that they could share and make sure that nobody was finding it impossible to make ends meet. It's in those verses at the end of chapter 4 that you find that lovely introduction of Barnabas (that was his nickname: it meant 'Super-high-powered follow-up man'): he sells a field and gives the money away. He's investing for the good of the church. Things are really happening. And amazingly wallets got converted, because conversion always had profound financial implications in the New Testament. In those days you couldn't serve both God and mammon.

And Ananias and Sapphira decided to give. It wasn't that there was a three-line whip in the church, decreeing that anybody who owned land had to sell it and give the proceeds away. Everybody in the church, the Scripture teaches us, had to make up their own mind, responsibly and personally before God, what they were going to give. That's very clear in verse 4 where you find Peter saying, 'Didn't it belong to you before it was sold? And after it was sold, wasn't the money at your disposal?' The church did not adopt a compulsory communism. But the trouble with Ananias and Sapphira was that they decided to give everybody in the congregation the impression that they were far more committed than they really were. And that was dangerous.

They sang with passionate enthusiasm, 'All to Jesus I surrender . . . I surrender all, I surrender all, I surrender all . . .' They keenly joined in with 'Take my life and let it be, consecrated Lord to' . . . 'me?' Must be a Freudian slip! But it's interesting that in our churches these days we don't talk about self-crucifixion, we talk about self-fulfilment; and we tend to prefer 'Take my life and let it be, consecrated Lord to me.' Certainly that was what Ananias and Sapphira were singing. But doubtless they went on to the next verse: 'Take my silver and my gold, Not a mite would I withhold.'

And God turned to them and said, 'You liars.'

And they dropped dead.

It's dangerous. Let's face it: we evangelicals, we Keswick people, we're good actors; we're good at giving the right impression. We know how to play our part. Indeed, we almost give the impression that we need a bit of hypocrisy, like oil to keep things rolling. Let's learn tonight from Ananias and Sapphira.

What can we learn? We can learn for a start that *Satan, the originator of lies, works very hard to get Christians pretending.* That's clear in verse 3. 'Ananias, how is it that Satan has so filled your heart that you have lied to the Holy Spirit?' There is an enemy, there is one who is more concerned than anything else to get us all playing the game that everything is going lovely; when we ask one another 'How are you?' and respond, 'Fine, praise the Lord!', whether it is or not. It's a very easy game to play. It's very easy for those of us who are preachers to play it, and some Christians actually encourage us to do it. I once got a letter when I was a missionary in the Philippines from somebody praying for me who said, 'I feel rather shy about praying for you, I imagine you must be ever so holy and that your life is one long quiet time.' She should have read the book of Jonah, shouldn't she! She'd have found out what a real missionary's like—real crummy stuff, at least I was. But when people stick you up on a pedestal we feel, don't we, that we have got to play our part. We feel obliged to give the impression that it's not just 'I surrender all', we've got to act it up.

We do so often play parts. And suddenly, every now and then, the Lord breaks through. I remember an elder saying to me, 'How can I talk about surrender to the Lord when in our family we are spending more on ice-cream and chocolate than we are investing in reaching lost people for Christ? How can I sing 'I surrender all', when ice-cream and chocolate matter more to me than a lost world?' But the devil is encouraging us to mouth the words and to say the right things, and it's not real.

But secondly, *though the devil is in this business, you and I are responsible.* In verse 9 Peter ask, 'How could you agree to test the Spirit of the Lord?' They agreed to do it. There was no way they could stand there and say, 'It wasn't my fault, Satan made me do it. This isn't a matter of repentance, you've just got to cast him out.' It was a matter of repentance. What we do with this awful temptation in our church is our responsibility.

Ananias and Sapphira had a jolly good marriage. Maybe they had a better marriage than you've got. There was none of this going their separate ways with their separate ambitions. Verse 2: 'With his wife's full knowledge he kept back part of the money'. In verse 9 we discover that this couple worked as a partnership, they discussed things, they agreed together about what they were going to do with that money. They had a good, real partnership.

But one of the problems with many of us is that when we get married as Christians we so easily start playing the game by new rules. How many of us, when we started buying our house and collecting things, suddenly changed our standards of Christian commitment? It's not just the married who have this temptation, though I think that those of us who are married have it especially. The problem is, nobody likes to admit that they have changed the rules. So in comes this awful pretence, that we've got the same old commitment. But I have to say to you, as I struggle with this message; the sort of sacrifice I was prepared to make when I was twenty-five I think twice about now I'm fifty. And so did Ananias and Sapphira. But they were neither honest to God about it, nor honest before their congregation.

I want you to see that God was affected. Verse 3 tells us that the lie was against the Holy Spirit. Not just against Christians, but against God (verse 4). In verse 9 they are described as testing the Spirit of God, trying their luck with God; chancing it, if you like, like children walking on thin ice. It never occurs to them that they might be the ones who will drown. Brothers and sisters, it's very easy to live a lie, isn't it? But God wasn't fooled, He saw through the lie.

Ananias and Sapphira dropped dead. Does that seem rather severe? It's not very nice and twentieth-century-tolerant, is it. I mean, drop dead—for *that*? But the integrity of the church matters to God, because hypocrisy, almost more than anything else in the New Testament, is a dreadful barrier to blessing. Christ can heal the sick, but those who go on claiming they are perfectly well are in trouble.

Just think of the ministry of the Lord Jesus for a moment: the sort of people whom He welcomed, whom He enjoyed, whom He shared with. They were not by and large the sort of people that we feel happy having around in the average evangelical church. Right? But the Lord Jesus didn't so much as raise an eyebrow at somebody who was sleeping around, who came to Him. The Lord Jesus welcomed into His kingdom somebody hanging next to Him on a cross, who had probably been involved in murder. Jesus went to have tea with a desperate extortioner who climbed on people, not just on sycamore trees. But what about the hypocrites? What about those who played a part, and were desperate to give the impression that everything was fine? Jesus does not have a good word to say for them.

So, brothers and sisters, let's start this week by being real with God and one another. You don't have to pretend before Him when He says to you tonight, 'How are you, lad? How are you, girl?' You can't con Him anyway, but that doesn't mean it doesn't matter. Do you remember how the psalmist put it in Psalm 32:3–5? 'When I kept silent, my bones wasted away through my groaning all day long. For day and night your hand was heavy upon me; my strength was sapped as in the heat of summer. Then I acknowledged my sin to you and I did not cover up my iniquity. I said, "I will confess my transgressions to the Lord"—and you forgave the guilt of my sin.' What a blessed release!

As those of you who are Anglicans hear so often, if we say we have no sin we deceive ourselves and the truth is not in us. But 'if we confess our sins'—if we stop pretending we are what we are not, if we come clean and agree with what God sees and play it that way—'he is faithful and just'—and will throw us out? and will discard us? No! I know that's what we deserve; but—'and will forgive us our sins and purify us from all unrighteousness' (1 John 1:9)—yes, even that which you didn't dare admit because they would throw you off the

Board of Deacons. There is no cleansing if you hold to your play-acting, there is no release of that guilt that you carry. It is dangerous to play the Ananias and Sapphira game.

Simon the Sorcerer (Acts 8:9–25)

In this story too we find that things are happening in the church. Many are becoming Christians in Samaria (verse 12). They were actually hearing the good news of the kingdom and the name of the Lord Jesus, they were believing and getting baptised. Men were doing it, women were doing it, it was happening. And there was evidence of the power of God, because everywhere that Philip went (verse 13) they were astonished by the great signs and miracles they saw. This was not simply a doctrinal revolution. God was there not just in theological books but in reality and in demonstrable power. And people were obviously getting blessed by the Holy Spirit.

Simon had been converted out of a wild background, which you can read about in verses 9–11. He had used supernatural powers, and had by his contact with the powers of darkness created for himself quite a following; people clearly thought he was fantastic. 'This man is the divine power known as the Great Power,' they said. The thing to notice here is that Simon had the same goals and ambitions after he was converted. You see it in verses 18 and 19: 'When Simon saw that the Spirit was given at the laying on of the apostles' hands, he offered them money and said, "Give me also this ability, so that everyone on whom I lay my hands may receive the Holy Spirit."' Lord, he was saying, I want to get blessed so that everybody can still think I am the Great Power, the dispenser of blessing, the indispensable guru.

We need to be aware of what we call 'old-life hangovers', the things that were typed into the computers of our lives before we were ever converted and which still keep popping up on the screen every time certain buttons are pressed; the things that keep coming back. We need to be aware.

I am amazed how many people read the story of Simon and say, 'Well of course, he wasn't really converted.' They haven't looked at the Scripture. It's quite clear in verse 13 that Simon was a baptised believer. You may not think that he was, but the word of God's Holy Spirit, who knows the inside out, says that he was a baptised believer. And yet in verse 21 we are told, 'Your heart is not right before God'; in verse 23 we are told, 'You are captive to sin.' Isn't that terrible? Here is a baptised believer, still trapped in sourness and selfishness.

Is there anybody here who knows anything of being trapped like that? Is anybody here bitter? There are a lot of bitter people in our churches. Are you bitter because God hasn't made you what He's made somebody else? Was that the bitterness of Simon? 'If only I could be an apostle, then it would be fine; why hasn't God chosen me to do this thing?' Or are you bitter because of what somebody did in the past that you are never going to forgive, and it's soured you up?

Simon was also described as 'captive to sin' (verse 23). That's an awful description for a baptised believer, because the lovely thing that we proclaim is that Jesus liberates. But that hadn't been made reality in the life of Simon. Isn't it terrible that again and again in our churches, because we don't take stories like this seriously, we are deeply shocked when it is revealed that believers—even Christian leaders —have become captive to sin? It started as a slip and now it's a bondage, the habit that you cannot get out of.

This is where Simon was. Did it matter? The answer is, yes it did matter, because it made Simon a useless Christian. And so you find this terrible statement in verse 21, 'You have no part or share in this ministry.' Simon, you are on the shelf.

I shall never forget hearing a Keswick sermon on 'Uzziah the King'[1]. It was about King Uzziah who was wonderfully helped—until he became strong. And he remained for the rest of his life with the name King Uzziah, but somebody else did the job. He was stuck on the shelf. It can happen to a believer. It was one of the things that the apostle Paul was talking about in 1 Corinthians 9:27, when he said this, 'I beat my body and make it my slave so that after I have preached to others, I myself will not be disqualified.' He was not thinking that one day, although he was a believer who led other people to Christ, he would go to hell. But he uses this little word that the King James Version translates 'castaway'; like a a cracked antique vase that I have in my study: not rubbish, but it cannot be used. Paul says, 'I will give myself a rough time, rather than be one of those.'

I believe that most of us have come here to Keswick this week because one way or another we long to be useful to God. Can you be? Can I be? In verse 22 Peter says to Simon, 'Repent of this wickedness and pray to the Lord.' Peter is saying to Simon, and I think to us as well, that the number one priority on our agenda must be to deal with God about the muckiness that there is in our lives. Peter tells him to repent, not to clean out his life, because poor old Simon would not have a hope of doing that. He doesn't call him to a clean-up campaign, he calls him to a change of mind. It is as if the Lord Jesus were to come to him and say, 'Simon, do you want to made different? Do you want to be healed, do you want to be clean?'

And Simon at least has understood that the Christian life is not a matter of 'me and God and everybody else is irrelevant'. He turns to Peter and says, 'Pray for me.' He has begun to plead for some brother to get involved with him, to help him out of the muck so that he could at last be useful to God.

It may be that there are some people here who have come here in deep bitterness and with hangovers of a past life; you long to be useful, and you wonder how you are going to sort it out. Don't go out of the tent tonight without getting somebody to pray with you. You see, although Peter says 'You are captive to sin', he does not say, 'So you have no hope', because Peter had been captive to sin. And the Lord Jesus had said to him, 'Simon, do you love me?' Peter had flannelled around three times and in the end said, 'Lord you know everything, you know I'm your friend.' And still the Lord Jesus set him free and used him, who'd mucked it up again.

Just as He did, indeed, with Jonah. You may be like Jonah tonight, bitter because the Lord has called you to something you didn't want to go to. Fancy asking an Israeli to go and evangelise Iraqis! Jonah was furious and fed up. But the word of the Lord came to Jonah the second time and the Iraqis were saved through him. He could be used again. So can you, so can I.

The sons of Sceva (Acts 19:13–20)

And that brings me to the last story. It is the story of what was going on in Ephesus. Once again, there were believers who had practices that belong to the past. The sons of Sceva (called here a Jewish chief priest, which wasn't actually what he was but what he obviously advertised outside his booth) tried to use the 'Jesus' formula. And the plain fact was that it didn't work, they got beaten up. It must have been a terribly embarrassing scene.

But it led to this most crucial reaction in the church: verse 17, 'They were all seized with fear, and the name of the Lord Jesus was held in high honour.' What a crucial reaction! I don't know how God might work in our hearts together tonight; we might even reach that point together where the fear of God would so come upon this place that we would say together, 'We must trust Jesus properly and not simply try to use Him. Jesus *shall* take the highest honour.' That's what they said, and for the first time in their lives those Ephesian Christians meant it.

They had things to deal with. Many of them had practised sorcery and they brought their scrolls. The Ephesians had occult practices where they dealt with spirits, and they had what were called 'Ephesian letters'. I didn't altogether understand this until I was counselling a friend from Malaysia and I looked at the thing hanging round his neck. I asked, 'What's that?' And he said to me, 'It's been prepared by a spirit master. My family used to have lots of problems from spirits, but one day we met this spirit master and he's prepared this thing with all this writing on it to protect us from the spirits.' I said, 'Does it work?' He said, 'Yes it's been wonderful.'

I said to him, 'That's one way with dealing with the spirits. You can make a pact with them. Then you end up belonging in the place where they belong. Or you can belong to the One who triumphed over the spirits and disarmed the principalities and powers and made a public example of them on the cross. And then you belong in the place where He belongs.'

Eventually that brother came to trust Jesus. And I began to understand the sort of thing that the Ephesians had here: the practised sorcerer had scrolls. They were very secret things, they didn't talk about them, but they part of everyday life in Ephesus. Perhaps they were so secret that the evangelists didn't think to ask any questions about them when they first evangelised them. But the trouble was that what was actually happening in Ephesus was that where practical everyday life was concerned people were dealing with the spirits and taking Jesus as a sort of extra insurance policy. He was not what He had to become: the Lord Jesus held in high honour. And so that night in Ephesus, they had a very expensive bonfire. I estimate that if the Ephesians were paid £2.50 an hour, that bonfire was worth £1,000,000. They didn't donate the bits and pieces to museums. They destroyed all of them.

Sometimes full surrender to Jesus is very expensive, isn't it? It was that night in Ephesus. But it was amazingly worth it. We are told in verse 20, 'In this way the word of the Lord spread widely and grew in power.' You could see that they took the book seriously because of the bonfire, because of what they said that night: 'We will not have any more truck with it. We will actually destroy it so we can't go back.'

It was very moving in our home when in a Bible study I asked that Malaysian man, 'What have you done about your things?' He said, 'It doesn't trouble me any more, but I'm afraid to destroy them because the spirits might take it out on my family.' We had a long discussion about it, and a little later we had a bonfire in our barbecue in the back garden. And the bits went in the bottom of the river. As we talked about this there was another brother in the Bible study who became very agitated. I thought it was because of the discussion about spirits, but it wasn't. He was hooked too as a believer, to practices that belonged to the past. He had a bonfire too. Not spirit charms, but pornography; things that had been kept in a cupboard that needed to be destroyed.

Notice the pattern of what happened at Ephesus. Verse 18: 'Many of those who believed now came and openly confessed their evil deeds', and they burned the scrolls publicly. That's what they did first, they believed. None of us is going to try tonight to deal with the problem of what is wrong in our lives by trying to pull ourselves up by our own boot-laces. We can't. Let's be honest before God. If we could deal with the muck in our lives, then we wouldn't have needed Jesus. But we can't change ourselves. And that is why the first thing these people did was that they reached out in trust to a rescuer from sin.

Then they confessed. 'Lord, I believe and You know all about me, but nevertheless I'm going to tell You myself that there's this in my life.' Things that belong to the past are brought into the present.

And then they had a bonfire. In other words, having reached out for the help of the one that we trust in, and having spoken frankly about the problem, with the help of God they sought to destroy the opportunity to go back. They had a bonfire.

I know only too well in my life, I expect you do in yours, it's so easy to keep rubbish from the past. Maybe in your baptism (I hope so) you were asked that most important baptismal question asked from the days of the early church and ever since: 'Do you renounce the devil and all his wicked works?' Maybe you said, 'I renounce them all.' Did you? Or did you take some back? Don't do an Ananias and Sapphira tonight.

As we come to the end of this meeting, the question is 'How are you doing in your walk with God?' Don't pretend. It's dangerous. Come clean with God, He sees you as you are. You may have been conning God with your finances —He knows. You may have been sleeping around—He knows. You may have been playing games with your congregation and giving the impression that you were a cross between the archangel Gabriel and the apostle Paul—but He knows. Come clean. He loves you, but He wants to deal with you, not your front. Don't do an Ananias and Sapphira. Don't do a Simon tonight. There is, profoundly, no need to be trapped in bitterness and selfishness. Jesus bore that bitterness, He died for our selfish ambition. And the gospel says, you can be set free if you change your mind; if you repent and say, 'Lord make me what You want me to be, so that I can be useful to You.'

Don't play at using Jesus. He is Lord. They made a bonfire that night, a million-pound bonfire. Is there something you've got to destroy tonight, literally or metaphorically? Is there some way that you've got to burn it from the past? The message of Keswick is, we have a Saviour from sin. Sin is dangerous. Playing with God is dangerous. But we do have a Saviour with whom we can come clean, and who was gloriously known as the Friend of Sinners.

Notes

1. This address was given by Dr Raymond Brown at the Keswick Convention of 1981.

'A FRIEND IN HIGH PLACES'

by Rev David Coffey

Hebrews 4:14–16.

As we turn to Hebrews 4 this evening, I want you to notice the two 'bookends' that stand at either end of the verses we are going to look at. The first is 4:13, 'Nothing in all creation is hid from God's sight. Everything is uncovered and laid bare before the eyes of him to whom we must give account.' It's a warning. All the verses preceding that are a warning to take God's word seriously. Why? Because to be exposed to the word of God is to be exposed to God Himself. The language used is that of nakedness. Everything is laid bare.

The other bookend is 4:16, 'Let us then approach the throne of grace with confidence, so that'—having been exposed and found wretched by God's word—'we may receive mercy and find grace to help us in our time of need.' Where do we turn in moments of wretchedness, when we are Ananias and Sapphira and we are still alive? Where do we go, when God's word has found us out? I give you two words to hang on to in the passage we're going to look at, and other words that will be built around it.

The first word is 'possession' (verse 14, 'Since we have . . .'), and the second is 'progression' (verse 14, 'let us hold firmly . . .').

Possession

It's a conscious possession. When the writer begins in verse 14 with 'Since we have', it's a great emphasis about present reality. It's not a wishful thinking. It's not a state of hope in God that it *might* happen. He is talking about that conscious possession of believers. So what do we possess? Read verse 14 again. We possess Jesus.

The best way to read those words, 'the great high priest', is 'the great great priest'. Go back to chapter 1 and read some of the amazing spiritual inheritances that we've entered into because we are the people of God, and we have been given as our possession this great great priest, the seven wonderful things that he opens his letter with (1:2–3). This is the great great priest, and this is our possession.

Then 2:9–10, 17–18 leads to 4:14: 'Since we have this great high [great great] priest . . . Jesus the Son of God.' The twin titles, Christ as fully man and fully God, Christ in His humiliation and exaltation. The Christ, in His sympathy and in His power and glory. No wonder the writer is inspired as he wants to inspire our hearts about what we possess! We possess Jesus, this great great priest.

We possess permanent access through Jesus

And by His shed blood on the cross and His mighty resurrection to glory, what further do we possess? We possess permanent access. This great great priest has gone through the heavens. We need to turn to the Old Testament for the background to this phrase. The high priest was allowed once a year to enter the holy of holies through the curtain, beyond the eyes of the people. And on the day that Jesus died that curtain was torn in two from top to bottom. The way to God's presence is now permanently open. So in 9:24 the writer explains that Christ did not enter a man-made sanctuary like the priests that have gone before. He entered heaven itself, and He now appears on our behalf in God's presence. That's what makes Him a great great priest.

And when he talks about going through the heavens, he's not giving you a cosmic geography lesson. He doesn't even want you to ponder as to where that might be. What he's really saying is that the one who's ascended is the one who has transcended all limits of time and space, so that in accordance with Scripture He is made higher than the heavens. And He ascended far above all the heavens so that

He might fulfil all things, in that place of rule and authority where the fight is over and the battle is won and the victory is secure.

Our great great priest has secured permanent access, having passed through the heavens as the transcended Lord. The same Jesus who was born at Bethlehem, walked in Palestine, died on Calvary, rose in Jerusalem, ascended from earth and is now crowned with glory and honour, is this great great priest who now appears on our behalf in God's presence. Brothers and sisters, we possess permanent access.

I was greatly blessed by Alistair Begg's Bible reading in Daniel this morning; however many times you have read a passage you always see new things. And whether it's Nebuchadnezzar or some other ruler—or you and me before we came to know Jesus—everybody wants to get to the centre of the universe in order to be like God. But what we are told here is that the permanent access that is granted to us, that will make us God-like, will never give us total rule, but will come as near as God intends His beloved people to be. What a possession and what a privilege, that by our great high priest we have this permanent access!

But we possess something further.

We possess a close identity with Jesus
Verse 15: '[He] has been tempted in every way, just as we are—yet was without sin.' I would imagine that in this area of temptation we are probably more secretive, even with those nearest to us, than in any other aspect of Christian living. There may be some temptations that we share; there are probably many more, even for the most holy man or woman here, known only to them and to the Lord, the friend in high places, with whom they may or may not share them.

This verse may be misunderstood in two ways, and because of this the devil seeks to come to divide and to destroy our faith. Firstly, *This verse does not say that Jesus encountered every conceivable temptation*. For example, He could not have experienced the temptation of those over forty. He could not have experienced the temptations of a married couple. He could not have experienced the temptations of being a single woman. And secondly, *This verse does not concede that if Jesus could be tempted and yet was incapable of sinning, His temptation in the wilderness and in other aspects of His ministry could not be anything other than a charade.* That is a ploy of the enemy to destroy your confidence in your great great priest! For the close identity with Jesus Christ as described here is as close as close can be. It's unthinkable that Jesus should have succumbed to that temptation which leads to sin, but never, ever, minimise the reality of the confrontation between Jesus and the tempter.

Bruce Milne helpfully points out that God restrains the power of temptation in the believer's life, so we are not tempted beyond what we can bear, but always there is a way out. The temptation which we meet is filtered through God's protecting hand: that's the way out. And in Jesus' case, the filter was removed.

His temptations were real. The forty days of unbroken temptation in the wilderness, where Satan offered the one who said 'Lo, I have come to do the will of God' alternative routes to the kingdom. The moment when Satan tempted Jesus through a friend who had just a little while earlier, under the inspiration of heaven itself, said what he would himself have conjured up the ability to say: 'You are the Christ'; and from those same lips came Satan's temptation, 'Don't take the road to Jerusalem.'

Or what about when He was tempted in the garden to let the cup pass by? Or even His last hours on the cross, the temptation implicit in the invitation, 'If you are the Son of God, then come down.' Read 5:7: 'During the days of Jesus' life on earth, he offered up prayers and petitions with loud cries and tears to the one who could save him from death . . .' My friend, have you, have I, any understanding of what took place in Gethsemane? Read the Gospels, read how this high priest was crushed in the wine-press of Gethsemane; how the blood was forced from His veins so that sweat fell to the ground like drops of blood. Never, ever, doubt His close identity with those being tempted. We give in, as someone has said, before temptation is fully spent in our bodies. Only the one who doesn't yield knows its full extent. What a great great priest we have in our possession!

We possess the gentle sympathy of Jesus

In verse 15 we have a high priest who is able to sympathise with our weaknesses. He uses this language because there are those who doubt that He could possibly be in such a high place and still be our friend. And so the way this writer puts his words together is his way of affirming that Jesus has a gentle sympathy with our weaknesses. In his description in 5:2 he describes the human tradition in which this great priest stands. There was continuity and there was discontinuity. But if a human priest is able to deal gently with those who are ignorant and are going astray, then how much more the great great priest.

He has a gentle sympathy with those who are ignorant of the way, and He has a gentle sympathy with those who are ignoring the way. My contact with people through the years suggests that more Christians are tempted to despair, and even quit, because of disappointment than because of almost any other temptation that besets us. And disappointment often leads if not curbed and dealt with, to disappointment in the Lord Himself. Be not ashamed, if that is the state of your wretchedness this evening. We have a high priest who is gently sympathetic to all conditions.

We all know too much about the Christian scene to know that disappointment can abound even in the Christian family. And I want you to know that the sufferings of this high priest while here on earth have produced such a sympathy in Him that He has never forgotten them. The friends who forsook Him in His hour of need, the family that thought He was mad at one stage of His ministry, the followers that deserted because they said, 'We can't cope with teaching like that.'

Do you understand what it says, this gentle sympathy? This is where you come this evening, to your great great priest. And you receive the gentle sympathy.

And what a title, 'the friend of sinners'. This high priest, with His gentle sympathy, one day stood between a woman who was guilty of adultery and the people who wanted to stone her to death. He defended the sinner and judged the sin: 'Go and sin no more.' And that friend of sinners is the high priest, gently sympathetic, in this tent this evening. Oh, 'What a friend we have in Jesus, All our sins and griefs to

bear.' Do you realise your possession in our Lord and
Saviour Jesus Christ?

Progression

Look at the second word. What must we do to enter into a
deeper fellowship with this great high priest? What holds us
back, now we know so much more about Him?

We progress by holding

Look at the second half of verse 14. We progress by holding.
'We hold firmly to the faith we profess.' That's why the
writer had to say to the Hebrews, 'Hold on to what you
possess,' because they were in danger of letting it drift. They
were in danger of saying, 'It doesn't matter to us.' I love that
phrase that appears about twelve times in the New Testament—'with Him'. It's one of the most intimate words used
in the New Testament concerning our relationship with our
Lord. Made alive with Him, buried with Him, dying with
Him, raised with Him, appearing with Him in glory, and
when His day of glory appears then it will be the day of our
appearing too. And then that great phrase, 'our lives are
hidden with Christ in God'.

And the writer says, 'Be fixated about this, set your hearts
and minds on this truth, hold firmly to the faith we profess.'

In the nearly 120 years of Keswick other generations have
faced their various challenges and had their own ways of
applying 'Hold firmly to the faith we profess.' But this is our
generation, and a very challenging one, and this is how I read
it.

First, we live in an age where great pressure is upon us
to be politically correct, ecologically sound, theologically
alert, socially active, ethically open and religiously friendly
... And I have to say, Where does God's word come to me
as I consider this phrase 'Hold firmly to the faith we profess'?
I said, in the ministers' meeting this week, that I would share
God's word to me. Similarly I am not saying that this is how
God will interpret this word 'hold on' to you. I am saying,

this is how He interpreted it to me. By His Spirit, let Him interpret it to you.

Now as I read these verses, and as we have seen the possession that we have, do you realise that this is a revolution in the fundamentals of how human beings relate to God? There are dozens of religions today that will say, 'We can provide access to God.' But there is something revolutionary about what the Hebrew writer has told us and what is recorded throughout Scripture, and that is the uniqueness of Jesus Christ to provide permanent access to God. It has never happened before, it will never happen again. He is once and for all now appearing in God's presence on our behalf. And I would say to you, friends, as I say to my own heart, expect no new revelation or discovery in this area.

How do I apply this to my own heart? For in the world in which I move, there are great pressures on us to be reasonable, arguing that in a multi-faith society it is not quite so important to hold so firmly to the faith we profess. In the Decade of Evangelism, when we are meant to be holding forth Jesus Christ and His good news, the good news of His kingdom, we have to tread very warily. Well, God says to me that we will not harbour racism in our churches. We will repent of racist attitudes. In our church communities we will promote harmonious community relations and we will respect those of other religious traditions, recognising the precious liberty of religious liberty. But when they appeal to our reasonableness, we will hold firmly to the faith we profess. We are going to have to make progression in that area, because I don't think it's been seen as a challenge to the people of God.

I was struck by the words of a Christian politician, not a member of our own House of Commons or House of Lords, but a Christian from another nation, whose great hero beyond the Bible is Sir Thomas Moore who died, he says, to prove he was not already dead. Whatever the views of Moore this politician draws this from him, how are we called to an obedience that is so easily misunderstood? He has four questions for himself as a politician, and for every man and woman who is involved in daily business.

1: Where do you locate that core of yourself that cannot be moved?

2: What wouldn't you trade in a world of barter?

3: What would you cheerfully die for?

4: In what cause are you willing to make war against the whole world—a holy war, a peaceful war, a war of God's kingdom?

Convictions like this he says, may lead you into conflict, even suffering. You may know a season of darkness, but without an uncompromising core of the self, introspection is endless and useless. Men and women become captive to their own doubt. Confusion is their native land, and finally they lose their ability to believe in anything, even their own courage. I say to you, hold on to the faith which we profess.

We progress by approaching

The way to read verse 16 is, 'Let us keep on approaching, again and again.' Approach the throne of grace with confidence. It's the throne of power and authority and dominion. It's a great place to bring human weakness. As I pastor I honestly don't have anywhere else to point you this evening, except to this place where this great high priest has enabled us to have permanent access to this throne.

Before it's a throne of grace it's a throne of power and dominion, and of course it's a throne of grace. What does the letter to the Romans say? 'Where sin increases, grace increases all the more'—the reign of grace in a world of sin. I think of some of you pastors and Christian workers who have had to maintain a holy war with the Lord and yet are in fellowships that have been contaminated by sin. You are broken up by the way sin has ravaged your unity. I want you to come here and realise that to come to the throne of grace is to come to that place where grace reigns in a world of sin. You come in all your need, and you say, 'Lord, this has happened to our community, the devil has come in like a fury, like a flood, and we are coming to that throne of grace because there we believe that where sin has increased, grace reigns.' You not only come to the throne and the throne of grace, you come with an attitude.

Let's then approach the throne of grace with confidence. In the original Greek language, that indicated bold frankness. It was the language of the Greek House of Commons. It was open free speech. And the Bible writers use this word. It means, come to the throne of grace and speak out everything; be unembarrassed, unrestricted, outpour the heart at this throne of grace. And you would say, 'Who would cope with my misery? Who would cope with the outpouring of my heart, with its intrigues and its jealousies and its pettiness, and how sensitive it is, and I'm a mature Christian and I should know better?'

Let me say, church workers are supposed to be transmitters and receivers. And very often, because we are so loaded down with care and counsel, we find ourselves simply in the receiving mode. People beat their way to our door and we become the depository for everyone else's despair. God says to you, Christian worker this evening: 'I want you to come to this throne of grace and with a bold frankness. You pour out to me all your needs.'

I love the way in which in the Gospel stories, people approached an earthly throne of grace boldly. Whenever it was noised abroad that Jesus was around, in the house, on the mountain, in the street, people boldly approached Him. 'Sir, my daughter is ill' . . . 'Lord, have mercy on me.' The woman who pushed her way through the crowd because she was haemorrhaging and no doctor could help her—that was a bold approach to the place of grace! Nicodemus and his question—a man who should have known better! And Mary comes boldly with her perfume jar, boldly approaching the place of grace. I say to you that you are to make progress, not only in holding to the faith, but in approaching the throne.

We progress by receiving

Look at that third expression in verse 16. You hold and you approach; and you receive mercy and find grace to help you in your time of need. Mercy to cover the sins of yesterday and grace to meet the needs of tomorrow—just like the Prodigal in his time of need. Has it ever occurred to you that the time the Prodigal set out to come home corresponded to the time the father expected him? If that's stating the obvious, why haven't you set out for home recently? What does it say at the end of verse 16? 'In our time of need'. And why, on this Tuesday 27 July 1993, knowing the state that you're in, knowing that you possess this great high priest—why shouldn't you move to Him at this moment in time?

What did the Prodigal receive as he set out for home, clutching his spiritual rags around him in his wretchedness and need? He was weak, he was friendless, he was far from home, and all he could do was cast himself upon the father's mercy. And he did, and he received a welcoming embrace. But it went beyond that. Here it says, we *receive* mercy, and —to our surprise—we *find* grace. Grace is the unexpected blessing. All the Prodigal asked for was that he might be able to find mercy. 'What shall I say to the father? I've sinned, I am no longer worthy to be called your son, I just want to be in the house, in the servants' quarters, but let me come home.' He received mercy and he found grace in ring and robe and shoes and banquet and blessing he never deserved and certainly never expected. Why don't you come and make progress to that throne of grace?

A month ago, in circumstances that don't matter, I actually met a prodigal. The Keswick programme was already at the printer and I knew I was going to be speaking on this subject. I asked him if I could tell his story to you without giving any details that might identify him. He gave me permission.

God had spoken to him after a serious failure and had wanted him home much earlier than he decided to go home. God began to speak to him through Scripture. 'I will not forget you . . . Can a mother forget a child? . . . Your name is engraved on the palm of my hand.' God actually went further and gave him what He does not always give, a vision of Jesus. It happened at his place of work and was very dramatic. And he heard the words of Jesus, 'Come home, just like the Prodigal.'

Six years went by. Then somebody in Scotland sent him a tape of gospel music. And I have in front of me the words he copied out from it, this prodigal who came home:

It's your kindness that leads us to repentance.
Oh Lord, knowing that You love us, no matter what we do,

Makes us want to love You too.
Waiting for the angry word to sear my soul,
Thinking that I don't deserve another chance,
When suddenly the kindest word I've ever heard
Comes flooding from God's heart.

I say to you, you need to persevere, because you possess a great great high priest. Hold on to it, hold on to the faith which we possess, and approach this evening, boldly, frankly, that throne of grace and you'll receive that mercy and you'll receive that grace to help in time of need. Make this your confession of faith: 'I've heard what I possess in Jesus my great high priest, this friend I have in high places; and I come and confess that faith afresh in Him now.'

'HOLD ON AND HOLD OUT'

by Rev Philip Hacking

2 Timothy 2

As we think tonight about the Lordship of Jesus, I wonder if I may point out to you, as the hymns we have been singing have already reminded us, that there are many aspects of that Lordship.

There are two words we mix up: 'evangelical' and 'evangelistic'. I often receive letters from Christian Unions at colleges and universities asking me to give an 'evangelical' talk. They mean 'evangelistic'. But what is the difference? For they both matter, and they both have to do with the Lordship of Christ.

An *evangelical* is a person who holds to the truth of the 'evangel', the gospel. I would go so far as to say that 'evangelical' equals 'Christian'; for me, the words are virtually synonymous. It's hard to find a Christian who isn't evangelical. Evangelicals don't always behave like Christians, that's a sad fact; but an evangelical is a person who holds on to the truth of the gospel.

An *evangelistic person* is somebody who holds out the gospel. Now, it is possible to be one without the other. Some people who come to the Keswick Convention are very evangelical and committed to the truth of the gospel, and they are rightly concerned that we should remain true to the message handed down to us. But they don't seem too concerned about sharing it with others. And there are those who have a real concern to reach out, who have a heart for the lost; they worry that 85% of children in this country never go to any place of worship or receive any instruction, they worry that 90% of people in this country don't go to any place of worship on a Sunday. They have a concern to reach out—but they're not sure of the message they want to give. How can you be evangelistic, truly, without being evangelical?

The theme of the Lordship of Christ fits both. You see, the evangelical believes that 'Jesus is Lord'—that great definitive statement: He is the Son of God, He is risen from the dead, He is returning, He is Lord. That's the heart of the evangelical message. But a person with an evangelistic heart is wanted to go out in obedience to the Lordship of Jesus.

I was moved this morning, I always am, at the World View meeting.[1] It's a privilege but also a challenge to make that awesome appeal; but to see all those people (not all young, but many were at the beginning of their lives) dedicating their lives to the Lord's service, saying to Jesus, 'Because You are Lord, I am going to obey You as Lord'—and of course that should be true of those who didn't stand up but in different ways want to obey Him as Lord.

So I come to this chapter, as Paul movingly writes the last recorded letter we have from him, to the comparatively young Timothy. He starts emphatically: 'You then, my son.' The emphatic 'you' is in contrast to the people in 1:15 who have deserted him. Oh, there were lots of people who were with Paul when the things were going well; but when the chips were down they wouldn't put their head above the parapet and Paul was an embarrassment and an encumbrance. 'Don't be like them!' Be more like Onesiphorus at the end of chapter 1, who was not ashamed, but was faithful.

What exactly does Paul want from Timothy? Why should Timothy be different? Paul wants him to be faithful both in his evangelicalism and his evangelism, and above all in response to the Lordship of Jesus. It's required of stewards that they should be found faithful. 'Well done,' says Jesus in the parable, 'good and faithful servant.' Not 'successful'. In that World View service this morning we heard of somebody

who spent ten years in Spain with very little 'success' in
worldly terms. But he's just as faithful as he ever was. He
may seem in earthly terms to be less successful that the
brother we heard who had a much larger congregation in
South America. But I've no doubt the Lord will say to him
too, 'Well done, good and faithful servant.'

During this past year since we last met at Keswick, three
great people associated with this Convention have gone to
glory. I'm sure there were more, but these three we know
well. Firstly Canon Tim Houghton and Canon Cecil Bewes,
who served the Lord on the Convention Council for many
many years and went to their reward full of years. We thank
God for every remembrance of them and for their obedience
and faithfulness; I know that particularly in their younger
days it wasn't easy to be an evangelical, especially in the
Anglican Church to which they both belonged. But of course
most of all we remember with deep affection, and in a way
with constant questions, our good friend and my own
personal good friend, George Hoffman. He was exactly my
contemporary. He spoke on this platform last year on this
day. And within weeks of the end of the Convention, he went
to glory in a tragic road accident in a country lane in
Gloucester. It was one of the strange ironies; a man who
travelled all over the world in dangerous places (including
Croatia, where he was very involved immediately after last
year's Convention), killed in a country lane in Gloucester.

What I remember about George Hoffman—and it links so
much to our theme tonight—is that he was a very faithful
man. I know of hundreds of people working hard in tough
situations who were enlivened by the fact that George
bothered to visit them, that he cared enough to travel, that he
was spending himself in the Lord's service. As a preacher he
was quite unique. His sermons would end suddenly. Some of
us coast to our conclusion for a very long time, but not
George. And I remember him standing on this platform last
year[2] and finishing with a most moving question. He'd just
related the parable of the talents: you remember our Lord's
words, 'Well done, good and faithful servant.' George ended
by asking, 'If you were to meet Him today, would the Lord

say to you, "Well done"? Or would He say, "Well?"' And George sat down.

And within weeks, he was hearing his Lord's 'Well done'.

George's death moved and challenged me deeply. I recollect on the day of his funeral I had to do an interview with Cliff Richard in Sheffield. Both of us would rather have been at the funeral service, but we had that prior commitment. Both of us had been deeply moved and challenged by the death of a friend. I bring you the challenge as I bring it to me: If we claim that Jesus is Lord, He asks of us that we should be faithful, and He challenges us in 2 Timothy 2:1 that we should be like Timothy, strong in the grace that is in Christ Jesus.

Note the balance: it's in the grace in Christ Jesus, that is, all of Him, that we must be strong. In Ephesians 6:10 Paul says, 'Be strong in the Lord' (literally, 'Be strengthened in the Lord) 'and in his mighty power' ('Make sure you are fit spiritually, be strong'); and if Christ is Lord, then He wants strong, faithful Christians.

May I urge you to keep fit spiritually? Keeping fit physically is a good thing, of course, but it's more important to keep fit spiritually. Out there they need Christians who go out from Keswick not as wimps. There are too many wimpish evangelical Christians today. When you hear, as we have heard this week, about the march of Islam, does it not make you want to be militant in the best sense, to have a new sense of dedication to Christ as Lord?

Do you know what that means? It means that on the one hand we must be evangelical, we must hold on to the truths that have never changed in all the 120 years' history of the Keswick Convention. We must even be prepared to be dubbed 'old-fashioned'. Jeremiah talks about going back to the old ways and the 'ancient paths' (Jeremiah 6:16). Every Christian in the true sense of the word must be conservative with a small 'c'. We must hold on to the truth of the gospel, because we know it matters.

May I suggest to you, then, just three aspects of the Lordship of Jesus which we must hold on to and hold out. First,

The message to be presented: the theological truth

What is the message? Let's note,

It is unchanging in its truth (2:8, 11–13)
Paul reminds Timothy (verse 8) that he must remember
Jesus who was raised from the dead, who was descended
from David. That's the heart of the gospel. 'You must
remember,' says Paul to Timothy, 'that Jesus is a real
person—our high priest sympathising with us, going through
all our needs and sorrows and yet without sin—but He's
raised from the dead, He's ascended, He is God.' Read
Romans 1:3–4: the same message. His human form descended from David, but declared to be the Son of God by
His resurrection from the dead.

In verse 8 Paul says 'This is my gospel'. Does he mean
there are lots of gospels and you can take your pick, as if
from some supermarket shelf? That's the idea today. There
are lots of gospels. The cults, sweeping into the areas where
Christians don't get in. The New Age. And within the
church there are many gospels. Paul would say, 'My gospel is
what's given to me, I received by revelation, and it's the only
gospel.' We saw last week in our Bible readings in Galatians
that anybody who preaches any other gospel should be
condemned even if he's an angel from heaven.

If you look at verses 11–15 you will see that the truth of
the gospel which is unchanging is all to do with dying with
Christ and being raised with Christ, enduring with Christ,
reigning with Christ. Verse 12, 'If we disown him, he will
also disown us.' I read just the other day a sermon from Dick
Lucas, who's preached often here at Keswick. And he said
something about a text that I hadn't spotted before: Mark
8:38, where Jesus said, 'If anyone is ashamed of me and my
words [I] will be ashamed of him.' Dick pointed out those
little words, 'and of my words'. Many people would say, 'Of
course I am not ashamed of Jesus.' They want their Jesus:
Jesus the liberator, the healer, the friend, the teacher—'Of
course I love Jesus.' But His words? 'Oh, I know better than
He does. I don't want to believe in hell, I don't believe in the

second coming, I don't believe He's the Son of God, I don't believe He was raised from the dead.'

I'm intrigued by the parable of the sower. Jesus gave His exact interpretation of the parable; He told us what it meant. Do you know, I read some commentators who tell me that Jesus didn't really mean what Jesus said He meant? That they know the parable better than He did? It's extraordinary! They say, 'Of course our Lord never allegorised in the parables.' But, you see, He tells us what it's all about, and He gives us the exact answer. It's desperately important: if you are ashamed of the words of Jesus, you are ashamed of Him. You cannot have a Jesus who didn't live. You cannot have Jesus as Lord without obeying His words. You cannot believe in Jesus and deny His resurrection, you cannot believe in Jesus and assume there's no final judgement in hell. If you're ashamed of His words, you're ashamed of Him.

And may I mention one of His words, most poignantly? We live in a multi-faith world. Now please, don't get me wrong. It's right that we should respect people of other faiths. I'm not suggesting for one moment that we should launch a great crusading movement against other faiths. But I am going to say that there are many people in our age who want to wish that Jesus never said, 'I am the way, the truth and the life, no-one comes to the Father but by me.' It's an embarrassment. How intolerant! But you can't have Jesus as Lord without accepting His uniqueness. And there are many church groups today who want to deny that uniqueness, for whom He shares the pantheon with many other lords and gods. You may not move the truth. You may not move the goal posts.

Unchanging in its truth: this is the truth of Jesus as Lord and we should rejoice that it's unchanging. And secondly,

It is unchanging in its power (2:9–10)
Paul points out that for that gospel, he's suffering. He's been chained like a criminal. It was costly to be a Christian for him. I still recollect that little letter I have back home, from one of our missionaries in Nepal. It was a year or two ago,

things have changed there since. The letter said that for every Christian in Nepal their baptismal birthright is a spell in prison.

The challenge that comes to us is that if we acknowledge Jesus as Lord, we may have to accept a response of suffering. And that may be called for increasingly in the days to come. 'But,' says Paul, in that lovely bit at the end of verse 9, 'God's word is not chained.' You can chain the preacher, but you can't chain the message. The message is let loose. And in the Acts of the Apostles it talks a great deal about the word of God personified, spreading, multiplying. And if I understand verse 10 aright, Paul can say, 'I'm enduring this, I'm prepared to go through chained as a criminal as a preacher, because I'm not just concerned about those here now, but I'm thinking about the elect, those who may yet one day obtain that salvation.'

Do you not care deeply for the future generations of this country? It's tremendous to see young people at Keswick this week and see what they are doing. They are doing the same things as us, they are going to the same messages we are going to. But in our country they are a tiny minority. How desperately important it is, that we should make sure that for them we hold on to the truth so that they grow up in a world where that truth is known. The mission field's on our doorstep.

As a Christian who believes the evangel, do you want to share it with others? Let me read you a little sentence from the great Bishop J. C. Ryle, the first Bishop of Liverpool (did you know, by the way, that he played in the first ever university cricket match, for Oxford against Cambridge?). Bishop Ryle in one of his books made this simple statement, 'No converted person is content to go to heaven alone.' It's so simple, and yet so profound. It's the mark that we do believe in the gospel. We are not ashamed of it, we want to share it. If you don't, it cannot mean much to you. If you are content to go out of this Keswick Convention tent tonight saying, 'Of course Jesus is Lord and I love to sing it, but I'm not prepared to suffer to share it,' the Lord doesn't believe what you say.

The message to be proved: the personal truth

Go back to verses 3–6. Here is the personal faith of the Lordship of Christ. And there are three significant metaphors, which I find personally difficult to preach on. The first is a military one. I was never in the army, and I only spent one month in the Boys' Brigade before they threw me out. So I don't have much to say on military matters. The second has to do with athletics, and though I love sport, athletics is not my scene. I can't imagine what compels people to run marathons! The third is a picture of a farmer, and I'm a city-dweller pure and simple.

But I do know the message of these three pictures that Paul brings out.

The soldier

First, the message must be proved in courage (verses 3–4). A soldier expects to serve. And when you join the Christian army, you have a fight on your hands, both internally and externally. It calls for courage, and we don't, says the writer, get entangled in civilian affairs. That means, because of our dedication to Jesus as Lord, because we have signed on in the army, we make sure that other things—that are not wrong in themselves—don't entangle us. How many I wonder are still holding back from a commitment to serve the Lord because civilian affairs matter. Security? Even, dare I say it, family? Families are very precious to us all, and Jesus said something about the family coming first in our lives.

There's that lovely picture in verse 4: 'He wants to please his commanding officer'. He longs for the day when the general, the master, will say 'Well done'. There is nothing wrong in wanting a reward in that sense, because unless we care about His reward we'll bother about the world's rewards, and if we bother about the world's rewards we'll never be a soldier of Christ. Let me give you a trivial illustration. Looking at an old school magazine some months ago, I remembered scoring forty-six runs in a school cricket match when I was fifteen (my playing deteriorated: by the time I was nineteen they only picked me for the team because I was the head boy and they didn't dare sack me). As

I went back to the pavilion, the captain, a senior man, put his hand on my shoulder. He didn't quite say, 'Well done, good and faithful servant,' but he said something appropriate and presented me my First Eleven colours. I remember that moment with great pride. I gained the captain's 'Well done'.

Let me bring you back to what the Bible says. I have a master, I have a Lord, who for my salvation went all the way to the cross. He won't say 'Well done' very lightly, but if those nail-pierced hands are laid on my shoulder and one day He should say, 'Well done,' I want nothing more. That to me is heaven.

The athlete

Secondly, discipline (verse 5). According to Paul, an athlete must run according to the rules. I understand that an athlete wishing to compete in the Olympic games of Paul's day had to produce a certificate confirming that he had prepared properly, before he was allowed to run.

You will know how Paul uses that analogy also in 1 Corinthians 9:25: 'Everyone who competes in the games goes into strict training.' To gain an earthly laurel, says Paul, an athlete will dedicate himself to discipline. And here to Timothy he is saying: 'There's a Christian race to be run. Are we ready to be disciplined in that?'

He is Lord.

The farmer

Thirdly, dedication (verses 6–7). Here is the hard-working farmer. May I commend to you Ecclesiastes 11? The dedication of the farmer: sow in the morning your seed, keep at it, keep at it. Farmers are the most dedicated people. It's a reminder to us that following Jesus as Lord means courage, discipline, dedication. Verse 7, 'Stop and think about it, reflect on what I'm saying'—you see there is a danger, even at the Keswick Convention, that I will imagine I can talk about the Lordship of Christ and so acknowledge Him as Lord, in a great company. I come in on Wednesday evening at eight o'clock and He's not really my Lord, and I go out at half-past nine and He is. Ah, there's some truth in that: but it will be proved if He's Lord not at nine-thirty tonight, but in the coming days and weeks and months when you are being challenged by many other lords. You cannot serve God and mammon. 'Reflect on these things.'

The method to be pursued: the experimental truth

Now finally (2:2) the method to be pursued. You all know this verse, don't you. It tells you that you must hold on and you must hold out. Let's look at it.

Paul says, 'The things you have heard me say in the presence of many witnesses . . .' What does that mean? One commentator says it has to do with Paul's ordination. I don't agree; I think that's making it too ceremonial. I think it simply refers back to 1:13, 'What you heard from me, keep as the pattern of sound teaching.' In other words, 'Timothy, you heard me say these things so often, with many witnesses. You know my message, keep the same.' But please note the phrase 'the pattern of sound teaching'. That means the outline, the architect's sketch. It does not mean that we should be preaching exactly the same way in Keswick in 1993 as our forebears did in 1893. It does not mean to say that we simply mouth scriptural words, whether of the AV or NIV or whatever. It means we must relate them to the world of today so that people understand them. It's the *pattern* of sound words—fill it in with your own words, but preach the same message: 'Hold on to the things you heard me say, pass on to others also.'

If you want another verse to take with you tonight, take Philippians 2:16. Paul writes to the Philippians from prison, saying 'in a crooked and depraved generation . . . you shine like stars in the universe as you hold out the word of life' (or, it can be interpreted, 'hold on to the word of life'). And you can't hold out if you can't hold on. That is the word of life which you hold out, it's the truth that we've received from the years gone by—the essence of Scripture, the unchanging message, the *evangel*. That's why you should be proud to be evangelical, not because evangelicals always behave properly, but because the gospel is something of which you should rightly be proud. Hold on to it, and secondly, hold it out.

Do you remember, in the parable of the Talents (Matthew

25) and the very similar parable of the Ten Minas (Luke 19), how in each case one of the servants buried in the ground what had been entrusted to him? They held on, but they didn't hold out. The safest way to make sure the gospel gets lost to the next generation is to keep it to yourself; to go into a holy ghetto, to be so frightened of the world out there and the church out there that we keep quiet and we wrap it up in a napkin and bury it. Oh yes, we remain true. Oh yes, we're evangelicals. But we don't say anything to anybody. The best way is to hold it out, to spread it out. If Jesus is Lord, then we must, as it were, make sure that that message and that truth go on being proclaimed.

We were reminded by Alistair Begg, at the beginning of his Bible readings in Daniel, of the importance of parents and children. Read Psalm 78 sometime, where it talks about fathers teaching children so they may teach their children, so that they may teach their children, so that the next generation may know the importance, the desperate importance of making sure the word of God goes on—hold on, hold out.

I am not a sentimental soul, but it is my last address as Chairman of this Convention. It's been a tremendous nine years, and this is not my swan-song. But may I say this, in my last address as Chairman? It has been a privilege to have been just one link in the chain by which the great message of Keswick, which meant much to me as a young man, goes on spreading. A tremendous privilege; and if, under God, I've been able to help it on a bit to become both the same message and yet to have a different or more contemporary emphasis, so be it; it's been a privilege. But we live in very urgent days, in church as well as nation, and God needs all of us, and the churches we represent, to hold on and to hold out.

The largest congregation I've ever preached to, or ever will preach to I guess, was in South India at a Keswick Convention not held in a tent but outside on a dried-up river bed. I'm told that there were 125,000 people in the congregation. I asked them, how on earth did they manage to preach before there were amplifiers? It was hard enough preaching to 125,000 with a microphone. 'Oh,' they said, 'no problem; this is what happened. The preacher delivered a sentence or two. Then a man a third of the way back picked up what he'd said and preached it, and a man two thirds of the way back picked up what he thought he'd said he'd said and he preached it, and when it got to the back they waved a red flag and the man at the front started all over again.'

Now can you imagine what difference there was between the message that started out and the one that ended at the back? The mind boggles. Well now, may I say, there is a day coming—we don't talk about it enough at Keswick—when the Lord will return. Until that day of triumphant victory when we reach, as it were, the end—or the beginning—it's important that the message that has started with Jesus, and gone on through Paul, Timothy, the Reformers, the people who led you to Christ, the people who started this great Convention, should go on; and it's vital that the message that reaches the back is the one that started at the front. The Lord wants you to be a link in the chain tonight. Hold on, hold out.

We shall shortly be singing a hymn that is always in my mind linked with that mid-century martyr, Jim Elliot. 'We rest on Thee, our shield and defender.' It's the hymn that Jim Elliot and his friends sang before he went out and was martyred. Jim Elliot wrote, 'He is no fool who gives what he cannot keep, to gain what he cannot lose.' That's the Lordship! He is no fool who gives what he cannot keep to gain what he cannot lose. Please, don't be a fool!

There are some people who hold on to things that do not last, and have no hand free to receive the only things that do last. Some people, even Christians, are so obsessed by the world and its transient pride and pleasure that they hold back from commitment to Christ as Lord, and they lose instead of gain. 'He is no fool who gives what he cannot keep, to gain what he cannot lose', which is life eternal with Christ.

Notes

1. This is a traditional Keswick Convention event, during which those present who believe that God is calling them to commit their lives to Christian mission are invited to publicly declare their conviction by standing up.

2. An address by Rev George Hoffman, 'The Sign of the Cross', is included in *The Cross and the Crown: 1992 Keswick Ministry* (OM Publishing, 1992). His address at the World View meeting, to which Philip Hacking refers, is available from the tape library as tape 1992/46. Tape ordering details can be found on p. 238.

KESWICK 1993 TAPES AND VIDEOS

Tapes

Here is a list of the tape numbers for each of the addresses included in this volume:

Rev Dr Donald English (Bible readings)	K1, K2, K3, K4
Rev Alistair Begg (Bible readings)	K31, K32, K33, K34
Rev Dr Donald English	K5
Mr Nigel Lee	K7
Mr Charles Price	K8
Rev Bob Key	K9
Rev Mark Ashton	K10
Mr Dick Dowsett	K38
Rev David Coffey	K39
Rev Philip Hacking	K40

Tapes cost £2.99 per cassette plus postage (UK rates: orders up to £6, p & p £0.75; £6–£15, p & p £1.50; £15–£25, p & p £2.50; over £25, post free).

Orders should be sent to:
ICC (International Christian Communications)
Silverdale Road
Eastbourne
East Sussex BN20 7AB

A full catalogue including previous Keswick addresses is available from the same address.

Videos

Video recordings are available as follows:

Rev Dr Donald English (Bible readings)	KES93/31, 32, 33, 34
Rev Alistair Begg (Bible readings)	KES93/50, 51, 52, 53
Rev Dr Donald English	KES93/35
Mr Nigel Lee	KES93/40
Mr Charles Price	KES93/42
Rev Bob Key	KES93/45
Rev Mark Ashton	KES93/47
Mr Dick Dowsett	KES93/57
Rev David Coffey	KES93/58
Rev Philip Hacking	KES93/60

Videos cost £10.50 each plus £1.50 p & p per video (in the UK).

A full catalogue is available from:
Mr D. Armstrong
STV Videos
Box 299, Bromley, Kent BR2 9XB.

KESWICK 1994

The annual Keswick Convention takes place each July at the heart of England's beautiful Lake District. The two separate weeks of the Convention offer an unparalleled opportunity for listening to gifted Bible exposition, experiencing Christian fellowship with believers from all over the world, and enjoying something of the unspoilt grandeur of God's creation.

Each of the two weeks has a series of four morning Bible readings, followed by other addresses throughout the rest of the day. The programme in the second week is a little less intensive, and it is often referred to as 'Holiday Week'. There are also regular meetings throughout the fortnight for young people, and a Children's Holiday Club.

The dates for the 1994 Keswick Convention are 16–23 July (Convention Week) and 23–30 July (Holiday Week). The Bible Reading speakers are Rev Philip Hacking and Rev Jim Graham. Other speakers during the fortnight are Rev Tony Baker, Rev Clive Calver, Mr Chua Wee Hian, Rev David Rowe, Canon Keith Weston and Rev Keith White.

For further information, write to:
The Keswick Convention Centre
Skiddaw Street
Keswick
Cumbria CA12 4BY